CANADA — THIS LAND,

THESE PEOPLE
A Reader's Digest Collection

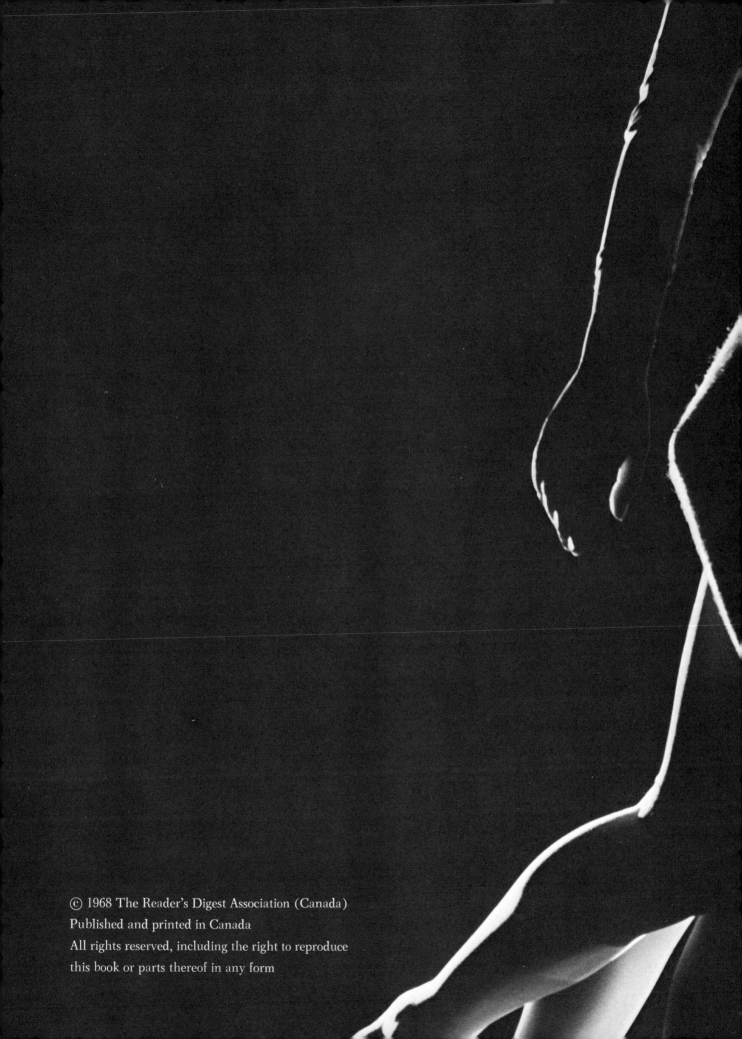

Introduction

Over the years Reader's Digest has carried many articles
about Canada's resources, her institutions, her men and women,
great and humble, and the fortunate land they inhabit. In this
volume we have gathered a rich sampling of what we have said.
We hope that it will achieve its purpose: to present a fascinating
portrait of a fascinating country.

The Editors

It is a goodly land; endowed with great recuperative
powers and vast resources as yet almost undeveloped;
inhabited by populations moral and religious,
sober and industrious, virtuous and thrifty, capable
and instructed—the descendants of a choice immigration,
of men of mark and courage, energy and enterprise,
in the breasts of whose children still should
glow the sparks of those ancestral fires.

Edward Blake, 1891

Contents

Contents (continued)

In Search of Canada

On a journey from sea to sea, a British writer
discovers a vibrant nation whose struggles
with history and nature have created
an identifiable, distinctive Canadian personality

By V. S. Pritchett

From San Francisco we flew north: out of the sunny city into the struggle with nature. Over the State of Washington, the rainstorms began and, below, the forests came tramping down in endless wet armies to meet us. The sea turned gray, and it seemed that it, too, had its forests, for when we looked over the water, innumerable wooded islands, like schools of whales, were nosing northward with us into dirty weather. The sea turned sallow and then rank ocherish where the silt of the Fraser River stained it far beyond its delta. Then, in a sudden vertical mixup of mountain, cloud, sea, forest and long, straight streets of bungalows and green lawns, we bumped down into Vancouver. From the runway nature lowered stormily on the city and looked stupendously rock-thighed and high. We were at the beginning of a journey from sea to sea across Canada, and the mountains stood like a lion in the path.

Were we in a new country? The immigration official had a Chinese face; the waiters at the hotel were Italian, German or Hungarian; there were Irish in the streets. So far, we might still be in the United States. But small things showed we were not: that first hot, full-bodied cup of tea in the hotel, tea drunk as a stimulant, not as a sedative; thicker, woollier clothes, provincial shops, an American accent softened by the quiet British intonation. A quiet, calm country, evidently not as rich as California. The girls with the "natural" European look, rather than the American artifice. Smaller cars.

In general, a mingling of British and American traits. One could say, outwardly American, inwardly British, yet perhaps Canada is the reverse of that. Perhaps Canada would turn out to be Canadian? Would this identifiable, distinctive Canada be revealed to us? Here is some of what I found.

Mountain, sea and forest—wrote V. S. Pritchett
—give Vancouver "a stupendous situation." One
favorite of lucky Vancouverites is Third Beach,
on the west side of Stanley Park. Just beyond
the beach is Siwash Rock, a West Coast landmark.
Across the First Narrows is West Vancouver.

15

Muskeg at Great Slave Lake
in the Northwest Territories.

Newsprint, wood pulp and lumber,
products of forests in many provinces,
have long been among Canada's top exports.

I found forest.
Forest everywhere,
forest at every turn,
forest behind forest,
mountain behind moun-
tain. And lakes.

Thousands of lakes,
gay eyelets of blue,
look out of the face of
vegetation, and you
realize how much of
Canada is wild water.
One understands why
this country was crossed
by water first, not by
land; and why now
it is the airplane that is
opening up the north.
How else could one
get to most of it?

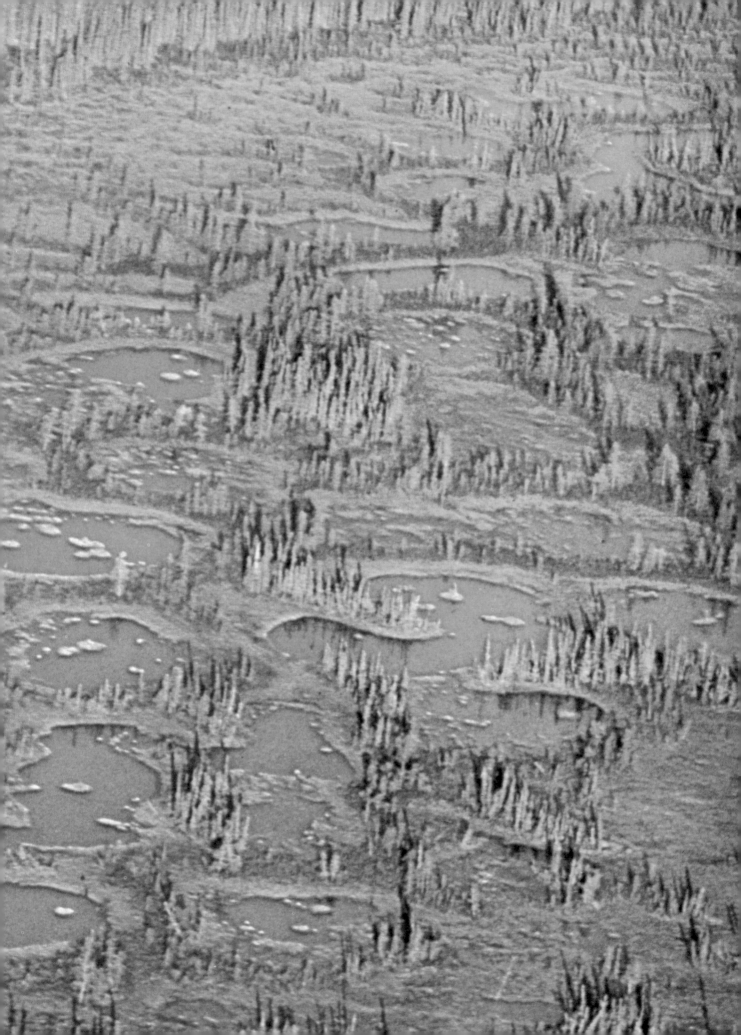

Wheat on three sides, railroad and elevators on the fourth, a Saskatchewan town nestles in the embrace of the bountiful prairie.

The City Hall (foreground) and the 56-story first tower of the Toronto-Dominion Center, symbols of the new Toronto, soar above the old streets of the Ontario capital.

The Canadian prairie, considered as a sight to the eye and an emotional experience, shares the spell of the Polish and Russian steppes. A human being is no more than a dot of a pencil. And the simple meeting of empty sky and lonely earth fills one with exaltation and fear.

Until the immigration of the last 20 years, Toronto was in the grip of Presbyterian rectitude. Perhaps new countries require this rocklike self-righteousness; it makes people work and saves them from moral collapse. But Toronto is obviously a gayer and livelier city than it used to be. Intellectually it has awakened. It has begun to laugh.

Almost brutal in their mass, but with the nobility
of massive cathedrals: the Rackla range
of the Selwyn Mountains in the Yukon.

One of the few Canadians who still makes
his living by hunting: Michael Kopak of Igloolik,
on Melville Peninsula in the Northwest Territories.

Until the great advance of modern technology,
Canadians were locked in a grinding struggle
with the climate, with exhausting distances
and, at last, with the Rockies. The Canadian
passes were almost insuperable: nature there
was at her worst.

Canada does not easily melt. Until now
its pride has been in *not* melting its population,
in letting the minorities go their separate ways,
in leaving people alone. The Canadian
is proud of his respect for individuality.

19

Winter in Canada is snow:
the cosy blanket on a Lake Louise roof,
a stilly cold Laurentian hillside at day's end,
the unspoiled new-white of a riverside village
basking in a strong February sun,
the challenge and the thrill
of a new mountain and that first long downhill run.

The escape is to the sea,
to the camp and to those
overwhelming Canadian passions —
skiing and fishing. Canadians
are men of the open air.
When nature relents in the struggle
she soothes them with sports.
The Canadians use their dry,
sunny winters as skillfully
as the Swiss use theirs.

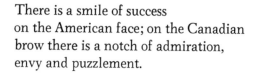

There is a smile of success
on the American face; on the Canadian
brow there is a notch of admiration,
envy and puzzlement.

He is not American. He is
not British (and in Quebec
he is not French), for the
attachment to Britain is no more
now than a respectful emotion;
nowadays the United States puts in
far more capital and takes out
more goods than Britain does
or ever did. Yet he is enough
British, American and French to be
lost when he asks himself
what a Canadian is.

Between Vancouver and Quebec you cross a continent of doubt. "We are a negative country" or "We do not know who we are," are remarks you will hear right across the continent until you get to Montreal. There the French Canadian — the *Canadien* — *does* know, but chiefly in a rhetorical way, who he is. The doubt sounds bad. But Canadians are proud of their doubt. It is the expression of that deep Scottish caution that is a marked strain in so many of them. In their dilemma they find a certain vanity and, it seemed to me, a certain strength as well.

Fresh-caught fish from the St. Lawrence
is cleaned and prepared for market
within minutes of being landed
at Grande Vallée on the north shore
of Quebec's Gaspé Peninsula.

Farms near Quebec City radiate
from a central village just as they did,
three centuries ago, from a fort.
In the event of Indian attack, settlers
could quickly reach the protection
of the fort. No man had to go farther
than another and none was
hindered by neighbors' fences.

The French Canadians are nearly
a third of the country's population,
the oldest historically established
in the northern part of the continent
and — here's the rub — they have
nothing like a proportional share
of economic power. Until only a few
years ago they were resigned to this.
Now they are not. Transformed since
World War II, the French Canadians
now are likely to change the balance of
Canadian life.

Abegweit, the Indians called the little island:
The Home Cradled by the Waves.
Prince Edward Island's long, sloping, sandy beaches
are among the finest in North America. This
is Cavendish Beach on P.E.I.'s north shore.

The Atlantic provinces, while aggressively
seeking and expanding industry, retain
old ways and an old simplicity of values.
Their way of life, V. S. Pritchett found,
is "un-American, un-Canadian, un-modern British."
It is their *own* way of life.

The Maritimes represent a happy indifference
to everything North America stands for;
these provinces boast that they produce more men
of brains, more leaders, than any other part
of Canada, that their culture is deeper
and that theirs is the happiest place
on the harassed continent.

In the last generation, the Canada which had been
written off as a stagnant playground has surprised
and disconcerted Americans by the strength
of its distinctive personality. At one time
it was possible for Americans to regard Canada
as an eccentric and touching survival
of British imperialism, a country fading until,
one day, it would become indistinguishable
from the United States. Older Americans —
and some older Canadians — still think
in this fashion. It is out of date.

MEN
OF
MARK

Men become great
as nations grow.
Prof. James W. Robertson, 1910

Sir John A.
Master-Builder of Canada

The dream of *the* Father of Confederation
was to shape one great and unified nation from
a handful of British colonies

By Bruce Hutchison

John Alexander Macdonald, one of the most decisive figures in North American history, was a magnificent paradox. As widely known for his scandalous public conduct as for his political acumen, he emerges in history as the Canadian counterpart of his great contemporary, Abraham Lincoln. For it was Macdonald who welded Canada into a union.

Today, few of the problems of Canadian-U.S. relations are understandable without some knowledge of Macdonald's life and work. It was he who permanently bisected the continent and made a separate nation north of the United States. Yet it was, in a sense, the United States that made Macdonald. This roistering public actor and melancholy private person might never have achieved his dream of a Canadian nation but for the upheavals of the American Civil War. He might, in fact, never have become more than a small-town politician except for an incident of American intrusion at the very beginning of his career.

In 1838, Macdonald, then a gangling homely lawyer of 23 in Kingston, Ont., already addicted to liquor, undertook the defense of a small group of Americans who had crossed the St. Lawrence River and invaded Canada to rescue it, as they thought, from the tyranny of Queen Victoria. Though Macdonald's principal defendant was condemned to death, the young lawyer's courage in taking a case that could ruin his budding political career won him the admiration of Kingston's voters. Moreover, the abortive invasion brought him the sharp realization that Canada must be united to resist the pressures of her powerful neighbor.

The Canada of those days was a British colony that consisted of a few muddy towns along the St. Lawrence, some half-cleared farms and, beyond them, the wilderness. It embraced the modern provinces of Ontario and Quebec, united in 1841. On the Atlantic coast there were still the four separate colonies of Nova Scotia, New Brunswick, Prince Edward Island and Newfoundland, which quarreled among themselves and regarded Canada as a remote foreign country. And by 1844 the colonial legislature of Canada was already coming to a dangerous deadlock between British Protestants and French Catholics.

The apprentice Conservative politician whom Kingston sent to the legislature was born in Scotland in 1815. When he was five, his parents brought him to Canada; he spent only about five years in formal schools. His chief qualification for leadership was what he had learned about his fellowmen in books, in the Kingston courts, in too many barrooms. His gaudy clothes and genial raillery, his addiction to bawdy jokes, made him seem a buffoon. Many saw only the mane of black curls, the disarming grin, the jaunty figure announcing from the platform that Canada preferred Macdonald drunk to his chief enemy, George Brown, sober. But others saw in the stricken eyes and prematurely lined face the lonely husband who sat at night beside an invalid wife, the distraught father mourning his first son, dead from a fall at the age of 13 months.

Progress toward Macdonald's goal of a great and unified Canada was slow and tortuous. In middle age, he was still in the political opposition. His work apparently had ended in failure. But over the years, with his great French-Canadian ally, Georges-Etienne Cartier, he had been quietly devising Canada's first coherent political party—an unwritten coalition between the British and French moderates —as opposed to the divided groups calling themselves Reformers.

Up to now he had worked largely by hunch and a strategy of postponement that had given him the nickname "Old Tomorrow," but in his Liberal Conservative Party, a loose union of the two Canadian ethnic groups, he had hit upon the only possible method of governing a future nation and a dual society. His ideas gradually won acceptance, and in 1857 he became premier of the colony.

Macdonald saw clearly that the scattered and divided colonies of British North America had no future apart. For different reasons, another frontier

Sir John poses with admirers
outside Ohsweken council
house near Brantford, Ont.,
as Indians make him a
chief of the Six Nations.

politician had reached a parallel conclusion about his own divided country. And the work of Lincoln was shortly to alter drastically the career of the Canadian.

Macdonald dreaded the new U.S. President's power as commander in chief of the world's largest army during the Civil War. What if the Union Army turned northward after defeating the South? The American government had quarreled, almost to the point of war, with Britain as the tacit friend of the Confederacy. Some senators in Washington proposed reprisals on the helpless British colonies.

This fear of the Republic in arms was now shared by Macdonald's political adversaries. The colonial legislature, meeting in Quebec City, had reached final deadlock. Macdonald held in his hand an order from the British Governor General dissolving the legislature when he learned that George Brown, lea-

der of the Reformers and his lifelong enemy, was now willing to join forces with him.

The two men had not spoken together outside the legislature for many years and loathed each other, but Macdonald did not hesitate. He thrust the royal order into a drawer and hurried to Brown's hotel room. An hour's talk created a joint government whose single purpose was to unite all the British colonies in some kind of confederation. The announcement of these plans turned the legislature into a riot of rejoicing.

For Macdonald, the stern puritanical personality of Brown was annoying but manageable. For Brown, the public morals and private habits of Macdonald were scandalous but endurable. With this understanding, the ill-matched pair barnstormed through the Atlantic colonies. In 1864, after months of speeches, banquets and promises of political patronage they assembled, at Quebec, the group known to history as the Fathers of Confederation.

The supreme turning point of Canada's affairs, and Macdonald's, had been reached. He knew it. As manipulator of the Quebec Conference he surprised everyone by his sobriety, eloquence and knowledge of constitutional problems. He used his legal skill to argue the details of a national constitution all day; at night he charmed the bickering delegates with his droll stories, promised them jobs in the future government or terrified them with threats of U. S. power. In the end, though he usually scribbled the notes for his speeches on envelopes, which he invariably mislaid, the Canadian constitution written at Quebec was almost all his work, set down in his untidy handwriting and carried away in his valise. It set the stage for a single country named after the largest colony—Canada.

Macdonald, Cartier, Brown and Alexander Galt took the draft of the constitution to London for cabinet approval. Brown discovered in his old foe an irresistible companion. Never a good hater, Macdonald flattered him, captivated him over the card table, almost grew to like him and wrote home

Macdonald's second wife, Susan Agnes, had been a family friend of his youth. They were wed soon after a chance meeting on a London street.

jokingly about "the old chap" who was three years his junior. The curious partnership of humor and righteousness quickly secured the assent of a British government as frightened as the Canadians of American power. This seemed to call for a celebration. Macdonald and Brown went off to the Derby where even the austere reformer enjoyed the refreshments. From their carriage they assaulted the race-track crowds with pea shooters and bags of flour.

Known as the British North America Act, when it was later formally passed by the British Parliament, the constitution was really the foundation of the modern Commonwealth, though no one then foresaw this long-range result.

The Dominion of Canada, proclaimed at Ottawa on July 1, 1867, amid cannon salutes, bonfires and orations, included only the four provinces of Ontario, Quebec, Nova Scotia and New Brunswick. The boy from Kingston who had become its first prime minister and a Knight Commander of the Bath— Sir John A., as he was known thenceforth—knew that his nation was as yet only a structure of paper documents.

Even at its birth, the Atlantic colonies had threatened to secede. On the western plains the halfbreed buffalo hunters who styled themselves the Metis Nation were linked by trade only with the American states to the south and seemed likely to join them. Beyond the Rockies the impoverished gold-rush colony of British Columbia, squeezed between the new American territory of Alaska and booming Oregon, had not entered the Confederation and was inclined to join the United States.

If the legal skeleton of Confederation was to be fleshed, its sovereignty must stretch from Atlantic to Pacific. The first step was to lure British Columbia into joining. Macdonald resolved to pay a high price for it—an impossible price, his opponents protested in panic. He would build a railway from the St. Lawrence all the way to the Pacific coast!

In an era of reckless chances the old gambler had

British Columbians hoped for no more than a wagon road through their awesome mountains. But Macdonald, with his dream of a nation coast to coast, offered a railway. Lord Strathcona drove the transcontinental Golden Spike at 9:30 a.m. November 7, 1885, at lonely Craigellachie in the Rockies.

"A railway to articulate the nation's disjointed limbs," Bruce Hutchison wrote of the CPR. Mountain Creek Bridge in B.C. contained 1,500,000 feet of timber.

taken his ultimate plunge. Fewer than four million Canadians were to finance North America's most difficult railway—around the badlands of the Great Lakes, across the prairies, through the unmapped Rockies, down to the Pacific. But, as he had expected, the British Columbians, hoping for nothing more than a wagon road, grasped his offer and joined Canada. It was to be make or break—a railway or no permanent nation.

It was nearly break. Unknown to Macdonald, his correspondence with the Montreal railway syndicate was stolen from a lawyer's safe and delivered to the opposition party in Parliament. To win the election of 1872 he had sought campaign funds from the syndicate and signed, probably while drunk, a fatal telegram: "I must have another ten thousand. Will be last time of calling. Do not fail."

The opposition leaped on that telegram. After many narrow escapes Old Tomorrow was now at last defeated. Although campaign funds from government contractors were nothing new in the sordid politics of the era, Macdonald's supporters abandoned him in pretended horror. The damning evidence was uncovered, letter by letter. The Pacific Scandal wrecked the government, apparently Macdonald's career, and the railway, too.

To the new government of Liberal Alexander Mackenzie the railway scheme seemed financial lunacy. It laid bits and pieces of track here and there, but British Columbia, regarding this temporizing as betrayal, was ready to withdraw from the Confederation. Was Macdonald's work of nationhood, like his career, to collapse unfinished? Sick at heart, he sat in the opposition benches, looking like a faded historical relic, a shrunken ghost of his great days, and watched the new government flounder.

His enemies said Old Tomorrow's day was done. What they failed to see was Macdonald's inner core of steel. They had never understood that all his jokes and persiflage, his ribald campaign speeches and his questionable backroom traffic hid a passionate resolve, a private vision of nationhood.

Reformer George Brown, long a political foe of Macdonald, joined Sir John in a "curious partnership of humor and righteousness"— and Canada was born.

Gradually this big dream of Canada returned to him with a new power born of mistakes and chastisement. The people felt it at once. From town to town the reviving warrior carried the battle into his enemy's camp. He made good use of the political picnic and, amid laden tables of country food, greeted local voters by their first names, remembered their wives and, from a rough platform or a wagon, aroused them with his word picture of a Canadian state stretching from sea to sea.

The gaunt, stooped figure, the mane of curls now white, the face more deeply lined, the bulbous nose redder, the eyes full of laughter and the voice of conviction, became a myth overtopping the man. His pranks were the street-corner gossip and family joke of the nation. It heard with delight that he had punched an opponent for questioning his word on the hustings, had been restrained by the sergeant-at-arms in Parliament before he could pursue a duel of honor, had shouted at a heckler, "I can lick you as quick as hell can singe a feather!"

These lapses were infrequent and generally exag-

Sick and spent, old Sir John fought the winter election of 1891—and won again. That June he died. Across the country and at his funeral in Ottawa (below) millions felt a great loss: "Their grief, their affection, their forgiveness of his frailties were the only monument he needed."

gerated. In fact, he was working harder and drinking less than ever before. A majority of Canadians soon forgave the Pacific Scandal. If anyone could save Confederation, its founder was the man. Within five years he was returned to power.

Macdonald realized that the railway must be pushed to the Pacific, whatever its cost. But he also knew that the unnatural east-west Canadian economy, erected against the north-south commercial pull of the continent, must fail if it could not be stimulated, and the stimulant must be drastic.

During his first months in office, tariffs were raised to protect Canada's "infant industries" and to encourage the movement of goods from east to west. These measures might be highly questionable economics in the long run but, in the short, Macdonald advocated them as the only chance for the nation's survival. Wise or unwise, what Macdonald called the "national policy" would live until our time as a key factor in Canadian-American relations.

A new syndicate was formed to undertake the gigantic task of completing the railway. Tracks were laid at breakneck speed across the prairies and through the Rockies. The last spike of the Canadian

Pacific Railway was driven on November 7, 1885. The prime minister was soon riding through the Rockies on the cowcatcher of a locomotive, and Canada could claim to be in business as a transcontinental state.

The old warrior died in harness. Ignoring his doctor's advice, the prime minister, then a man of 76, depleted and sick, dragged himself through the hard winter election of 1891, marched with the bands and the torchlights. But even as the voters gave him another term of power he lay paralyzed in his house beside the Ottawa River. The Canadian people, who had learned to love him as much for his faults as his virtues, could hardly imagine their nation without him. Expectantly they waited for some final word from Sir John A.

None came, and perhaps none was needed. The message of his long, triumphant but tortured life was known to all Canadians. He had conceived his own dream of Canada and bequeathed it to his countrymen.

Ottawa
A Queen's Choice

By Gustave Lanctôt

Ottawa was a rough, tough lumber town when Queen Victoria picked it in 1857 to be the capital of her united colony of Canada East and Canada West— today's Quebec and Ontario. To the fewer than 14,000 Canadians who lived there, the former By- town seemed an unlikely choice, but the exercise of the royal prerogative in faraway England had a double advantage. It eliminated capital-city rivalry between Toronto and Montreal, both of which coveted the honor, and it located the government of the would-be nation relatively far from the United States border, safe from military invasion. Even so, Canada's MP's were far from unanimously enthusiastic about Victoria's decision: Parliament ratified it by only 64 votes to 59.

But that was enough. Now, where would Parliament meet? On the hill at the center of the town a handsome stone building was started in 1858. Eight years later, on June 8, 1866, Parliament moved in. Twelve months after that, Confederation: the first of many great occasions celebrated by a larger Canada on the lawns of Parliament Hill.

In 1916, disaster. On February 3 fire destroyed everything but the walls and the library of the proud first home of the Canadian Parliament.

But on the same lofty site there soon arose a big- ger, six-story building cut by a multitude of win- dows, bristling with gargoyles and dominated by the 300-foot Peace Tower with its carillon of 53 bells pealing across the historic Ottawa River and beyond to the green hills of the Gatineau.

The vaulted Hall of Honor (upper right) leads from Confederation Hall to the door (background) of the Parliamentary Library. The beauty of the stonework and intricacy of the carving is shown in a wide-angle view (right) of Confederation Hall, just inside the main entrance of the Houses of Parliament.

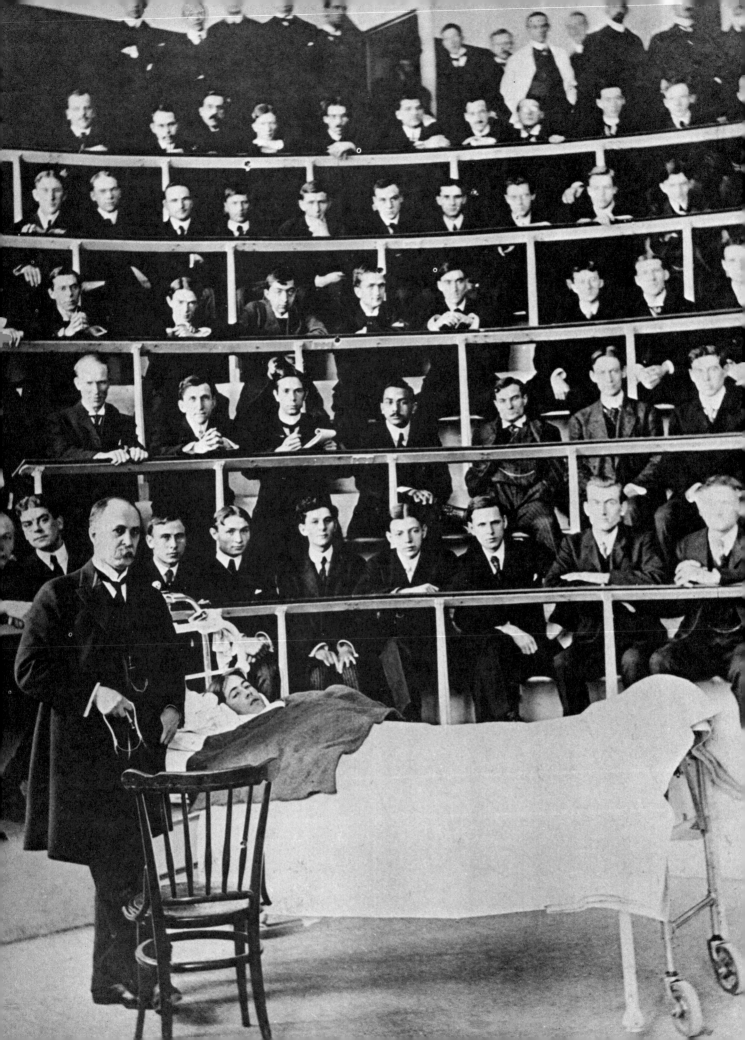

"The World's Best Doctor"

Among his many innovations—bringing medical students
to the patient. But William Osler was great not only for what
he did but for what he *was*

By Richard Match

William Osler discovered no miraculous cure or wonder drug. Yet at his death in 1919 he was the most beloved physician since Luke. And 30 years later an article in *The Journal of the American Medical Association* said: "The years have added to his glory. No one has in any way taken his place as the world's best doctor."

Diagnostic wizardry, brilliant research, writing and teaching—these constituted Osler's tangible achievements. The revolutionary methods he brought to medical schools have probably saved as many lives as the conquest of typhoid. He was great not alone for what he did, however, but for what he was: he was master of the art of ministering to a patient's troubled mind as well as to his sick body.

William Osler (the first syllable rhymes with *dose*) was born in a Bondhead, Ont., parsonage in 1849, the last of eight children of the Rev. Featherstone Osler. At 15 he was expelled from the village school for unscrewing the desks from the floor one night and piling them in the attic. Transferred to Trinity College boarding school, he came under the influence of two remarkable men: the school warden, W. A. Johnson, an Anglican clergyman who studied natural science as a hobby; and the school physician, Dr. James Bovell, a medical man who late in life entered the ministry. The examples of these men provided the two main streams of influence in Osler's life: unswerving devotion to science and profound religious faith.

Few medical schools of the time owned a microscope, but Dr. Bovell did. He and Dr. Johnson trained the eager young Osler in its use. Shortly after he entered Trinity College proper to study for the Anglican ministry, Osler published several authoritative articles on microscopic fresh-water animals. A year later he told his disappointed father that he had decided to become a doctor.

Graduating from McGill Medical School, in Montreal, Osler went to Germany, Austria and England for further study. In a London laboratory he became fascinated in the study of irregular clumps which form in blood after it is drawn from the body. Others had noticed the clumping, but Osler was the first to observe that in circulating blood there were colorless globoid bodies which he called "the third corpuscle." Since these globes clumped after exposure to air, he concluded accurately that the bodies (now known as blood platelets) played an important role in clotting. Announcement of this significant scientific discovery brought him so much acclaim that McGill called him home to become, at 24, professor of physiology.

The "boy professor" immediately converted a cloakroom into a laboratory, McGill's first. Then he spent $600, half of his annual income, to buy a dozen microscopes for his students. Without appearing in the least rushed, he took on innumerable extra jobs, including those of librarian and registrar of the Medical School. New medical journals and societies seemed to sprout in his path; he probably founded more of both, and attended more meetings, than any other doctor in history.

Trichinosis was considered a rare disease in Canada—there were then only four cases on record. But from his boyhood examination of farm animals' viscera under the microscope Osler knew that the trichina worm turned up more often than his elders suspected and was probably sapping the strength of countless Canadians. Now, with his own laboratory, the young professor decided to attack trichinosis; he volunteered to perform autopsies for any doctor who would let him. Soon he was averaging 100 post-mortems a year.

Infected pork had been found to be the source of trichinosis in Europe, so for eight months Osler and a student veterinarian, A. W. Clements, haunted Montreal's slaughterhouses, performed more than a thousand autopsies on hogs. Finding dozens infected, they demanded that municipal meat inspection be instituted and that the public be educated to cook pork thoroughly. This was the first of many campaigns which were to make Osler the most effective public-health crusader of his time.

Through his autopsies young Osler was acquiring

a training in pathology that few practicing physicians could match. He reasoned, however, that he could accomplish more if, in addition to studying the organs of those who died, he could study living patients and link their outward symptoms with an abnormal condition of some one internal organ. But living patients were hard to come by; McGill considered young Dr. Osler purely a laboratory man and would not permit him to examine patients in the wards of the affiliated hospital.

The smallpox ward of the hospital was then being supervised on a rotating basis by several all-too-reluctant physicians. Osler volunteered to take charge of it —and thus got his first opportunity to work with sick people. (He also got smallpox—a mild case, fortunately.) Soon he talked his superiors into giving him charge of a noncontagious ward as well.

Hospitals were expected to be gloomy buildings in those days. Osler changed all that. He began by ordering flowers and a coat of pastel paint for the wards. Then he went to work on his patients. He gave them little medicine but "lavish doses of optimism," practicing psychosomatic medicine long before the term was invented. "The miracles at Lourdes and Ste. Anne de Beaupré," he once wrote, "are often genuine. We physicians use the same power every day. It will not raise the dead; it will not put in a new eye or knit a bone; but the healing power of belief has great value when carefully applied in suitable cases."

"To the astonishment of everyone," recalls a Montreal doctor, "the chronic beds at McGill, instead of being emptied by disaster, were emptied rapidly through recovery, and new cases stayed but a short time. It was one of the most forceful lessons in treatment ever demonstrated."

Innovations like these spread Osler's reputation beyond Canada and he was offered a medical professorship at the University of Pennsylvania. Undecided, he flipped a coin; it fell "heads" for Philadelphia. Thus, casually, American medicine was set on the road to its present excellence.

Osler's students at Pennsylvania hardly knew what to make of this medium-sized, athletic-looking Canadian with receding black hair, a big drooping mustache and a taste for brilliant neckties. Instead of mounting a lecture platform, as was the professorial practice, he hitched himself up on a handy table, confessed that he hated to prepare lectures and announced that he couldn't teach without a patient for a text anyway. "To study the phenomena of disease without books is to sail an uncharted sea," he stated; "but to study books without patients is not to go to sea at all."

Accordingly, he introduced a thin young man and told the class to see for themselves what a real live case of anemia looked like. Patients illustrating other diseases followed, all lucidly analyzed by Osler. The medical students were electrified; it was the first time most of them had ever tapped a patient's chest, listened to a heartbeat or examined blood under a microscope. For at that time (1884) no medical school in the United States offered effective "on-the-job" bedside teaching. "It makes one's blood boil," Osler fumed, "to think that there are sent out year by year scores of men called doctors who have never attended a case of labor or seen the inside of a hospital ward."

Not content with bringing patients to his students, Osler now brought students to patients. For the first time anywhere, medical students entered hospital wards freely, as much a part of the team as interns, nurses or attending physicians. They took case histories, examined patients (under close supervision, of course) and made tentative diagnoses which were confirmed or corrected by the experienced doctor in charge.

As Osler had predicted, the patients received better, more alert care than ever before, with fewer mistakes, thanks to the constant stimulus of inquiring young minds for whom diagnoses had to be checked and counterchecked. The cornerstone of all medical education today, William Osler's bedside teaching pays dividends in better medical care to every human being now alive.

Osler was a founder of the Johns Hopkins University School of Medicine in Baltimore, Md. He wrote 1200 books and articles—one every two weeks of his adult life.

In Baltimore the trustees of the will of a merchant prince named Johns Hopkins were now building the finest hospital and medical school on the continent. Searching Europe and America for physician-teachers, they chose William H. Welch to head their pathology department; Howard Kelly, gynecology; William Stewart Halsted, surgery; and William Osler, internal medicine. Of Johns Hopkins' famed "Big Four," the oldest, Osler, had not yet reached his 40th birthday.

From the day it opened in 1889, brilliant youngsters flocked to the new Baltimore center, and within a few years Osler's trainees in particular were eagerly sought from New York to San Francisco.

Dr. Osler's ward rounds, starting promptly at 9 a.m., were the high spot of the hospital day. Nurses, interns and visiting doctors made an admiring procession in his wake. Patients knew (they were supposed to know) a great man was coming to help them, and they smiled. For the children, to whom he was particularly devoted, he had a "secret" whistle, a prearranged signal to warn them of his approach.

Osler was an uncanny diagnostician, a bedside sleuth with few equals. He knew what to look for, and he took the time to find it. In one patient, for example, he suspected the presence of an arterial aneurysm—a dangerously dilated blood-vessel sac which, if it could be located, might be removed surgically. If not, it might hemorrhage fatally. Repeated physical examinations had failed to turn up the elusive sac when Osler appeared at the bedside.

For an hour, while interns grew restless, the Chief just sat there watching the sick man's chest and abdomen. Finally he said, "Let's try swinging the bed around to the far wall." Puzzled, the interns complied.

Lifting the window shade high, Osler studied his patient only a moment in the new light, then pointed to a spot on the chest wall. There, faintly but unmistakably shadowed by the slanting afternoon sunshine, was the telltale pulsation of the aneurysm no one else had been able to find.

Often Osler could diagnose quickly. Leading his students through a ward one morning, he passed the bed of a patient whom he had never seen before. Grasping the man's toes for an instant he waved good-by, and as soon as they were out of earshot he informed his startled retinue that the owner of the toes suffered from leakage of a heart valve. No undergraduate who saw him pull that diagnostic rabbit out of the hat ever forgot that this particular heart condition causes a distinctive jerky pulse, easily observed in the big toe.

Among the visiting doctors who followed Osler through the wards one day was an unknown young country surgeon from Minnesota. Osler's thorough study of patients, the constant use of scientific diagnostic aids like the microscope made a deep impression on him, and he came back many times with his brother. The brothers' name was Mayo.

Another young man used to wander over from the surgical department to watch Osler—a young man so impatiently outspoken about the work of other

39

A brilliant pathologist and diagnostician,
Osler knew what to look for, and how—
and that it might take time to find
it. This historic series of photos
is called "Osler at the Bedside."

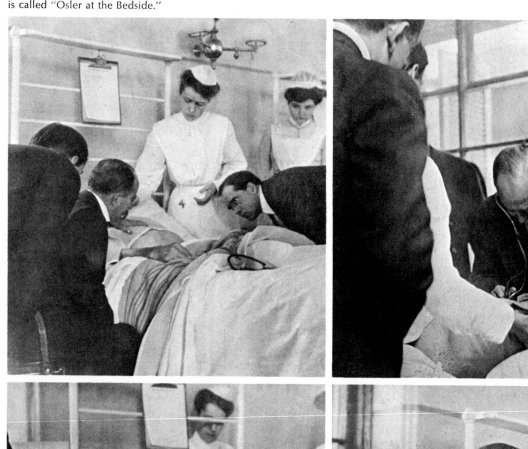

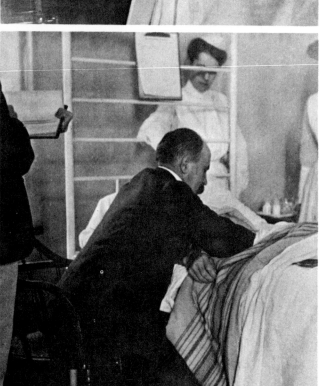

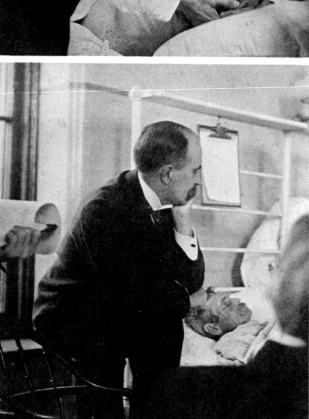

staff surgeons that rumor said his days at Johns Hopkins were numbered. Sensing his potential greatness, Osler gently suggested self-restraint. The hotheaded young man offered to resign. Next morning he had a note from Osler. "Do nothing of the kind" it said. "Who is free from faults? Your prospects here are A-1 and we need you." So it was that Harvey Cushing stayed at Johns Hopkins to blaze new trails in brain surgery and to become William Osler's devoted son in all but name.

Duties at Johns Hopkins were just part of Dr. Osler's activities. He was also president of the American Pediatric Society, author of a neurological study of cerebral palsy, an authority on angina pectoris and certain other circulatory ailments (one is still called Osler's disease), co-founder of the National Tuberculosis Association, of Christmas Seal fame. He was a crusader against malaria, typhoid and syphilis, and a pioneer advocate of better mental hospitals. Meanwhile, he wrote no fewer than 1200 books and articles, an amazing average of one every two weeks during his adult life. Some of them remain classics in their field, unexcelled even after years of medical advance.

In 1897 a Baptist minister in Montclair, N. J., read Osler's *Principles and Practice of Medicine* and was both enthralled and appalled. In it Osler had summed up all that medical science knew at that time, then bluntly declared there was much more it should know and didn't. The minister was Frederick Gates, who was an adviser to John D. Rockefeller, Sr. He discussed Osler's book with the great philanthropist and out of that conference grew the Rockefeller Institute for Medical Research and, later, the Rockefeller Foundation.

By 1905 Osler, besieged by sick people, working at a killing pace, concluded that if he were to retain his own health he would have to find a quieter post than Johns Hopkins. Medical schools all over America sought him; a Canadian millionaire offered McGill $1,000,000 if it could get him back. But his choice was made when King Edward VII appointed him Regius Professor of Medicine at Oxford. A few years later the King conferred on him the baronetcy which made him Sir William.

His first move in England was to make peace between London's two rival medical societies, which had not spoken to each other for 50 years. His second was to reintroduce bedside teaching to a nation which had neglected its potentialities. Osler took Britain to his heart, and she took him to hers.

Too old for front-line duty in World War I, Osler went into uniform as medical consultant to the Canadian and American Army hospitals in England, and unofficially earned the title of "Army Consoler General." He received hundreds of anxious cables from next of kin whose wounded soldiers were hospitalized in Britain. In each case he located and examined the wounded man. The Canadian Medical Corps adopted for parents the most reassuring form cable it could think of: "Your son has been seen by Osler and is doing well."

In August 1917 Sir William's own son and only child, 21-year-old Revere Osler, was gravely wounded at Ypres. Half a dozen of the American Army's greatest surgeons—Harvey Cushing and George Crile among them—sped to the scene. An operation was performed, but in vain. With heavy hearts they watched as the Chief's beloved boy was lowered into the earth of Flanders.

Following the Armistice, Sir William spent a year raising money to save the war-ravaged libraries of Belgium and to give aid to the starving children of "enemy" Austria. Then, in December 1919, worn out by his wartime activities and by grief for his son, he was unable to withstand an attack of pneumonia that followed recurrent attacks of bronchitis. Knowing more about the disease than his attending physicians, he realized how it would end for him, and faced death serenely.

After he died a slip of paper was found by his bed. On it he had written: "The Harbor almost reached after a splendid voyage, with such companions all the way, and my boy awaiting me."

41

Alexander Mackenzie
First Across Canada

This intrepid explorer changed the map and the future. Before the age of 30, he had discovered the mighty river system that bears his name and had blazed the first overland trail to the Pacific

By Bruce Hutchison

While his companions watched in silence, the 29-year-old Scot mixed some vermilion pigment in melted grease, then scrawled across a rock his title deed to the most prodigious feat of exploration in North America's history: "Alexander Mackenzie, from Canada, by land, the twenty-second of July, one thousand seven hundred and ninety-three." Though the words would soon be expunged by the Pacific gales, they proudly proclaimed that, for the first time, white men had crossed the continent.

No one can identify Mackenzie's rock today. It stands somewhere in Dean Channel, a coastal inlet north of Vancouver. It marks the end of an odyssey little known to most North Americans; yet it shaped the continental future. Thenceforth Britain could claim and hold the north Pacific coast by right of overland discovery.

Alexander Mackenzie was born on the Scottish island of Lewis in 1764. His mother died when he was still young, and his father took him to New York. At the beginning of the American Revolution the boy was moved to Montreal, where he attended school briefly and became an apprentice in the fur trade. His lean figure, handsome face and shrewd talent for business impressed his employers, and they sent him to Fort Chipewyan, their far western peltry of Athabasca, in what is now northern Alberta.

Soon after he arrived there, by canoe, his restless mind turned to the geography of the Canadian vasts. As a 25-year-old trader of the North West Company he shared its ambition to reach the Pacific and reap a precious new harvest of sea-otter pelts then being monopolized by Russians from Siberia. But he wanted more than that: he must see the ocean for himself. For other men, snug in distant cities, the Pacific was a commercial opportunity. For Mackenzie it was an obsession. He pored over the vague, chaotic charts drawn by his predecessors from Indian legend and their own wild guesses. Surely, he thought, the rivers flowing northward eventually turned west and emptied into the sea where four powers were about to collide. Russia held Alaska. Spain was in-

stalled in California. Seagoing Captain James Cook had claimed the whole shore line for Britain. An American, Captain Robert Gray, had sighted the mouth of the Columbia. If he, Alexander Mackenzie, could unlock the secret of America's interior, he might change everything.

Thus, on June 3, 1789, with 13 companions in three canoes, Mackenzie started north on a stream ending no one knew where. His surmise was false: the stream did not turn west. Instead, it took him to the Arctic Ocean. The vast Mackenzie river system had entered the world map.

This discovery—a voyage of nearly 3000 miles in 102 days—should have been sufficient achievement for one man's lifetime. It only tormented Mackenzie. His road to the Pacific still evaded him. Back at his fort for another winter of exile, he realized that if he was to reach the Pacific he must learn to calculate latitude and longitude, must know, every day, where he stood in the unmapped continental vacuum. With the consent of his employers, he paddled to

Lean, handsome Alexander Mackenzie made two momentous voyages into the unknown—to the Arctic Ocean in 1789 and through the Rockies to the far Pacific four years later.

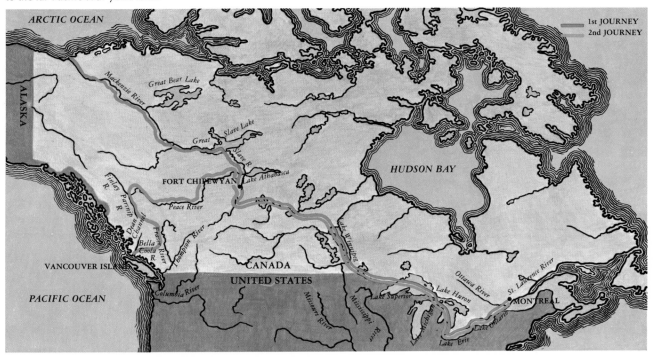

Montreal, sailed to England and spent half a year in study at his own expense. Returning to Canada in the spring of 1792, he brought with him some instruments and a heightened resolve to complete his search.

By autumn he was installed again at Fort Chipewyan and, on October 10, his party paddled out of Lake Athabasca into the current of the Peace River, which penetrated the high dike of the Rockies. At its headwaters they hoped to hit the unknown rivers flowing westward.

This time he had planned well. During the previous summer his men had built a camp on the bank of the Peace, and he wintered there. As soon as the ice broke in the spring, on May 9, he launched a single canoe into the brown swirl of the Peace. This shell of birchbark, affectionately described in his diary, was 25 feet long and "so light that two men could carry her on a good road three or four miles without resting." The men who climbed into the canoe with Mackenzie were Alexander Mackay (his

second-in-command), six French-Canadian paddlers—Joseph Landry, Charles Doucette, François Beaulieu, Baptiste Bisson, François Courtois and Jacques Beauchamp — and two Indian hunters.

At first the going was easy. Then, around the middle of May, the party encountered some of the worst water in America—the swirling vortex of the Peace River Canyon, a ditch 300 feet deep and 25 miles long. The canoe could not be paddled against the furious current; it had to be poled or dragged by a rope. Often it was unloaded and carried around the slippery cliffs from which large stones kept rolling down.

It took four days of toil to carry the canoe around Portage Mountain. The men, drenched with rain and numbed by constant wading in icy water, began to mutter among themselves that Mackenzie was leading them to certain destruction. Mackenzie himself was full of doubts.

At last the canyon was passed and the canoe relaunched. Only a few miles upstream, Mackenzie

43

beheld the river's great fork. Here was the largest decision of his voyage. Should he continue north-westward on the main channel, now called the Finlay, or turn south on its tributary, the Parsnip? Which would take Mackenzie to the fabled River of the West and on to the sea?

The men held for the Finlay—it was broad, smooth and safe, whereas the Parsnip looked narrow, swift and dangerous. But Mackenzie remembered the warning of an old Indian who had told him that the Finlay poured out of impenetrable mountains where no man could travel. The word of one nameless Indian was little enough to go on, but Mackenzie had no other clue. Against the unanimous advice of his crew, he chose the Parsnip. It was one of the most fateful choices in North American history.

The current of the Parsnip was too fast for paddles, too deep for poles; so, tortured by mosquitoes, alternately soaked by rain and stifled by heat, the voyagers clutched the overhanging branches and slowly pulled themselves upstream. Mackenzie heard his men whispering to one another that their only chance of success had been missed at the fork. He was almost ready to turn back and ascend the Finlay.

The questions were soon answered, by accident. As the canoe inched up the Parsnip, it was sighted by a hunting party of the Sekani Indians. They threatened the canoeists with bows and arrows. Ordering his men not to touch their guns, Mackenzie beached the canoe and, in sign language, invited the Sekanis to parley. They approached dubiously, bows taut and arrows pointed. At the sight of a few glass beads and other trinkets, however, their humor changed, and they talked to Mackenzie through his Indian interpreters. Where, he asked, would the Parsnip take him? They gestured toward the south. There another river flowed onward to the "stinking lake."

This was the party's first rumor of the ocean. They pushed on.

The Parsnip ended in a maze of little brooks, which could be the long-sought western watershed. On June 12 the canoe was taken from the water and carried 817 paces over a low hill to a small lake. White men had finally surmounted the Continental Divide north of the American plateaus.

But the River of the West still eluded them, and the fierce current of its tributary smashed their canoe on a rock. Nearly all their musket balls were lost, along with other equipment. The canoe was a wreck. Once again the men turned mutinous. Mackenzie said nothing until they had cooked a good meal and warmed themselves with rum; then he began to talk quietly. As to what he said, we have only the stilted record of his diary—"the honor of conquering disasters" and "the disgrace that would attend us on our return home without having attained the object of the expedition." But his actual words must have been something else. Once more his men were shamed into obedience.

Next day they stitched the canoe together with new bark and dragged through "a dreadful country" of morass and underbrush until, on June 18, they came to a broad current. The Fraser, as it is known today, bore them safely west.

Suddenly a flight of arrows showered from the bank. Again Mackenzie ordered his crew not to shoot, and stepped ashore alone. His daring gamble succeeded. After a brief argument among themselves, some of the Indians followed him back to the canoe, where he gave them presents of beads and knives. Mackenzie had discovered the warlike Carriers, a nation whose widows carried their dead husbands' bones on their backs.

The Carrier chief said that the river was long and treacherous and emptied into the "stinking lake" far to the south. But there was a trail to the west, he said. Four days by canoe and two days of easy walking, he suspected, would take the white men to the coast.

On July 4, the expedition started overland, each man carrying a pack of about 90 pounds. From Mac-

kenzie's notes it is impossible to fix his route. It turned out to be far longer than the Carrier chief had said. The weather turned cold and wet. The high mountains of the Rainbow Range loomed on the western horizon. The trail climbed upward across the divide where the snow was packed hard. Though it was midsummer, the men shivered under a wintry wind until they began moving downhill into the warm valley of the Bella Coola River, only 31 miles from the sea.

Late on the evening of July 17, they sighted a large encampment of Indians. They approached it cautiously. There was no need for alarm. The Indians were apparently expecting strange guests and had prepared a banquet of roasted salmon.

Despite his hospitality, the chief was anxious to get rid of the visitors. Their presence, he said, would frighten the salmon then surging up the river to be caught in huge traps of woven cedar roots. Mackenzie gladly accepted the loan of two dugout canoes, with crews to paddle them. These stout craft swept down the Bella Coola at a surprising speed.

Midnight sun highlights the wild labyrinthine beauty of the delta at the end of the vast river system that bears Mackenzie's name.

On July 19, Mackenzie arrived at the river's mouth. He tasted the water. It was salty; apparently they were in a long coastal inlet. At this point, the Indians refused to take their canoes farther. They put the white men ashore and paddled back up the river.

Mackenzie would not turn back: he was determined to see the ocean of his dreams. In a nearby Indian village, he was able to buy another canoe, leaky but serviceable. On July 20, the ten men in their clumsy craft lurched through a labyrinth of islands into Dean Channel. Suddenly, however, three canoes shot out of a hidden cove, and 15 Indians, all shouting angrily, overtook them.

In the wrangle that followed, Mackenzie gradually learned the cause of their hostility. The Indians said they were of the Bella Bella nation and had seen other whites in giant canoes at sea. Their chief complained bitterly that a white chief named "Macubah" had tried to kill him with a gun. For such a crime he intended to have his revenge. (Doubtless "Macubah" was the British navigator Captain George Vancouver, who had sailed up this coast not

long before, although Mackenzie knew nothing of this incident.) The Bella Bella chief ordered the white men ashore. Mackenzie had no option. Ten more canoes now appeared from nowhere. Mackenzie's men paddled to the beach, primed their guns and prepared to defend themselves. But the attack never came. At sunset the Indians unaccountably paddled away.

Mackenzie waited the night through. The next morning, he mixed his pigment of grease and red mineral dust, scrawled on the southeast face of the Dean Channel rock his "brief memorial." Then he led his men to the canoe and started home.

The return journey took only 33 days. On August 24, the inhabitants of Fort Chipewyan saw a canoe racing down the Peace River. Mackenzie had triumphed again. He had beheld both the Arctic Ocean and the Pacific Ocean, and he had come back without loss of a single life.

After wintering at Fort Chipewyan, Mackenzie paddled to Montreal in the spring, sailed to England and left the wilderness forever. The King of England knighted him. Ample profits from his partnership in the fur trade made him rich. A wife and children and a manor in Scotland made him happy.

Yet the wilderness had taken its full toll. The only living man who had touched both the northern and western shores of America became an invalid before middle age. He died on March 11, 1820, at the age of 56, while traveling home from Edinburgh. His signature on the Pacific rock had long since disappeared. But he and nine comrades had permanently changed the map and future of the New World.

He Discovered the Treasure of Great Bear Lake

Gilbert LaBine's persistence and imagination made
uranium available at a crucial moment in world history

By Francis and Katharine Drake

The arctic landscape sprawled under a pale May
sky. In the foreground lay a lake face, frozen like
flint. All around it saucers of snow sunk in prehis-
toric rockbed stretched to the horizon. In all this
harsh, brooding emptiness one solitary thing was
moving—a man in parka and steel creepers, clam-
bering up the rocky cliff which fringed a frozen inlet. Once on the summit the man settled his gaze on
the rocks around him, on a jet-black vein splashed
with green, orange and canary-yellow stains. He
picked up a fragment and stared at it, shook it,
tossed it aloft, felt its weight as the small black
lump thumped back in his mitt. In a second he had
unbuckled his miner's pick and raised it aloft. . . .

That solitary figure, pacing his claim across the
rooftop of the world on the morning of May 16,
1930, could not possibly anticipate the monstrous
forces dormant in those misshapen rocks, the staggering events that were to flow from their discovery.

And yet, but for this man and this moment, the
Atomic Age might have dawned elsewhere than on
this continent.

Gilbert LaBine, the man with the pick, was born
on his father's farm near Pembroke, Ont., in 1890.
His earliest memories were colored by prospectors
returning from the fabulous Klondike with tales of
bonanzas. Prospecting, he decided, was the life for
him.

LaBine was barely 15 when he kissed his mother
good-by and hastened after the throng that milled
around Cobalt, Ont., during the rich strikes of 1905.
In a few months, contrary to every law of probabil-
ity, he made a silver strike. Moreover, he sold it for
$5000, and old-timers were saying he had that lucky
instinct, a "natural nose" for ore. He was still not
17 when, uncovering a second silver strike, he
spurned an offer of $25,000, only to find his vein too
low-grade to repay extraction. Ignorance of geology

The Eldorado mine in the
1930's. It was built soon after
Gilbert LaBine's discovery.

had led him to miscalculate. He needed something more than a natural nose, he realized. He needed a mining education.

Earning his living from camp to camp, young La-Bine edged into field lectures by government experts, fingered samples in assay offices, memorized the multicolored mineral maps of Canada, studied every pamphlet and textbook he could lay hands on. Before others of his age had finished college he had acquired a practical and scientific background rare among Canadian prospectors.

In 1913 a famed geologist, Dr. W. G. Miller, was trying to arouse interest in a newly discovered ore, pitchblende—the source of radium. The price of radium was then $120,000 a gram, the entire world supply measurable in ounces.

Miller had identified pitchblende in Canadian ores, but in infinitesimal amounts. LaBine sent for samples from abroad and studied the physical properties of this strangely heavy mineral, remarking the bubble structure and the queer green and yellow alterations of its uranium component.

It took more than 15 years to put this esoteric knowledge to use — but the miracle *did* happen. La-Bine had done well in those years. With substantial successes in gold, silver and copper, and a reputation second to none in Northwest mining circles, he had become president of Eldorado Gold Mines Ltd. In 1928 LaBine outlined a daring proposal to the stockholders.

For years he had figured that the rich lodes covering Ontario and the awakening Great Slave belt swept on through the uninhabited Northwest to the frozen fringes of the Arctic Ocean. Directly in their path slumbered the Lake of the Great Bear, a land-locked basin almost the size of Newfoundland. Indian trappers had brought back tales of cliff formations — and cliffs, LaBine knew, suggested outcrops. But outcrops of what? Gold, silver? Perhaps another Klondike?

Moreover, LaBine informed his stockholders, he believed it possible to penetrate the area by plane. It

Ten tons of concentrated ore, treated with 50 tons of chemicals, produce this handful of radioactive crystals containing one-28th of an ounce of radium.

is a measure of his reputation that the company approved the first air prospecting in the Northwest Territories, an unprecedented venture which involved the mushing-in of Indian teams months in advance to plant fuel caches, following wilderness maps so vague that they omitted bodies of water wider than the English Channel.

The one-man scouting expedition was landed on Great Bear Lake in the summer of 1929. When veteran bush pilot "Punch" Dickens returned for his lone passenger some weeks later, he found La-Bine tired and baffled. He had followed outcrops along the 80 miles of shore line—copper, lead, cobalt, a little silver. But nothing to stir the blood. Westward, through Fort Norman, lay the route back. LaBine gazed, however, as though mesmerized, toward Great Bear's faraway eastern shore. "How's the gas?" he demanded suddenly. One

Governor General Lord Tweedsmuir
(standing) addresses an Eldorado
banquet in Ottawa in 1936. From left:
Maj. Gen. A. G. L. McNaughton,
president of the National Research
Council; Dr. Charles Camsell, deputy
minister of mines and resources
and commissioner of the Northwest
Territories; Lord Tweedsmuir;
Harry M. Snyder, treasurer of Eldorado
Gold Mines; Prime Minister
Mackenzie King and Gilbert LaBine.

cache still untouched, Dickens reported. "Let's take a quick peek over there," LaBine said.

Buzzing the eastern shore line from 500 feet La-Bine saw, almost in the last mile, an abundance of colorations which swarmed out of nowhere and abruptly vanished—green, yellow, orange, *black!* He could almost swear to it — a ribbon of black, across a neck of land near a small island.

"I'll spend next year making a systematic survey of that eastern shore," LaBine told his stockholders. "If you want to fade, okay. It will cost real money." Again his backers gave him a green light.

It was March 28, 1930, when LaBine, with his old friend and fellow prospector, E. C. St. Paul, returned to Great Bear Lake. An account of the next seven weeks belongs in another story. To the prospector it is all in a lifetime — the cold, edged like a knife, the mushing over snow and ice, the perilous inland sorties, the endless disappointments.

On the morning of May 16 St. Paul awoke to feel a stabbing at his eyeballs, his vision a pain-filled blur. He was snowblind. It might last days or weeks. Hurriedly applying tea-leaf poultices, LaBine spent

hour after hour battling the inflammation; finally the treatment showed results. St. Paul was still blind, but the pain was lessening. He could be left for an hour or two.

LaBine decided to cross-section the area around the camp. It lay in the shelter of a promontory that tapered westward to the lake. Moving cautiously on steel creepers, LaBine began to cut across the frozen hogback. He reached the top without incident. Then, all at once, his heart was hammering. A few hundred feet beyond him lay an inlet with a little island. And there, skittering across a long-remembered headland (now famous as LaBine Point) shone anew that bedeviling streak of black.

Half an hour later LaBine's impatient pick dislodged a chunk of pitchblende the size of a wastebasket. Clear across it loomed its credentials—the bubble-like structure, the orange, green and yellow alterations of uranium. The seam on which he stood was nearly two *yards* wide, a prodigal contrast to the tiny samples he had studied. All around him lay rocks shot with the eerie cobalt "bloom" of intense mineralization. As LaBine began to trail the

Gilbert LaBine's accomplishments helped change history and the lives of all men.

winding vein, he came suddenly across a cliff of copper nearly 100 feet high. In another 50 paces he had uncovered sprawling lodes of cobalt, manganese, nickel, incredible clusters of pure bismuth.

Moving like a man in a dream, he came on a vein of high-grade silver ore, 20 feet across. And there, beyond it, was suddenly not just one black ribbon but another! And still another! Three pitchblende outcrops! He had discovered the richest source of radium and uranium in the world.

LaBine dropped his pick and took a deep breath. At long last a dream come true — radium for everybody. He did not realize, of course, the further power locked inside this ore; he could not know that on the strength of this black rock billions of dollars would be spent, vast plants would be built.

During the '30's, this man who pioneered the Western Hemisphere's first pitchblende refinery broke the international radium monopoly single-handed and forced a $45,000 reduction in the price of every gram of radium. Then, in 1939, the splitting of the uranium atom sounded the start of the big race among nuclear physicists to fit a key into the lock of atomic fission. By 1940 Nazi institutes had swept aside other projects, spurring their top-flight researchers to furious efforts. By 1941 British and American scientists were close behind them. In 1942 Enrico Fermi and his Chicago group shot triumphantly ahead, achieved the first nuclear chain reaction. Now only one vital question mark barred the undertaking of the United States atomic energy program. Where was the necessary quantity of raw material?

Amazingly, it was at hand. As early as May 1942 practically pure uranium oxide was ready for delivery from LaBine's Arctic mine — several tons a month then, and soon the amount was doubled.

Realizing the critical importance of a uranium stockpile in the international race, LaBine, even before the chain reaction was effected, had started full-scale production. To carry out this plan over the disapproval of banks and stockholders, he and his brother Charles put up all of their private fortunes, nearly a million dollars. The extent to which this patriotic action speeded completion of the atom bomb has never been disclosed.

In January 1944 the Arctic holdings (now depleted) and the secret refineries at Port Hope, Ont., had been expropriated by Ottawa from the 3500 stockholders of Eldorado Gold Mines Ltd. to become the exclusive — and most powerful — property of the people of Canada.

In the summer of 1952, LaBine's company, Gunnar Gold Mines Ltd., laid claim to another rich pitchblende deposit. This time it was uranium.

The years brought LaBine many honors. A former governor of the University of Toronto, he was awarded the Curie medal for the fight against cancer, and the Order of the British Empire and he received an honorary doctor of law degree from the University of Western Ontario.

But the treasure of Great Bear Lake remains his greatest monument. In all history there have been few cases where the actions of one individual affected the lives of so many of his fellow men.

"In Flanders Fields"

In three immortal verses, Col. John McCrae
voiced the war dead's challenge to the living

By Bernhard Ragner

On January 28, 1918, three years after being gassed in the Second Battle of Ypres, the man who wrote World War I's greatest poem in English died of pneumonia and meningitis in a British military hospital in northern France. Next day they buried Col. John McCrae among his comrades in the military cemetery at Wimereux, his immortality and theirs assured by the three sublime verses of "In Flanders Fields."

McCrae, born in Guelph, Ont., in 1872, served as a gunner in the South African War, then was a doctor in Montreal and a lecturer at McGill University before rejoining the Army in 1914 as a medical officer. He reached Flanders in 1915 as Major Mc-Crae, brigade surgeon of the 1st Brigade, Canadian Field Artillery.

His superb poem was penciled during a lull in battle on May 3, 1915, on a page torn from a dispatch book. McCrae sent the poem to *Punch* anonymously and the editor, recognizing its beauty, printed it in heavy-leaded type, which *Punch* used only on great occasions. As if by miracle the verses reached the outer fringes of the earth in record time.

McCrae's commanding officer, Maj. Gen. E. W. B. Morrison, wrote:

"This poem was literally born of fire and blood during the hottest phase of the Second Battle of Ypres. My headquarters were in a trench on the top of the bank of the Ypres Canal, and John had his dressing station in a hole dug in the foot of the bank. During periods in the battle, wounded men actually rolled down the bank into his dressing station. Many times during the 16 days of battle he and I watched the chaplains burying their dead whenever there was a lull.

"Thus, the crosses, row on row, grew into a good-sized cemetery. We often heard the larks in the morning singing high in the air, between the crash of the shells and the reports of the guns in the battery just beside us. John told me that he had written the poem between the arrival of batches of wounded."

John McCrae's grave is No. 3 in Row 4 of Plot 4 in the military section of Wimereux Communal Cemetery near Boulogne. In the cemetery is a memorial stone seat erected in the mid-1920s by the Canadian Clubs and friends of McCrae in Canada and the United States. McCrae House, the Guelph (Ont.) cottage in which the soldier-doctor-poet was born, was acquired in 1966 by the Colonel John McCrae Birthplace Society and is now a national historic site.

John McCrae was a gunner
in the South African War,
a medical officer in World War I.
He wrote his immortal verses during a lull
in the Second Battle of Ypres.

IN FLANDERS FIELDS

In Flanders fields the poppies blow
Between the crosses, row on row,
That mark our place; and in the sky
The larks, still bravely singing, fly
Scarce heard amid the guns below.

We are the Dead. Short days ago
We lived, felt dawn, saw sunset glow,
Loved, and were loved, and now we lie
In Flanders fields.

Take up our quarrel with the foe:
To you from failing hands we throw
The Torch; be yours to hold it high.
If ye break faith with us who die
We shall not sleep, though poppies grow
In Flanders fields.

John McCrae

In his original, Colonel McCrae wrote,
"In Flanders fields the poppies blow."
Later, in a signed copy, he changed
"blow" to "grow." There were also
minor changes in punctuation.

"He Taught Us How To Live"

At remarkable, ragtag Notre Dame College in Saskatchewan,
Father Athol Murray's classes hum with informality
and blunt talk and boys learn to major in life

By Frank Germann

On a soft July morning in 1936, I knelt reverently in a Roman Catholic confessional in the small Saskatchewan town of Rouleau. I was 13 then, and scared stiff of the tough little priest in front of me. Not that I'd done any grievous wrong; it was just that you never knew what to expect from Father Athol Murray.

People said he had "the mind of a Greek scholar, the vocabulary of a dock worker and the soul of a saint." We boys worshiped him and stood in awe of him. He knew everything about sports; he was handsome, short but with powerful shoulders and thick black hair; he could cuss and fight; and he could size you up at a glance.

Now those knowing eyes were fixed on me as I timidly began the ritual words, "Bless me, Father, for I have sinned . . ."

"Hold it, Frank!" cried Father Murray. "Have you ever thought of coming to Notre Dame?"

I stopped, aghast. *Nobody* should interrupt confession. Anyway, his question was preposterous. Of course I'd thought of Notre Dame. Everyone in western Canada knew about Athol Murray's miracle: how, in the heart of the Depression, he'd built a high school and college on the bald prairie in the neighboring village of Wilcox, 30 miles south of Regina. Any boy or girl lucky enough to be admitted could get a sound education. You didn't have to be Roman Catholic or a genius, but you had to convince Father Murray that you truly *wanted* to make something of your life. I was eager to continue school, but I knew I would soon have to quit and find work.

"We can't afford it," I told him.

Father Murray smiled. "At Notre Dame," he said, "we don't let money worry us. Pay what you can. God will take care of the rest." Full of enthusiasm, he talked of his college and my future. Within minutes, I was on fire with his dream. Athol Murray had forever changed my life as he has countless others.

That autumn, carrying my own bedding as required, I entered Notre Dame of Wilcox. I'm still there, as a teacher, and still my awe grows daily for the priest we all call "Père."

His campus is a ragtag collection of buildings among dirt streets and scrub grass in a windswept town of 300 people. We haul our drinking water ten miles by truck. Food is so plain that one newcomer called it "good preparation for a concentration camp." Yet none of us, old grads or freshmen, would trade rough-and-ready Notre Dame for any other college in the land. "Whatever Father Murray sets out to do," a University of Ottawa rector once said, "is always so great, so profound that you never forget."

Ken Kerchner remembers. His parents' home had been sold for taxes and the family was on relief when Père admitted him. Now a prosperous building contractor, he says, "I love the man. It's as simple as that."

The college was full when another priest brought in Ed Grant, 14 and penniless. "Find the little mucker a bed," Père said. When Grant got his Bachelor of Arts degree, Père scratched up money to send him to law school. Ed now has his own law firm in Regina. "Everything I am," he says, "I owe to Father Murray."

Indeed, most of us owe whatever we are to Père. He goaded us into getting higher degrees, scrounged money to help us through, found us jobs. But his gift to us was much more than the tools for making a living. He taught us *how* to live.

Hunched and white-haired now in his late 70's, he still majors in life. Roaring with laughter, eyes darting with excitement, sipping Scotch from an unwashed glass, his inevitable cigarette dripping ashes down his paunch, he demonstrates the ancient art of conversation day and night. He reigns in a tiny office as richly assorted as he is: walls lined with pictures of family, churchmen, Jimmy Durante;

"Polmaise," one of the oldest buildings in Wilcox, Sask., was Father Murray's rectory, then a boys' residence. It was destroyed by fire during a blizzard in 1947.

desk littered with mail, books, cheese, crackers, his troublesome upper plate.

His students file in with respect and affection, as I once did, to be scolded, lectured, comforted or filled with his own joy at the beauty of the ages. "Look!" he gloats over a photo of a Michelangelo sculpture of a father and newborn son. "After all these centuries, look at those eyes, the stunned wonder in them over the miracle of life." He talks eloquently of hockey, art, Plato, plumbing and politics. He worries aloud about what he calls the "new religion," science, but stoutly maintains that it has only helped enhance the wonders of God. "I say the Our Father a damn sight better," he affirms, "since I saw those pictures of earth from outer space."

Père frets at the tendency to mass thinking; he rages at socialism. He waged a personal vendetta on the then-socialist government of Saskatchewan, the Coöperative Commonwealth Federation, when it was ramming a compulsory medicare plan through the legislature. Like most other free-enterprisers, Père hated the compulsion. In a speech, he cited the Boston Tea Party, concluded that maybe again it was "a time for muskets." Some government officials talked of charging him with inciting a riot.

Père consulted his archbishop and friend, The

Most Rev. M. C. O'Neill. "Athol," said the archbishop gently, "if *only* you hadn't mentioned the muskets!" They decided that Père should leave quickly on vacation.

Medicare was enacted, but Père stayed unrepentant. After the CCF was defeated by the Liberals in 1964 he was asked to deliver the invocation at a Liberal rally. "Oh Lord," he prayed with fervor, "we thank Thee for letting the sunshine of free enterprise shine again on this province." Later, visiting the Toronto Maple Leafs' dressing room, he spied goalie Johnny Bower, a Saskatchewan native. "You can come home now, John!" he bellowed, while reporters eagerly scribbled. "We got rid of the socialists!" And Père was in the news again.

His talent for making headlines is sometimes a trial to fellow clerics. His young and devoted assistant, Father Jim Weisgerber, has lost friends in the priesthood for defending his exuberant boss. And the patient Archbishop O'Neill once said wryly of their relationship, "I play it by ear with a bit of help from the Holy Ghost!"

Père believes in religious individualism, too. "There *is* a God," he rasped from the pulpit in Wilcox. "And I don't much care if you're a Catholic, Buddhist or Mohammedan, as long as you believe in Him." His particular campus pride is the Tower of God, a 55-foot stone structure decorated with symbols and relics of the Christian, Hebrew and Muslim faiths.

He has built many other monuments to God, most of them human, in his years as a priest. Yet he entered the Church almost by chance. Athol Murray graduated from Quebec's Laval University, studied law and worked on Toronto newspapers. Then, one day in 1913, he picked up a ten-cent copy of St. Augustine's *Confessions* in a Toronto bookstore. One sentence particularly stirred his soul: "To him who does what in him lies, God will not deny His grace." Suddenly Athol Murray knew what was within *him*. Still clutching the book, he hurried to his local archbishop. He wanted to be a priest.

From the beginning, his heart went out to young people. When he was assigned to Regina in 1923, one of his first acts was to found an athletic club for underprivileged boys of all creeds. In the tradition of his hero, Knute Rockne of the *other* Notre Dame, he trained clean, tough players. By the time he was offered his own post in 1927, Père was committed to his boys and the prairie. He asked to be sent to Wilcox, which had no parish priest. Then he learned that its patron was St. Augustine—surely a sign from God!

Several of his boys followed him from Regina— "You're the only father I have," said one—so he found beds for them and looked to their education. There was a convent in Wilcox. With the nuns' consent, it became the nucleus of Notre Dame, probably the world's only coeducational, nonsectarian college under Roman Catholic auspices. For a motto, Père chose *Luctor et Emergo*: "Struggle and Come Through." It couldn't have been more apt.

A small, unused furniture factory became a class-room. The church basement was turned into a kit-chen, the rectory into a boys' dormitory. Then came the Depression and after it years of crippling drought. Our wheat crops withered, and dry wind whipped our starving livestock. Worst of all was the depression of the spirit as parents watched chil-dren leave school to seek work.

In the midst of this, Notre Dame remained a beacon of hope. Its instructors were glad to teach for their bed and board. And when the word went out that youngsters could pay in cash, coal, meat, vege-tables, eggs—or not at all—they came, mostly boys, from everywhere.

Père's talent for handling tough cases became a legend. At night when some boys barricaded them-selves in their huts, defying the "lights out" rule, he crashed the door with his thick shoulders and chased them to bed.

In my student days the sheer challenge of living

was enough to tame most delinquents. The dormi-tories included two old bunkhouses and one aban-doned icehouse. We were generally hungry. The staple diet was bread with gravy, peanut butter or bologna.

There was never enough fuel. Père burned stacks of old magazines; we students foraged. Spring thaws revealed great gaps in the village's board sidewalks.

Père was a scrounger extraordinary. When a Re-gina hotel installed new beds, he got the old ones, cheap. And when the local auto plant was reno-vated, Père salvaged lumber to build a "stadium"— a few windblown bleachers.

When ingenuity failed, Père would say, "Gang, there's no food, no money and no credit. We need a miracle. Get down and pray." We did, and time after time, "miracles" seemed to happen. Cash trickled in with the next mail; somebody donated meat; a total stranger stopped in with $100. Some-times Père gave the miracles a little push. Once a

In the Christian wall of the Tower of God
is this three-by-eight-foot Window
of Christ donated to Notre Dame
by French artist André Rault.

Notre Dame's special pride is
the Tower of God, "built by
Muslims, Hebrews and Christians,"
said Father Murray, "in a
consensus that *there is a God.*"

businessman came by. Père told how we were broke
and hungry—as usual.

"What're you doing about it?" the man asked.

"We pray every day."

"You don't really believe that'll work, do you?"
scoffed the businessman. Yet as soon as he got home,
he sent the college $200. Père immediately wired
back: NEVER UNDERESTIMATE THE POWER OF PRAYER.

Tiny as the college was, our various teams could
hold their own. We'd play anyone, anywhere and,
with Père egging us on, we generally won. We
traveled up to 8000 miles a season, through bitter
cold and choking dust, in the boxed-in back of a
truck called the "doghouse." We often slept in it,
and Père, hatless and shirt-sleeved in summer,
swathed in buffalo coat and aviator's leather helmet
in winter, always took the hardest bed himself.

The best part of the trips was the talk on the long
ride home. Conversation is Père's nourishment. On
public platforms he is witty and outrageous. He
may remove his troublesome upper plate and plunk
it on the podium, muttering clearly, "Damn Protes-
tant teeth!" Or strip off his clerical collar, revealing
a soup-stained shirt of flaming plaid. His lectures
are reinforced with dramatics, for Père is an incur-
able ham. Once, while discussing Greek mythology,
he produced a small statue of Bacchus, god of wine,
with bowl uplifted.

"Gang," he announced, "the Greeks claimed if
you prayed to Bacchus he'd fill your bowl. Let's give
it a try." They prayed, then one peeked in. "Father!" he shouted. "It's full of wine!"

"It's a miracle, pass it around!" cried Père. A
thoughtful man, he had stocked the bowl the night
before.

They were rich, exhilarating days. Père stretched
our minds and fired our imaginations. After graduation, two advanced degrees, and three wartime years
in the RCAF and Army, I returned as a teacher. I
hoped it would still be exhilarating; it was, and has
been ever since. We don't merely teach a philosophy
of life: we try to live it. We work twice as hard as
most college teachers. We coach teams, train air
cadets, attend bull sessions, meet parents and girl
friends. We know all of our few hundred students
and we watch their minds and characters grow.
But there is no doubt that Père is in charge.

In 1966, his friends and associates launched a
$750,000 drive to build a library, sports arena and
men's residence. All of his mixed bag of acquaint-
ances shelled out—the first donation, $250, came
from a Regina bookie. To open the campaign, there
was an 1800-plate testimonial dinner, with speeches,
cheers, tears and eulogies. Père loved it all, but was
glad to get back to Notre Dame.

A few days later, he trudged into a classroom for
a farewell lecture to one of our graduating classes.
Cigarette bobbing in his lips, he scolded them for
breaking cups and wasting the precious water.
"You're soft!" he said. "Yours is an age of reckless
irresponsibility." But a moment later he burst out,
"God, I love you kids!" He cautioned them against
developing parochial minds, reminded them that
the "light and grace of the human mind make for a
great civilization." Finally he said, "Every human
life is insignificant unless you yourself make it
great."

Then he stumped slowly from the room, and
every youngster there must surely have realized that
here, by any standard, was a truly great human life.

Wilder Penfield
Explorer of the Human Brain

A great surgeon relieved the suffering of hundreds of epileptics
and gave us rare insight into the mysteries of the mind

By Murray Teigh Bloom

Surgeons consult with Dr. Penfield prior to an operation.

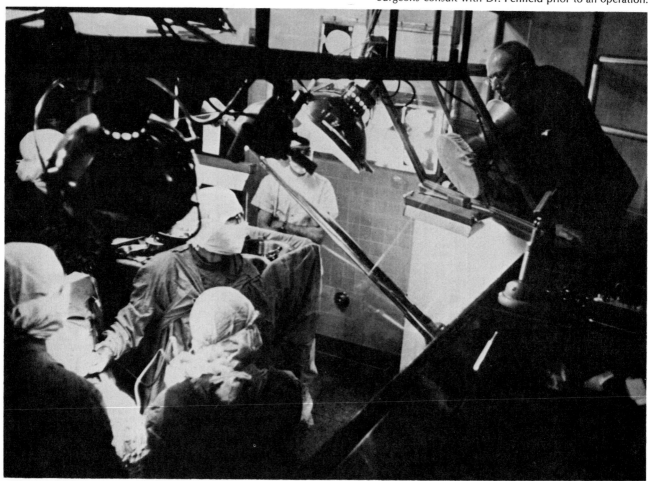

From the gallery of the Montreal Neurological Institute's main operating room I witnessed a seven-hour brain operation performed by one of the world's great neurosurgeons, Dr. Wilder Penfield, whose work has uncovered important clues to the intricacies of the human nervous system.

The patient this day is a 29-year-old New England salesman whose severe and frequent epileptic seizures have prevented him from working regularly. Dr. Penfield is his last hope.

The pace in the operating room is deceptively relaxed and leisurely. Under a local anesthetic a flap of the patient's shaven scalp is formed by a curved incision, a door of skull is sawed out, and turned back with the scalp flap and held by retractors. Now the dura, the filmlike covering of the brain, is opened and a section of the brain about the size of a saucer lies exposed, convoluted gray traversed by throbbing red arteries. The brain itself is a three-pound mass of pink-gray jelly, composed of some ten billion cells.

Sitting nearby, when he is needed, is a key member of Dr. Penfield's team, Dr. Herbert Jasper, a leading electroencephalographer. It is his job to interpret the hill-and-dale lines inked by the pens of a machine registering electric currents generated by the brain as the surgeon touches it at various points. The patient is conscious throughout.

Dr. Penfield's probing electrode touches a spot on the cortex, the gray matter. "I felt something in my thumb and forefinger," the salesman says. A tiny sterile tag numbered 1 is dropped on the spot on the cortex.

The electrode touches other spots, and tags are dropped in place for each reaction. Thus the brain areas controlling the patient's lips, jaws, eyelids, nose and chin are identified. The gentle but relentless probing goes on. Suddenly at tag 26 we hear the epileptic say, tensely: "I had a warning of an attack just then—the strongest one yet."

With tag 30 the electrode probes deeper into the yielding gray matter. "This is it," the patient gasps as he stiffens. On the electroencephalograph we can see the vivid "spike" markings produced by a small epileptic seizure. In a minute it is over.

The hours pass. Gradually the area of the brain's temporal lobe in which this man's attacks start becomes clearly defined. Fortunately it does not include any areas of important or vital functions such as sight, hearing or breathing. Now the diseased tissue, hard and rubbery, is carefully removed with a metal suction device.

Seven hours after the operation began Dr. Penfield sews the dura with a curved needle. An assistant takes over to replace the retracted skull flap. Another epileptic has a good chance of being reclaimed for normal living.

Dr. Penfield, as director of the Montreal Neurological Institute, probably the world's leading center for neurological surgery and research, performed that operation hundreds of times. During one of his early pioneering operations, in 1931, he stumbled upon a patient's invisibly recorded past—his probing suddenly brought forth from the patient an account of a long-forgotten experience. The incident has led to new insight into the strange mechanisms of human memory, of how the brain records every waking sight and sound and, literally, how we profit by past experience. This unique knowledge, developed patiently over the years by Dr.

Dr. W. V. Cone (right) had been at New York's Presbyterian Hospital with Dr. Penfield. Both neurosurgeons went to Montreal in 1928.

Penfield, has been called "a turning point in the study of mankind."

Some members of the class of 1913 at Princeton University are still surprised that "Pen" Penfield of Spokane, Wash., became a surgeon. At college he was mainly interested in playing football. (Not until his junior year did he decide to study medicine.) In the autumn following graduation he coached the freshman team. The following year he was head field coach of the varsity. He won a Rhodes scholarship, and left after the season was over to begin his medical studies at Oxford. He taught himself to be ambidextrous and started using a straight razor to help develop a steady hand for surgery.

At Oxford he met the man who influenced his life vastly: the famous Canadian, Sir William Osler, then Regius Professor of Medicine. In 1916 Penfield returned to the United States to complete his medical studies at Johns Hopkins. When he graduated he had a wife, a child and no money. But he still had one unused year of his three-year Rhodes scholarship. Borrowing money, he returned with his family to Oxford to study with Sir Charles Sherrington, the greatest living expert on the human nervous system. After that Penfield knew what his lifework was to be: neurosurgery.

In 1928 came another turning point in his life. He was offered the chair of neurosurgery at Montreal's McGill University because of his growing reputation as a surgeon and experimenter in the nerve cell laboratory he had founded at New York's Presbyterian Hospital. In Montreal, Penfield dreamed of a vast new institute devoted exclusively to the study and treatment of brain ailments. He is a persuasive dreamer. Contributions from the Rockefeller Foundation and wealthy Canadians enabled the vision to come to life. In 1934 the Montreal Neurological Institute, an eight-story limestone building on the slopes of Mount Royal, opened its doors.

Today half or more of the institute's patients are without funds and Dr. Penfield's only income is from a comparatively small group of private patients. But there are other rewards. Though he is a naturalized Canadian citizen, he has been at or near the top of popularity polls of "greatest living Canadians." He has also been awarded the Order of Merit. (Dwight D. Eisenhower and Winston Churchill are two of the 24 members of the order.)

These honors surprise no one, but they underline an almost incredible irony. This unorthodox, trailblazing surgeon was once regarded with pity by his colleagues for his perseverance. The British neurosurgeon, Sir Geoffrey Jefferson, said of him: "Penfield devoted his life to epilepsy research at a time when the subject was regarded by the medical pro-

fession as fruitless and time-wasting. He persevered for 20 years in a medical desert, in the face of every kind of discouragement."

Penfield believed epilepsy was not a disease but a symptom of something awry in the brain. And his persistent investigations have shown that epilepsy is literally an electrical explosion brought on by a too heavy charge accumulating frequently in a damaged part of the brain. The damage in more than half of his patients is attributable to inadequate oxygen or improper head compression at birth.

The surgical procedure Dr. Penfield developed is known as the Foerster-Penfield operation. It was first performed by Dr. Otfried Foerster in Germany. Dr. Penfield helped Foerster to analyze his results while he was studying neurosurgery there. Until 1934 the results were not promising but today half of the patients selected for operation from among

Believing epilepsy not a disease
but a symptom of brain damage,
Wilder Penfield devoted
his life to relieving the suffering
of epileptics. Here he and
neurosurgeon Lamar Roberts
discuss neurograms of an epileptic
patient prior to an operation.

those not responding to the anti-convulsant drugs are cured by operation. In another 25 percent the operation cuts the number and severity of seizures.

On recommendations of their physicians, patients come to the MNI from all over the world. One of the earliest of these was a middle-aged housewife, and it was halfway through this operation that the historic incident took place which has helped us understand the miracle of human memory.

Dr. Penfield's probing electrode touched a spot on one of the two temporal lobes, above the ears. At once the housewife exclaimed in surprise that she seemed to be having her baby all over again. She went on to describe the sights and sounds of the delivery room — vividly, exactly and in detail, as if the events were taking place again before her eyes.

Dr. Penfield knew that when certain parts of the brain were touched with the electrode he could cause a leg to jump, an eye to wink. Such responses had been carefully plotted on an atlas of the cerebral cortex showing which parts of the gray matter governed different body functions. But the vivid recall of an incident that had happened years ago was completely unexpected.

Soon a succession of similar incidents occurred. A young South African suddenly saw himself back in a family gathering, heard the piano playing.

"No, doctor," he exclaimed in wonder, "I am not just remembering it. It is happening again in this room. I know I am in Montreal but I seem to be with my friends too. I can see and hear them."

A secretary recreated a period when she once had to wait hours in a snowbound station. A businessman relived a forgotten moment of his childhood when he saw a strange man coming through the fence at a baseball game.

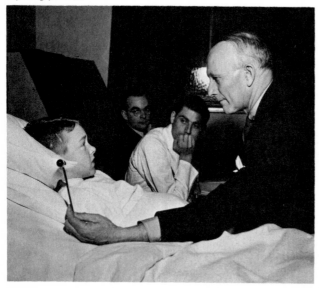

Other doctors look on as
Dr. Penfield examines
a young patient.

Dr. Penfield would tell his patients he was going to touch the same spot with the electrode again and then ask them what they saw or heard now. Since the brain itself is incapable of feeling anything, the patient had no way of knowing that Dr. Penfield was deliberately withholding the electrode. Yet each time, the patient would report that he saw and heard nothing. But when Dr. Penfield did retouch the spot, he would get a repetition of the sights and sounds the patient had reported previously.

One young woman reported she was in the living room of a house her family had lived in more than 15 years before and that a phonograph was playing the march from *Aida*. She hummed it as she listened inwardly. When the electrode was removed the music stopped. When it was reapplied she heard the music again—where it had begun previously. Dozens of similar instances finally convinced Dr. Penfield that he had stumbled on a completely new phenomenon.

Every day our eyes take a half million snapshots. Our ears bring the accompanying sound to an adjoining part of the temporal lobes. Somehow the sound is synchronized with the "film" so that the two are always together when there is a memory

playback. Two experiences ("strips of time," Dr. Penfield calls them) are never activated at the same time.

"Among the millions of nerve cells that clothe parts of the brain there runs a thread," Dr. Penfield says. "It is the thread of time, the thread that has run through each succeeding wakeful hour of the individual's past life. When my electrode activates some portion of that thread, there is a response as though the thread were a wire recorder, or a strip of movie film on which are registered all those things which the person selected for his attention in that interval of time."

Simultaneously as the "film" and sound track are permanently recorded in the brain several "indexes" are probably also created, Dr. Penfield believes, so that the mind can find a particular living memory quickly.

How does this "indexing" system work? You suddenly meet a friend you haven't seen for years. As he turns and looks at you there is a sense of familiarity. Suddenly you recognize him. But even as you focus your attention on him you realize he is changed in little ways.

"There is a difference," Dr. Penfield explains, "between this moving, talking individual and the detailed record of him that is preserved in your brain, a record you could not have conjured up voluntarily. Now you see the new lines in his face, an altered stoop to his shoulder. Actually, on seeing him again you have reopened the old 'file,' rediscovered its contents, compared past with present."

These quick reviews of old "files" take place many times a day, Dr. Penfield believes. Whether we are approaching a dangerous traffic intersection or trying to find a name for a face seen in a crowd, the brain's marvelous review mechanism will automatically call up long-forgotten incidents and details for comparison and interpretation.

Dr. Penfield's monumental work has immediate applications for all of us. It tends to confirm, for example, the effectiveness of audiovisual methods of education. Lessons are learned better when facts are recorded simultaneously by eye and ear on our minds. Dr. Penfield also believes that foreign languages should be taught in childhood when the mind is most receptive to a second tongue. He points out that although the language learned then may be forgotten with lack of practice, only a few weeks in the land where it is spoken will bring back the former ability. For the mind has *permanently* recorded the early lessons.

Controlling the vast network which feeds information to our memory storehouse and brings forth interpretations and answers is the upper brain stem, which links the brain's two hemispheres. This may well be the true seat of human consciousness, Dr. Penfield thinks.

"The slightest injury to the upper brain stem usually produces deep unconsciousness. This is not true of the cortex, the brain's outer covering, or of the lobes. Such a headquarters switchboard as I believe the upper brain stem to be is so delicate, so complicated, as to stagger the imagination."

The mind itself may never have the wisdom to comprehend fully its own workings. But thanks to Dr. Penfield and his hundreds of epileptic patients we now have some key clues to explain what makes the human brain the most marvelous machine on earth.

Dr. Penfield now is retired from medicine but the Neurological Institute he founded continues its work under the brilliant leadership of Prof. Theodore Rasmussen. Following his own advice, Dr. Penfield has embarked on a second career, as a writer, and has produced a number of books. "In the field of would-be authorship," he says, "there are many things I long to do and the art of creative writing fascinates me as much as medicine did." He is also president of the Vanier Institute of the Family and a recent winner of an award from the Society for the Family of Man.

The Man Behind the New Montreal

Thanks to hard-driving, fast-moving Jean Drapeau, Canada's longtime
"sin center" has been bursting with progress and pride

By David MacDonald

There is an adage which says you can't fight City Hall. And then, *au contraire*, there's Jean Drapeau of Montreal, a remarkable little French-Canadian lawyer whose career clearly demonstrates that you can—and win great victories.

When Drapeau began battling civic corruption in Montreal, in 1949, Canada's largest city was a gaudy, bawdy metropolis that harbored 250-odd gambling joints and more than 100 brothels in one of North America's biggest, most blatant red-light districts. Raking in millions of dollars yearly, the dens openly defied the law and a strangely myopic police force. As the gutsy young attorney for a reform-minded citizens' group, Drapeau set out to prove that organized vice in Montreal enjoyed—and paid for—official protection in high places.

Today, Drapeau himself occupies a high place—the mayor's office. Not only has his reform campaign succeeded, but he has gone on to prove himself one of North America's most enterprising mayors. Among his projects: a 16-mile subway, Expo 67 and the $25 million *Place des Arts*, a glittering cultural center. But most striking of all is the renewal of midtown Montreal, where a two-billion-dollar building boom has transformed seedy sidestreets into broad boulevards, handsome plazas and soaring skyscrapers. "Montreal is becoming one of the truly great cities on this continent," says U.S. town planner Vincent Ponte, "and it's largely due to Jean Drapeau's vision and drive."

Short and bald, with a tiny mustache and thick spectacles, M. Drapeau looks as mild as Mr. Milquetoast. But behind his bland façade is a man of many parts, all moving. Brisk in public, but warm and bouncy in person, he works 16 hours a day with full Gallic gusto. In the interest of saving time, Drapeau favors black suits; for formal functions he simply clips on a black tie and —*voilà!*—he's ready to go. "I don't know how Jean does it," marvels Lucien Saulnier, chairman of the city's executive committee. "He never seems to sleep."

Once, after a full week of dawn-to-midnight toil, Drapeau actually fell into bed at 10 p.m. He awoke, fresh, at 3 a.m. Within an hour he was back at his desk in the rococo *Hôtel de Ville*, dictating letters in both French and English. "For me," he shrugs, "it is a labor of love."

Jean Drapeau has always been ardently fond of Montreal—but not always proud of it. The son of an insurance agent, he was raised in the city's solidly French east end. By the time he had worked his way through law school in 1942, Montreal had long since become the sin center of Canada. As a student, Drapeau saw men queuing outside one bordello— which solicited business through *loudspeakers*— while policemen strolled by, eyes front. "Such mockery of the law made me furious," he recalls.

He wasn't alone. In 1944, alarmed by Montreal's venereal-disease rate, the Canadian Army threatened to put the city off limits. Police and City Hall officials professed all innocence. Yet overnight, as if by remote control, every *bordel* temporarily shut down.

Two years later, after a public outcry over police bungling, the Morality Squad chief was fired. Later it was discovered that he'd picked up at least $20,000 in his work, including a large payoff from unknown sources not to contest his dismissal.

Pacifique Plante, a junior Crown attorney and friend of Drapeau's, was given the Morality job. Plante raided brothels and books with handpicked men, even jailed a longtime gambling kingpin who'd never before been prosecuted. In the gambler's address book was the private phone number

The Royal Bank Building, part of *Place Ville Marie,* soars into Montreal's skyline. But the best of the past has been retained to complement and be complemented by the new.

Not fight City Hall? Jean
Drapeau, who looked as mild
as Milquetoast, took on fat
Mayor Camillien Houde *and*
Quebec Premier Maurice
Duplessis—and won. With
crimebuster Pacifique Plante
(center) and Pierre Des Marais
of the Civic Action League,
Drapeau acknowledged
admirers' cheers when
first elected in 1954.

of Montreal's perennial mayor, Camillien Houde, a fat and flamboyant old pol who ran the city just as he pleased.

In short order, Plante was charged with insubordination by Police Director Albert Langlois—formerly an inspector in the red-light district—and Houde's executive committee sacked him.

But then a few indignant Montrealers formed the Civic Action League to seek a judicial probe into vice conditions. As legal adviser they recruited Jean Drapeau, an up-and-coming *avocat* with a penchant for underdog causes.

While his law practice dwindled, Drapeau and Plante pored over court records of all police raids on brothels and gambling joints since 1941. These showed that such disorderly houses were struck with clocklike regularity. Yet even places supposedly padlocked by the police stayed open. Moreover, the actual owners were never charged. (Among other things, this concealed the fact that two brothels paid rent to a city health officer whose job was—lo!—combating V.D.) "The whole system," says Drapeau, "was a huge, sordid hoax."

So Drapeau and Plante drafted a petition making charges against five civic politicians and 58 policemen. But many Montrealers were too cynical to sign it. Others feared reprisals: one builder who signed lost city contracts; a doctor was savagely beaten up. "Of almost 1000 people we asked," Drapeau remembers, "only 74 joined us."

But that was enough. In May 1950, Quebec's superior court assigned Mr. Justice François Caron to hold a full inquiry.

While Drapeau and Plante prepared files on 4000 underworld figures, civic officials and cops, they were constantly followed by hoods and/or detectives. *"Eh bien,"* Drapeau cracked, "what's the difference?"

Good question. For the two-and-a-half-year Caron probe uncovered police villainy that shocked even blasé Montreal.

As co-prosecutors, Drapeau and Plante built their case around the Morality Squad's own ledgers. While giving the *appearance* of vigorous law enforcement, these proved that crime paid well in Montreal, and why.

For instance, 53 of the city's bookie joints remained in operation despite over 5000 convictions; cops had obligingly fixed padlocks to their side entrances, broom closets—even on doors nailed to blank walls—so as not to interfere with business. Though gambling rings took in over $100 million a year, money seized for prosecutions averaged 50 *cents* per raid. One big-time gambler, asked how long he could have carried on without such coöperation, replied candidly, "Maybe 24 hours."

Raids on *bordels* were always tipped off; when Morality officers were due, the madam would take most of her girls out, leaving one to pose as the keeper and pay a slight fine. One such "straw woman" amassed 112 convictions in ten years. "Everything was protected," Drapeau summed up, "because everything was paid for."

Five times defense lawyers stalled the probe with legal writs; Drapeau fought each of them . . . and won. Then threats were made against the judge, Plante, Drapeau's attractive wife Marie-Claire and their three sons. Drapeau narrowly escaped a late-night ambush. Twice, rocks shattered windows of his modest stucco home. "It was a war of nerves," Drapeau says now. "If I had quit, it would have looked as if I'd sold out."

Witnesses told how underworld intermediaries, or "edge men," collected dues for police protection, and how one city councilor tried to bribe another to ignore a gaming house in his district. A police captain swore he was reprimanded for arresting a dues-paying gambler. "We've followed this system for 40 years," his inspector declared, "and you're not going to change it."

In 1954, the Civic Action League asked Drapeau to run for mayor. "The only way to clean up City Hall," one friend argued, "is from the inside." When he agreed, the CAL put up a slate of 35

council candidates. Then came Mr. Justice Caron's long-awaited decision. Finding that "the police constituted a silent union (with) commercialized vice," he fired Director Langlois, who was later reinstated by an appeals court, fined 19 other officers and barred 16 of them from public office for varying terms.

With that, Drapeau stumped the city, denouncing the "rotten, corrupt, inefficient" regime of Mayor Houde, who had decided to retire. Racketeers threw money and hundreds of hoods into the election fray. Goon squads wrecked CAL committee rooms, beat up helpers. But Drapeau won by 54,000 votes over eight other candidates. At 38, he became the youngest mayor in Montreal history and was named Canada's Man of the Year.

Under his administration, police closed betting and bawdy houses, smashed lottery and slot-machine rings, clamped down on bars and nightclubs that had long flouted a 2 a.m. curfew. They also drove out five big U. S. gambling syndicates. As many mobsters fled Drapeau's jurisdiction, or were deported, honest cops took heart.

At City Hall, Drapeau swept out a graft-ridden tax-assessment office and set up a patronage-free personnel department to keep political appointees off the payroll. He pushed through street-widening projects, started town-planning surveys, even slapped down some of his own CAL supporters, who sought kickbacks on city contracts. "All that talk of honesty," Drapeau fumed, "—I *meant* it!"

But he also made mistakes—notably by failing to seek rapport with Montreal's influential English minority. Most damaging of all, he angered Quebec's dictatorial premier, Maurice Duplessis, who was not at all reform-minded. When Drapeau stood for re-election in 1957, Duplessis' party fought him with a sum said to be $250,000. The *Union Nationale* machine was put behind Sarto Fournier, a ward politician who offered to make Montreal "wide open but honest."

The campaign was the roughest on record. Dra-

Among the glittering show-
places of Jean Drapeau's vibrant
new Montreal is the
$25 million *Place des Arts*.

peau's family was threatened, and thugs broke a CAL official's legs with tire irons. On election day, ballot boxes were stolen in pro-Drapeau districts. As he learned later—too late—paid impersonators cast 20,000 phony ballots against him. This, plus a weak showing in the strongly English west end, cost him the election by 5000 votes. The verdict was almost unanimous: "Drapeau's finished."

Far from it. As Montreal backslid into an unprecedented crime wave, the little lawyer returned to the attack. In 1960, after Duplessis had died, he again ran for mayor—and won by 30,000 votes.

Drapeau promptly hired Commander Andrew Way of Scotland Yard and André Gaubiac, ex-chief of the Paris *Sûreté*, to help remake Montreal's police department. (After obtaining leave-of-absence from the outgoing regime, Director Langlois retired and later died.) "I want a police force," Drapeau told them, "—not a political farce." Way and Gaubiac assembled a top-notch flying squad to tackle major crime, which fell 50 percent in one year; promoted bright young men, weeded out the inept and dishonest, raised pay for recruits.

Then, as one citizen recently observed, "After the cleanup, Drapeau began the buildup." Following 50 years of talk about a subway, for example, he hustled off to study the world's best subway systems, then sold the city council on one using rubber-tired trains, the $213,700,000 Montreal *Métro*.

Symbol of downtown Montreal's dramatic renaissance is *Place Ville Marie,* with its 48-story cruciform Royal Bank Building—four gleaming skyscrapers in one. Equally striking is *Place Victoria,* the world's tallest concrete tower and, according to British architect Sir Basil Spence, "the most beautiful of all big buildings."

Then he scored another coup. When Moscow dropped plans to hold a world's fair in 1967, Drapeau quickly talked the federal and provincial governments into backing Montreal's successful bid to the Bureau of Exhibitions in Paris. That was all he needed.

For a half-century Montreal *talked* about constructing a subway. Drapeau talked it into being— a $213,700,000 rubber-tired *Métro*. No two stations are alike. Each, like Crémazie (below), is a colorful showplace in itself.

While land speculators grabbed up possible sites, he secretly pondered an "impossible" one—two islands smack in the middle of the St. Lawrence River. One already belonged to the city; the other, nonexistent, had to be created. When surveys proved it feasible, at a $10 million saving over other sites, Drapeau caught the speculators flat-footed. "The debate," he announced, "is now closed."

On a thousand acres of lagoon-laced parklands just minutes from downtown Montreal, Canada and some 70 other nations spent almost $700 million to stage the biggest fair in history: the Canadian Universal and International Exhibition of 1967. Many Montrealers called it simply "Drapeau's show." Fifty million people saw it.

In Drapeau's resurgent city are several new high-rise hotels, a National League baseball team, more and more underground shopping malls and *Place Bonaventure*, a $75 million trade center. For the near future: a vast slum-redevelopment project and a permanent opera company. "When Drapeau says he'll do something," remarks Walter O'Hearn, executive editor of the Montreal *Star*, "he usually does it—even if he has to batter down doors and trample on a few toes. Before he came along, Montreal was in a bad way. Now he's got it bursting with confidence."

At a university convocation, before he left to work among the lepers of Africa, Paul-Emile Cardinal Léger listed and lauded the mayor's many achievements.

"It would not surprise me," the prelate added, "if he tried to move our next Vatican Council to Montreal!"

"Your Eminence," Jean Drapeau replied, deadpan, "that is the last time I shall confide in you."

DRAMATIC HOURS

**Difficulties do not crush men,
they make them.**

Rt. Hon. Arthur Meighen, 1942

How We Discovered Insulin

The story of one of the great medical
feats of all time

By Dr. Charles H. Best
as told to J. D. Ratcliff

The man who came into the laboratory the morning
of May 16, 1921, didn't look like a medical immortal. Few do at age 29. Dr. Frederick Banting looked
more like a farmer—powerful, with slightly stooped
shoulders, blue-green eyes, big nose and jutting,
stubborn chin. His voice halting, quiet, betrayed
an inborn shyness.

"Let's get started, Mr. Best," he said. "We really
haven't much time." What an understatement! He
had asked the University of Toronto for the use of a
laboratory for eight weeks, for ten dogs, and for the
help of someone who knew chemistry and physiology. The money value of his request was at most
$100. With this he thought he could conquer a
disease that had always baffled medical men: the
merciless killer, diabetes!

"You read French, don't you?" Banting asked. I
did. "Let's go to the library then," he said, "and look
up how a Frenchman named Hédon took a pancreas out of a dog."

That was the beginning.

We both knew the horror of diabetes—described
by a Greek physician 2000 years earlier as a "disease in which the flesh melts away and is siphoned
off in the urine." Somehow the bodies of stricken
people stopped burning sugar into energy. Instead
their bodies turned cannibal, consuming stored fats
and proteins. There was always unquenchable
thirst—victims often drinking several gallons of
water a day while losing a like amount of sugary
urine. And their appetite was ravenous. The only
treatment was a rigid diet designed to correct the
patient's disrupted chemical balance. Severely
stricken victims were offered a grim choice: eat well
today and die tomorrow, or cut down to a few
hundred calories a day and linger for a while in
weary befuddlement.

Banting had seen diabetes convert a vivacious 15-
year-old girl classmate at Alliston, Ont., into a
pathetic child for whom death came swiftly. At my
home in West Pembroke, Me., I had seen the same
happen to my Aunt Anna. A stout, vigorous woman

in her early 30's, she wasted to 80 pounds before
she died.

The world would have considered us a most unlikely pair to match wits with this killer. I was a
22-year-old graduate student, working for my master's degree in physiology and biochemistry. Banting's experience in research was virtually nil. At
his family's urging he had started out to study for
the Methodist ministry. But, a halting speaker, he
changed to medicine. He had been an average
student.

After serving as a surgeon in the Canadian Army
in World War I, and winning the Military Cross for
bravery, he set up practice as an orthopedic surgeon
in London, Ont. He waited for patients who never
came. One month his income was four dollars. His
fiancée could see little future with such a man, and
they parted.

Now this man was staking all his meager resources on his hunch that he could cure the sugar
sickness. He gave up his little practice, sold his office
furniture, books, instruments, everything. Banting
couldn't afford another failure.

It was known that the pancreas—a pale-yellow,
pollywog-shaped abdominal organ that produces
digestive juices—was somehow involved in this
disease. In 1889 Oskar Minkowski in Germany had
removed a dog's pancreas, mainly to see if the animal could get along without it. Next day he noted
flies clustered around puddles of the dog's urine.
The urine was sugary; the dog, in normal health
the day before, now had diabetes.

Did pancreatic juices, then, contain a factor that
normally regulates the metabolism of sugars? To
test the idea, research men tied off the ducts that
carry these juices to the intestine. When dogs got
this surgery, their pancreases shriveled and degenerated—but they did *not* get diabetes! The shriveled
organs, unable to send digestive secretions to the
intestines, were still producing the antidiabetic
factor. But, if it wasn't in the pancreatic juices, where
was it?

Dr. Frederick Banting (right) and Dr. Charles Best in the summer of 1921, during a pause in their round-the-clock search for a cure for diabetes. The dog was one of the first to have its life prolonged by insulin.

Attention shifted to the thousands of mysterious little "islet" cells scattered through the pancreas and surrounded by tiny capillaries. Did they secrete some "X" stuff, perhaps a hormone that regulated the burning of sugar? And did they empty it, then, not into the intestine but into the bloodstream? Several research men had suggested as much and had gone hunting for the elusive hormone. But all had come home with empty game bags.

Now it was our turn.

"Maybe it's this way, Mr. Best," Banting said—not for several days would we become Fred and Charley. "Maybe when the researchers remove a healthy pancreas and grind it up to extract this X stuff, enzymes in the digestive juice mix with the X stuff and destroy it—just as they break down proteins in the intestine. Maybe that's why no one has been able to find it."

Knowing that when the pancreatic ducts are tied off the cells which secrete digestive juices degenerate faster than do the islet cells, we would tie off these ducts in dogs and wait. "In seven to ten weeks the pancreas will degenerate, stop making digestive juice—and there will be nothing to destroy the X stuff. You extract it. Then we'll give this extract to a diabetic dog and see if it lowers the sugar in blood and urine."

I did my chemical work in our cubbyhole lab. Dog surgery was performed two flights up in the skylighted attic. Before summer was over, that attic became as steamy as any Turkish bath. To get some relief we wore little or nothing under our white lab coats. Since money was short, we ate in the lab. Eggs and sausage fried over a Bunsen burner became diet staples.

One serious problem was a scarcity of dogs. When the situation became acute, Banting said, "Crank up The Pancreas, Charley, and let's go." (This was our name for his Model T Ford.) We rattled through the poorer parts of Toronto, hunting for dogs whose owners would part with them for a dollar.

We had tied off the first pancreatic ducts in May, and in early July we expected the pancreases to be shriveled, the X stuff accessible. We opened one of the animals—and found the pancreas blooming with health, no atrophy, no shriveling. Banting and I had tied the ducts incorrectly.

Our eight weeks were almost up. This would have been as good a time as any to accept defeat. But Banting was a stubborn man. During the war he had got an ugly shrapnel wound in his right arm. Doctors had wanted to amputate. Banting refused—and nursed the arm back to health. Now we were going to nurse our sickly project back to health.

Prof. John J. R. Macleod, head of the physiology department, who had provided us with work facilities, was on vacation in Europe. "He won't know the difference if we stay on," we decided.

Leonard Thompson, who had been given only a few weeks to live, was the first diabetic human to receive insulin, in January 1922 at the age of 14. He recovered—and died 13 years later after a motorcycle accident.

We began reoperating on the dogs, tying off ducts, correctly this time. On July 27 we got the beautifully shriveled, degenerated pancreas we wanted. It should contain the X stuff—if the X stuff existed.

Now we sliced the pancreas into a chilled mortar containing Ringer's solution and froze the mixture. We allowed it to thaw slowly, ground it up and filtered it through paper. A dying diabetic dog was waiting, too weak to lift his head. Fred injected 5 c.c. of the filtrate into a vein. The dog *looked* a little better—but self-delusion is easy at such times. Blood tests were needed.

I drew a few droplets from the dog's paw and began testing for blood sugar. Banting hovered over me. If sugar were heavily present the reagent in the test tube would turn deep red; little sugar and it would be a pale pink. There was a new test every hour and the reagent was getting paler, paler. Blood sugar was going down—from 0.20 percent to 0.12 percent, to . . . It was headed for a normal 0.09 percent! This was the most exciting moment of Banting's life or my own.

Life now became a blurred nightmare of work. This thing had to be nailed down. Dogs had to be injected, blood had to be drawn for testing, urine collected. It was an hourly, round-the-clock schedule. We stretched out on lab benches to get what sleep we could.

But there was an ever-reviving miracle for us to behold: dogs glassy-eyed with the sleep of death upon them; then, a few hours later, they were up, eating, tails wagging. Jolted back to life, one dog lived 12 days, another 22 days.

Our pet was Marjorie—dog number 33. Black-and-white, vaguely collie, she learned to jump up on a bench, hold out her paw to give us a blood sample and keep still to get the shot on which her life depended. For 70 days she was alive and well. Then we ran out of the extract, isletin, as we then called it. (Only later did Macleod persuade us to change the name to insulin.)

It took almost all the isletin we could extract from a degenerated pancreas to keep one dog alive for one day. How far would this go toward keeping alive millions of diabetics around the world?

Fred remembered reading that the pancreas of an unborn animal was mainly islet cells—since the digestive juice wasn't needed in the womb. As a farm boy, he also knew that farmers frequently bred cows before sending them to the slaughterhouse, to hoist weight. Wouldn't pancreases from the unborn calves be rich in isletin? We cranked up The Pancreas and headed for a slaughterhouse. Later, back at the lab, we ground up the salvaged pancreases, extracted, purified and reaped a rich harvest of isletin.

We could now keep dogs alive as long as we wanted. Eventually, of course, it was found that with improved extraction methods any animal pancreas—sheep, hog, cow—provided insulin. There was going to be enough for all needs.

By November 14 we were ready to share some of our excitement with the world. Before the Journal Club of the Department of Physiology, Banting and I gave our first paper—complete with lantern slides showing blood-sugar charts. But the crucial ques-

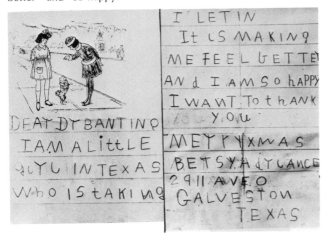

tion still had to be answered. *Would insulin work in human beings?*

Across the street in Toronto General Hospital was 14-year-old Leonard Thompson. After two years with diabetes, he was down to 65 pounds, and could scarcely lift his head from the pillow. By the usual criteria he would have, at most, only a few weeks left.

We had established that an insulin "cocktail," taken by mouth, did not work. So now Banting and I rolled up our sleeves. I injected him with our extract and he injected me—we had to be sure it wasn't too toxic to be tolerated by human beings. Next day we had slightly sore arms, that was all.

So in January 1922, the wasted little arm of the dying boy was injected. Testing began. All over again, it was the story of our dogs. Blood sugar dropped—dramatically. Leonard began to eat normal meals. Sunken cheeks filled out, new life came to weary muscles. Leonard was going to live! (He lived another 13 years and died in 1935—of pneumonia following a motorcycle accident.) He was the first of dozens, then hundreds, thousands, eventually millions to get insulin.

Honors began to shower on us. For the best piece of research conducted at the university that year we were awarded the Reeve Prize—a welcome $50. A grateful Parliament voted Banting a life annuity of $7500. Then came a great research institute named for him, and later one named for me. When Banting won the Nobel Prize in 1923 he shared the money equally with me.

Both of us stayed on at the university, and through the succeeding years concentrated on our individual research projects. But the excitement of the old days was missing. Then on a wintry February day in 1941, we were walking across the campus. "Charley," said Banting, "let's start working together again. You handle the chemistry, and I'll . . ."

It was not to be. Three days later Banting—now Major Sir Frederick Banting, working on problems of aviation medicine—was aboard a two-engine bomber bound for England. The plane crashed in a snowstorm in a forest near Musgrave Harbor, Nfld. Banting, severely injured, tried in his delirium to dictate something to pilot Joseph C. Mackey, the only other survivor, to whom the technical medical phraseology was unintelligible. "This may well have been the struggle of a great mind to fight against death in a race to record his last thoughts," said Mackey. Soon the great man died.

Of all eulogies, perhaps most moving was the one spoken five years later at a London gathering of the Diabetics Association: "Without Banting this meeting could have been only a gathering of ghosts bemoaning their fate."

Sheepdog Navy

A report on Canada's little ships when the
Battle of the Atlantic was at its worst

By J. C. Furnas

She wasn't much to look at. The grimy motley of camouflage made her appear dingy and mid-winter weather on the North Atlantic had gnawed away half her red-crossed White Ensign—not white any more, but dirty gray. Regulations said ensigns should be washed regularly but this crew, like many another, firmly believed laundering would mean bad luck.

As she stuck her nose deeper in the mounting swell, spray froze on her in an ever-thickening weight of ice. Officers and men in hooded duffle-coats looked like a frostbitten congregation of monks. One seaman was muffled in a lady's discarded fur coat, rebuilt for male shoulders, and a signalman wore a leather windbreaker still bearing his high-school football letter. Dungarees were the nearest approach to a uniform.

This was a typical unit of the Royal Canadian Navy in mid-war, one of scores of plucky little ships battling the twin enemies of U-boats and weather, doing a seamanlike and dirty job in obscurity born of an overriding need for security.

The RCN's specialty was submarine-hunting and the submarine threat was at its peak that winter of 1942-43. By then the Canadian Navy handled nearly half of the whole North Atlantic convoy

job—No. 1 lifeline of the war—plus numerous other missions around the globe. Not bad for a navy which in 1939 consisted of six destroyers and five mine-sweepers. By mid-war more than 300 fighting ships were in service. There had been losses, but victories too, as the RCN learned by doing what had to be done.

A realistic willingness to specialize in dirty work and never mind big-ship glamour made it all possible. The miscellaneous character of the fleet was evident almost any day in Halifax or St. John's, Nfld., or Sydney, N.S., or Londonderry. Alongside an old English-built Canadian destroyer might be a revamped U.S. "four-stacker," acquired in the destroyers-for-bases deal between Washington and London in 1940. A graceful craft with sawed-off clipper bow, looking queer in her gray war paint, would be a millionaire's yacht hastily converted for minesweeping or patrol. Just behind her might be a "killer boat"—one of the dogged little vessels that used to go whale-hunting in the Antarctic.

But the real miracle was the way Canadian shipyards, which in 1939 had no major facilities, supplied new and specialized escort craft to make up the bulk of the sheepdog navy. "Why," said an admiring Canadian officer, "they're turning them out like

The doughty little corvette was
sturdy, dependable, a good sea
boat—and wet, inside and out.
Seamen counted the Atlantic
an enemy hardly less
formidable than the U-boats.

sausages." Chunky and well-armed minesweepers that doubled as escorts, big wooden gasoline-powered Fairmile motor launches for harbor-and-river patrol and convoy of small coasters, and, most plentifully and usefully of all, corvettes—husky little ladies not much bigger than sweepers but packing plenty of punch. They carried light deck guns, rapid-fire Oerlikon dual-purpose guns, heavy machine guns and depth charges. Sometimes these corvettes went all the way across, sometimes only as far as Iceland, where similar ships based on Britain took over.

The corvettes' breeding was out of the sturdy North Sea fishing trawler by the whaler's killer boat. Broad beam and bluff bow enabled them to ride the heaviest weather with ease. Skippers found them better sea boats than many vessels 20 times their size.

Shallow draft made them difficult to torpedo because a torpedo would not run accurately unless set too deep to catch a corvette's keel. And they could turn on a dime for repeated depth-charge attacks or for ramming a surfaced submarine. One skipper, making use of his corvette's great maneuverability, rammed a submarine three times running, risking his own ship but finally sinking the enemy.

Canadian shipyards were producing so many escort ships by mid-war that some could be given to Britain, the Free French and the United States. They also built close to a million tons of merchant ships.

That rate of production naturally meant a dearth of skilled shipbuilding labor. Expert mechanics, shipfitters and the loftsmen who translate blueprints into vessels can't be trained in a hurry. Canada advertised for "lost" skills, men who had left such trades for other jobs, and turned up an unexpected gold mine: hundreds of skilled veterans of Scotland's Clydeside shipyards who, finding things tough in the old country when shipbuilding slumped after World War I, had migrated to Canada. These middle-aged Scots remembered just how to do it.

The dufflecoated lookout—
"like a frostbitten monk"—and
the "chief" bound for his engine
room both wear lifejackets.

One Canadian ship, *Kitchener*,
won additional fame as the star
of a wartime Hollywood
movie, *Corvette K225*.

Earphones tuned to the
"pingggg" of the Asdic
(antisubmarine detection
device), a seaman does his
trick at the wheel.

The Canadian Navy grew in war
from 1800 men to close to
90,000. Most recruits to the
messdeck had never seen
the sea before joining up.

Canada's Navy had no recruiting problem. It was able not only to man every ship Canada could launch, but to supply thousands of men to the Royal Navy. The RCN was largely officered by reservists from the Merchant Marine and fishing fleets and the RCMP patrol fleet. But there were many officers from the Volunteer Reserve—sea-minded young fellows who had long been encouraged to take Navy-sponsored courses.

However, when an organization expands from fewer than 2000 men to over 50,000 in three years, a lot of officers must be raised from absolute scratch. Fresh-water yachtsmen—several yacht clubs joined practically en masse—and kids just out of college were fed into the Volunteer Reserve. In time dozens of commanders of fighting vessels were men who had never been to sea before the war.

The skipper of an escort vessel I sailed on was experienced in merchant shipping but the lanky gunnery officer had only recently graduated from college. As "action stations" sounded, he appeared to enjoy himself hugely scrambling forward to muster his crew at the deck gun with a half gale from the North Pole playing tunes on his teeth and freezing the six-day beard on his chin. It was another ex-college boy on the bridge who rang action stations. He did it on his own, not waiting to ask the skipper, and was tickled down to his half-frozen toes when the "old man," scooting up to the bridge like a squirrel, agreed that the Asdic gave every indication Jerry was off there to starboard in the howling gloom.

The ship swung hard astarboard in an astoundingly sharp curve, the telegraph jangled for full speed ahead, and sparks poured from the funnel. The kid beside me tinkered hopefully with the magazine on his submachine gun. A year earlier he'd been driving a truck in a small Ontario town. Even under his shrouding dufflecoat you could see his shoulders sag in disappointment when the "old man," saying something sulphurous, had to admit the quarry was lost—this time.

The corvette *Pictou* fires a depth charge, one of the sheepdog navy's main weapons against U-boats.

Canadian losses in the never-ending battle were considerable. In one black week the RCN lost a destroyer, a corvette and a converted yacht by enemy action.

Accidents aboard ship were frequent. A centipede dipped in glue could not keep his feet on the slippery steel decks of a corvette showing off in a heavy sea. That meant broken legs, fractured skulls—usually without a doctor to help. And there was the ever-present chance of being washed overboard. The boys all knew what that meant in northern latitudes in winter:

"So far as I'm concerned," the gunnery officer would say, " 'abandon ship' means pick up a big chunk of iron and dive overboard. I'd rather get it over with." But in the next breath he'd be discussing what he planned to do after the war, back home in British Columbia.

A Million Fingers in the Dikes

When the Red River jumped its banks, a nation's heart
went out to a city battling to save itself

By Carl B. Wall

To the 100,000 men and women manning the 30 long miles of dikes protecting Greater Winnipeg from the turbulent flood waters, this night of Friday, May 5, 1950, is zero hour. For nine days now the Red River has been on foaming rampage.

Between the U. S. border and Winnipeg, it has become a vast, churning lake submerging 600 square miles of land. Before the torrential, frigid water, farmsteads of the rich Red River Valley have crumbled and fallen. On ever-shrinking patches of high ground, cattle, horses, wild game await starvation or drowning. So great is the threat that Colonel H. W. Harich of the U.S. Army Engineers' Flood Control reports: "This may well be the worst flood North America has ever known."

With temperatures close to freezing and 50-mile-an-hour winds whipping across the plain, thousands of homeless stream into Greater Winnipeg, now a dike-encircled fort. Here, where the Red coils like a snake through the city, the water is 25 feet above normal, seven feet above flood stage.

Greater Winnipeg is a metropolis of 300,000. Now the hardihood that comes from wrestling with 50-below-zero winter temperatures is released against the common enemy—the river.

A vast volunteer army sloshes through knee-deep mud to strengthen dikes with sandbags: men in their 70's, girls in their teens, Wolf Cubs. Army searchlights stab through sleet and rain to seek out sagging points. Giant bulldozers and draglines rip through landscaped lawns, golf courses, terraced gardens, throwing the precious earth against the rim of the rising river. Houses close to the bank, buried by dirt and sandbags, become a part of the dikes.

In St. Boniface, on the east bank of the Red, a million dollars' worth of earth-moving equipment is thrown into the fight on the massive Lyndale Dike. Behind another dike is St. Boniface Hospital with its 520 patients. In this area Canadian soldiers work furiously, their language restrained by the presence of Grey Nuns who are amazingly enduring at filling sandbags.

His clerical collar concealed by overalls, the Most Rev. Georges Cabana, Coadjutor Archbishop of St. Boniface Diocese, industriously begins shoveling six shovelfuls of sand per bag, instead of the customary four. An Army private, who has been toting bags for hours, protests. "Look, you big lug," he growls, "it's four to the bag or I'm going to plug you into the dike." "Okay, Bud," says the Archbishop.

In the predawn hours of Saturday, May 6, the wail of the evacuation sirens sounds over dike after dike. The river has approached disaster stage—27 feet above normal! A state of emergency is declared. Flood Control Headquarters are set up under Brig. Ronald E. A. Morton. Like a wartime command post, it operates in three shifts around the clock.

From all Canada, reinforcements speed to the battlefront: hard-rock miners, Royal Canadian Navy frogmen and divers, Army engineers, specialists in bridge work and dike construction, fishermen and rescue boats. Highball railway freights are

King George and King Edward
municipal hospitals were
isolated by the swollen Red
River. Ambulances, automobiles
and a Navy-manned duck
evacuated 212 patients.

A government airplane (top) drops
hay for animals stranded on a sliver
of land south of Winnipeg.

dispatched to pick up thousands of tons of food supplies, pumps, carloads of sand, millions of sandbags from all available sources.

In the next nine days, the RCAF air shuttle will bring in more than a million pounds of flood-fighting equipment. A million and a half of the six million sandbags used on the dikes will be airlifted. Emergency generators, rubber boots, vaccine, medical supplies will pour in by air.

The industrial center of Winnipeg, built on a plain, is an easy target for the swirling waters. In downtown areas, 200-pound iron manhole covers pop like corks under the tremendous pressure from overloaded storm sewers. Radio station CKRC is forced off the air because of short circuits caused by water lapping against towers and transmitters, normally three quarters of a mile from the river.

In residential areas, as sewers back up through toilets, homeowners pour linseed oil into the traps to form a heavy glob which acts as a plug. Others use putty, rags, newspapers. Some homeowners purposely flood the basements of their homes to equalize the pressure exerted by the river. One rigs a block and tackle around the family car, hitches it to a sturdy tree, and raises it above the water. Here and there empty oil drums, tied to axles, serve as buoys for cars completely submerged.

As the Wildwood and Riverview dikes begin to crack, the order is given to evacuate the King George and King Edward municipal hospitals. There are 212 patients—and only ten regular ambulances in the entire city. Volunteer drivers appear with their own cars, and ambulances from Fort Osborne barracks and Stevenson Field are pressed into service. A Navy-manned duck carries two polio patients and their 600-pound iron lungs to safety.

As heat fails and sewage backs up into basements, other hospitals and nursing homes are evacuated. A group of temporary wartime buildings is quickly readied for the seriously ill, and complete surgical field equipment is flown in to be available in case of power failure. By air and rail, 1424 patients are transported to safe zones, miraculously without loss of life.

By Sunday, May 7, the boiling waters, churning along at 25 knots through the suburbs where the river loops in tight turns, have hurdled the banks to short-cut their northward race. Overnight, 4000 are homeless.

To care for these and 4500 evacuees from rural sections, the Red Cross and civic clubs set up bunks

Soldiers and civilians fill sandbags
to build up the riverbank (top)
in hard-hit East Kildonan.

Soldiers and civilians fill sandbags
to build up the riverbank (top)
in hard-hit East Kildonan.

in the civic auditorium. In the railway yards, sleeping cars shelter hundreds. Hotels put Army cots in lobbies and banquet rooms.

Despite heroic efforts, the implacable river penetrates to the very vitals of the city. Two key electric substations are threatened. Hundreds of men are deployed to throw sandbag ramparts around them. Behind these dikes, pumps are set up to hurl back the seeping water. Deep in the bowels of the buildings, engineers perform ticklish miracles restringing high-voltage cables. Navy frogmen lower themselves through manholes to plug 240 power conduits through which flood waters are seeping into subterranean installations.

Rock causeways are hurriedly built on top of flooded city streets to bring in vital supplies, particularly coal, to the electric and gas plants. Hundreds of trucks are commandeered to haul in rock and ballast from a quarry 12 miles outside Winnipeg.

As the river continues its inexorable rise, engineers are faced with the job of keeping open the bridges which connect Winnipeg with municipalities east of the Red. Over these vital transportation links come such essentials as bread, meat, milk. Debris crashes and jams against the bridges. Thousands of tons of steel girders, rails, anything available, are dumped on the bridges to save them.

But one by one, four of the five great spans over the Red must be closed. Only the 50-year-old Redwood Bridge to the north is open. Army engineers dynamite derelict houses and barns logjammed against its foundations.

To meet the threat of disease from floating sewage, thousands are inoculated against typhoid. Flooded cellars are doused with chloride of lime. Chlorination of drinking water is increased, raw milk banned.

With the Red now nearly 30 feet above normal, the Assiniboine River on the west and the Seine on the east suddenly back up under pressure of the Red. Brigadier Morton advises immediate evacuation of all women and children.

So begins the exodus of 120,000 persons. Roads out of the city are black by day and brilliant by night with traffic. Planes carry capacity loads to Toronto, Montreal, Vancouver. Hundreds of aged and sick are stretcher-borne to planes or sleeping cars. From throughout the country come thousands of telegrams offering shelter. Owners of summer cottages in resort towns outside Winnipeg mail keys to the Red Cross, asking that their places be used for the homeless.

On the night of May 18, the Red reaches the incredible height of 30.3 feet above normal. At Flood

At the height of the flood, never-say-die Winnipeggers hoisted their flood slogan on the City Hall.

WE'RE WEARY AND WET -BUT WE'LL WIN!

Headquarters, two alternate plans are readied. One is Operation If—a disaster plan for the evacuation of the *entire* city if the river rises another two feet. The other plan is Operation Rainbow—rehabilitation of the flooded city.

For long days, the fate of the city hangs in balance. Finally, on May 25, with the river at 28.85 feet, and slowly inching downward, Brigadier Morton relaxes the evacuation order.

Thus end 20 days and nights of constant siege and exhausting effort to conquer a river and save a city. So remarkable was the rescue work in those 20 days that only one man was drowned. So thorough were the sanitation measures that not one case of illness could be attributed to the flood. In all the shuffle of evacuation, there was not a single traffic fatality.

By early summer, Winnipeg's citizens were driving into Operation Rainbow. On the City Hall the flood slogan "We're Weary and Wet But We'll Win" was replaced by "Let's Look Nifty in Fifty."

"They say that Winnipeg was saved from complete disaster by a miracle," City Engineer William Hurst told me. "It was—a miracle of guts and hard work."

He held up both his hands. "The miracle of 100,000 multiplied by ten. A million fingers in the dikes."

A huge five-year construction job ended the threat of flooding in Winnipeg. In 1967, with removal of the last 100 million cubic yards of earth, the $63-million Red River Floodway was completed to steer flood water harmlessly around the city. Thirteen bridges carry railway and highway traffic over it, ten electric power lines span it and two pipelines dip under it.

Linked with the Floodway are two projects to control flooding on the Assiniboine River, which joins the Red in Winnipeg: a dam on the Assiniboine at Shellmouth near the Saskatchewan border and a diversion into Lake Manitoba near Portage la Prairie. These two projects cost $20 million.

The Floodway posed unusual difficulties. The Red River Valley is not a true valley but the wide, shallow basin of a long-vanished glacier lake. Its overburden of clay or "gumbo" soil retains moisture, and sudden weather changes can cause piers and foundations to slip. To minimize this problem, gentle slopes were constructed on the sides of the 30-mile-long Floodway channel, which has an average depth of 30 feet and a top width of 1000 feet.

The project was built by Manitoba, with Ottawa sharing the cost. A direct offspring of the 1950 disaster, it provides security not only against floods of that magnitude but against substantially larger ones.

Fighting the Wild Atoms at Chalk River

That day in 1952 something went wrong inside Canada's nuclear reactor. It touched off an epic of courage and ingenuity in the first test of man's ability to handle a major peacetime atomic emergency. In more than two decades of steadily-growing atomic activity, it was the only Canadian accident of any consequence

By David O. Woodbury

The frosty air of a mid-December afternoon in 1952 hung motionless over Chalk River, Ont., Canada's atomic-experiment station 130 miles northwest of Ottawa, where 1700 men and women were winding up their week's work. Within the red-brick building that housed "NRX," then the world's most powerful atomic-research machine, scientists were conducting an experiment. Suddenly, in the control room, alarm bells jangled, instrument pointers leaped off-scale. Deep inside the massive concrete shield something had gone wrong.

The moment dreaded by every atomic scientist had overtaken Chalk River. Would this multi-million-dollar atomic giant burst its bonds and become contaminated with deadly radioactive dust?

Inside the reactor's eight-foot-thick shield was an aluminum tank filled with precious heavy water. Submerged in this were 176 long thin rods of uranium, sheathed in aluminum tubes that circulated water from the nearby Ottawa River to keep them cool. For the experiment that afternoon it had been necessary to cut the cooling water around some of the uranium rods to a trickle and to turn off some other controls.

"We were taking a calculated risk," Fred Gilbert, manager of reactor operations, said later. "But our calculations weren't good enough. It was a million-to-one gamble that the remaining emergency devices wouldn't all fail at once. But they did."

In one enormous burst, the atomic chain reaction burgeoned to a hundred million watts of heat, blasting molten metal, radioactive ashes and steam through the bottom of the machine into the basement.

Every employe at Chalk River had been alerted by years of drill for just such an emergency. As soon as the siren cut loose, doors and windows were

Surrealist blue glow is caused by gamma radiation from spent fuel rods hanging in a pool of water called a rod bay. Spent fuel from Canadian nuclear reactors contains fission products such as Barium and Krypton isotopes and plutonium. Some is melted and reused, some exported as fuel for breeder reactors.

An aerial view of the Chalk River Nuclear Laboratories, Canada's atomic station 130 miles northwest of Ottawa on the Ottawa River.

slammed shut in offices and laboratories, cafeterias and guardhouses. Telephone lines were cleared for emergency use. Then down the deserted street strode Dr. A. J. Cipriani, Chief of Radiation Hazard Control, adjusting his respirator. Behind him teams of monitor men fanned out among the buildings, Geiger counters in hand. The watching employes knew that this was not just another drill.

Radioactive ash had already escaped through the tall stack into the winter air. The siren wailed again, this time the long sustained note that meant *evacuation*. Holding handkerchiefs to their faces to keep from breathing radioactive dust, workers filed out to long lines of buses. In a few moments they were rolling away through the snow.

Chalk River was deserted—save for the handful of men converging on NRX to fight this first major battle against atoms that had burst their bonds. Thereafter, for 14 dangerous months plucky pioneers were to stage a cleanup under constant menace of deadly radioactivity. These ingenious men established once and for all that human beings can safely build, repair and maintain useful peacetime atomic engines saturated with death.

The crew on duty that afternoon had done the one thing left to do when all normal controls go. Opening valves under the machine, they had dumped the heavy water out of the reactor tank. This stopped the wild chain reaction and ended the first threat of general conflagration. But the emergency had not passed. The cooling river water was still flooding down through the breaks, spreading radiation far and wide through the building.

As supervisors rushed into the control room, muffled in their masks, they faced a critical decision. Overheated uranium may ignite and burn like gunpowder beyond all stopping. If those remaining rods of the unruly metal kindled, nothing could prevent a holocaust. "Keep that cooling water going!" was the only possible decision.

For three days they kept the water going, till a million gallons of radioactive liquid had nearly submerged the basement, contaminating everything in its path with radioactivity nearly seven times as strong as that of all the radium produced since the Curies discovered it 50 years before.

The contaminated water obviously could not be returned to the river. Yet every day it remained in the building it carried radioactive mud deeper into floors and walls and equipment. The only answer was to run a pipeline for about a mile into the wasteland and pump the water into pits in the sand.

Welders and pipefitters worked around the clock laying the pipe over frozen ground. By Christmas Eve the work was done. The water was pumped away to seep harmlessly into the forest sands. But the worst job was still ahead. Radioactive material covered every inch of machinery, floors and walls; atomic dust coated beams and ceilings. Worst of all, the interior of the wrecked reactor was thoroughly saturated.

Many atomic experts believed a cleanup was impossible. Heavily radioactive materials ordinarily must be handled by mechanical robots behind thick lead or under many feet of water. The Canadians knew all that; yet they said, "It is important to prove that this job can be done without robots. The only way to prove it is to try."

They knew that as long as the exposures to radiation were kept within limits no undue risk would be involved. After all, damaged cells tend to be replaced by the body. The chief dangers arise when the radiation dose is big enough to interfere with cell replacement.

If workers took turns, a man could absorb three months' dose in a few minutes and still be all right, provided he took no more during the three months. The work thus could be precisely budgeted in estimated units of human exposure. But there were not enough men to do it.

Calls for help went out; response was fast. Skilled radiation-control groups from Canada's Army and Navy flocked in. Fully 200 U. S. technicians, skilled artisans and specialists came north—atomic submarine crews-in-training, experts from the U. S. Navy's Radiological Defense Laboratory, experi-

Decontamination of the main floor in Building 100 after the 1952 NRX incident.

Rehabilitation included this removal of a damaged fuel rod from NRX. These men work deep inside the reactor.

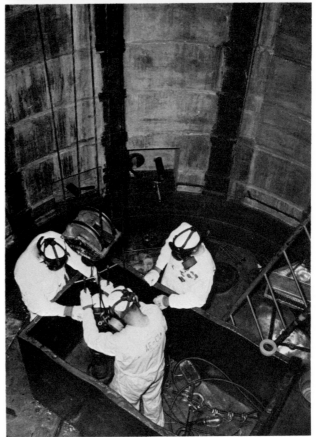

This was the main reactor hall during the 1952 clean-up. As long as exposures to radiation were kept within certain limits, workers ran no undue risk.

enced people from Westinghouse, General Electric and Electric Boat Co.'s atomic projects.

Meanwhile, at Chalk River, janitors, guards, chauffeurs, even clerks and accountants went to work with mops and vacuum cleaners. In the first week there was a setback. One of the pipelines sprang a leak. Repairing it used up the radiation allowance of 17 skilled mechanics and put them off the job for months.

Workers had to be thoroughly briefed in every move. There must be no idle seconds in the presence of the deadly radioactivity. Every person wore white coveralls, hard shoes and rubbers and a respirator mask. Sometimes the masks leaked, no matter how thoroughly inspected; one time 80 men were temporarily off the work list for overexposure. Everyone wore the standard film badge, fitted with a photographic negative to record the amount of radiation received. Every man had a card which told exactly how much of his precious exposure time he had used.

Some pockets of radioactivity were so "hot" that even to find them by Geiger-counter search was too dangerous. An ingenious camera, sent from the Knolls Laboratory in the U. S., mapped their location by remote control. To clean out these pockets, specially trained workers were sent to the "firing line" for a few minutes at a time. These men wore plastic suits into which clean outdoor air was blown to prevent any possible dust from leaking in. Coming off the job, the wearer went straight to the showers to be washed down thoroughly, suit and all. He was then stripped by a special undresser to keep the man's hands from tracking contamination to his own skin, and showered again; then he was thoroughly explored with a counter. If any trace of radiation was found he was showered over and over.

Supervisors for the cleanup were essential, and their exposure allowance had to be conserved at all costs. The U. S. Atomic Energy Commission sent a portable television outfit, so cleanup crews could be directed from the safety of the control room.

From January to June the cleanup went on. In some places radioactive liquids had gone so deep that inches of concrete had to be chipped off and replaced. Meanwhile, behind massive lead shields, skilled workers began gingerly lifting the scrambled wreckage from within the NRX machine itself. At last they exposed the heart of the great reactor, the central tank called the "calandria." This ten-foot-high aluminum drum, weighing two and a half tons, had been the center of the uranium "meltdown." It would be the largest and heaviest radioactive object ever handled. The gamma rays were so intense that to approach to within 50 feet was hazardous.

The removal plan was worked out to the finest detail. Automatic grappling hooks would be lowered on cables from an overhead crane; the tank

Canada now has a second big reactor, NRU (below and right) and three small support reactors, in addition to rebuilt NRX.

would be lifted out, swung over the open floor, then lowered into a canvas dust bag on a wooden sledge. Drawstrings would tightly close the bag to prevent lethal dust from escaping. Then the sledge would be towed to the woods and buried. The whole procedure was run off in advance with a dummy tank. A single slip among the 70 men involved might mean death or months of extra work.

On the fateful evening of May 22, 1953, all was ready. High under the roof sat the crane operator in his heavily shielded cab, awaiting orders for his delicate maneuvers from a distant observer. Monitors stood ready to check the exact strength of radiation at every moment. Over loudspeakers the announcer's voice begins to drone the 28 steps of the action. "Number one. Attach hook. Align for lifting." There is a whir of gears as the big hook slowly descends into the reactor. Tense minutes pass. Then, without a hitch, the big, innocent-looking calandria rises into view.

"Health men take survey readings." Out from behind their shields hurry the instrument men, quickly checking, dashing to safety again. Then the ponderous mass of aluminum swings out over the room and sinks slowly into the yawning canvas bag. Another crew jumps out, snatches the draw ropes

and pulls hard. There is an audible sigh of relief.

But then comes trouble. The sledge has been held by cables attached to it by a long steel pin, which must now be removed. But the pin refuses to pull out! It is jammed tight.

"Stand-by crew!" the loudspeakers bellow. "Move out. Relieve that pin!"

Like hunters stalking prey, the scientists slip from their protecting screens, eyes glued to the canvas bag with its lurking death. They seize the ropes leading to the pin. "All together now! *Heave!*" For a second they strain. The ropes are taut. Imperceptibly the pin begins to slide. All at once it is out and the calandria is free to start its journey to the burial ground.

"Cut all trailing ropes!" sings out the announcer as a tractor picks up the tow rope.

Axes flash, the last tie is gone and the sledge begins to move. (As it lumbers past the buildings, recorder needles inside jump off-scale.) Out across the empty plant the procession moves like some strange funeral cortege, supervisors in cars ahead, the tractor driver sitting stolidly behind his thick lead shield.

Half an hour later, deep in the woods, the deadly object is brought to rest. Methodically, bulldozers heap sand around and over it till the last vestiges of its lethal rays are permanently imprisoned. Not a single spectator attends the final rights.

NRX, rebuilt with increased power in 1954, its strength boosted again in 1961, is still in service, three times as powerful as before the accident. It completed 20 years of operation in July 1967. In addition, Chalk River now has a second big experimental research reactor, NRU, and three small support reactors. NRX itself is still one of the world's most useful reactors for fuel development and material testing. Information and experience obtained from it have influenced the building and operation of 100-odd power reactors around the world.

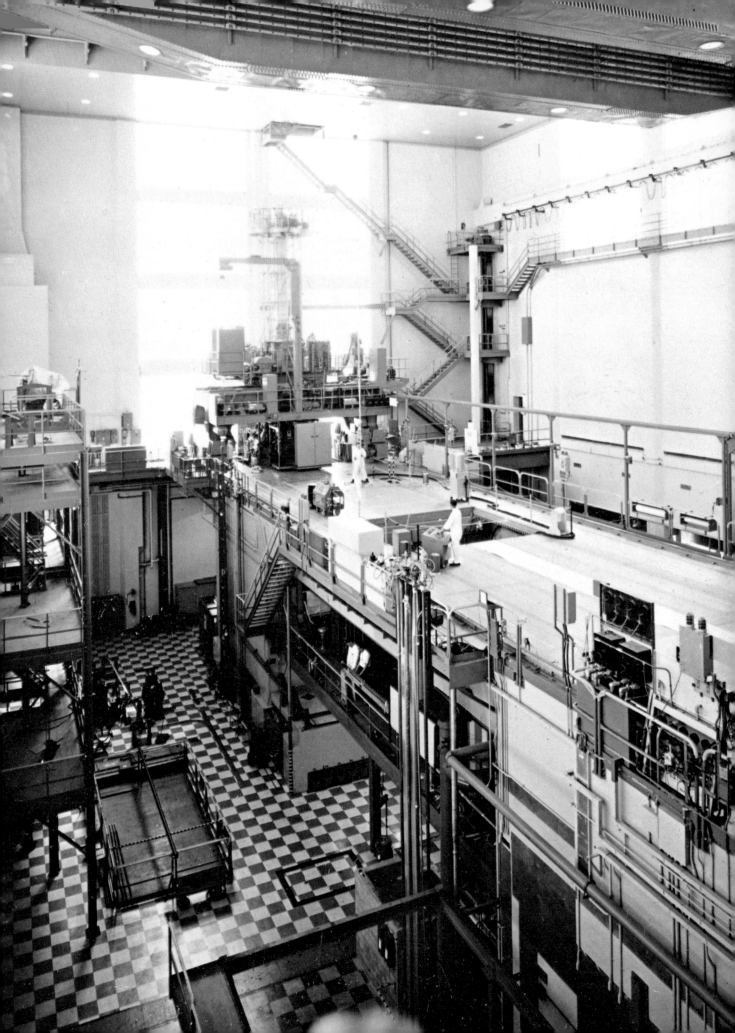

The Big "Bump" at Springhill

Trapped in one of the world's deepest coal mines, given up for dead
by many, a little group of survivors waited in darkness and despair

By Joseph P. Blank

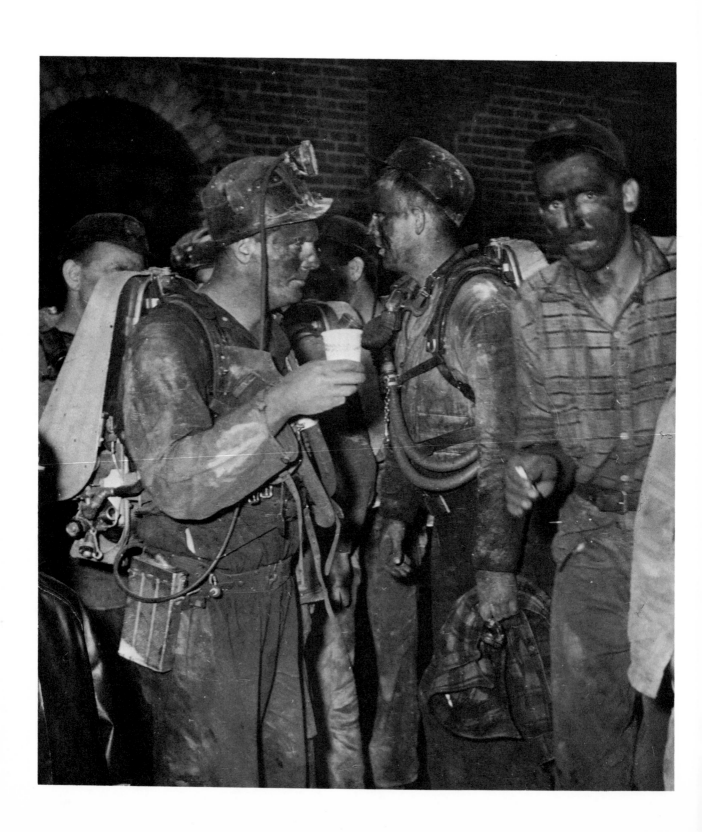

No one in Springhill, N.S., will ever forget that Thursday—October 23, 1958. It was a beautiful Indian-summer afternoon as the 174 men scheduled to work the three-o'clock shift in the No. 2 mine at the edge of town donned their mining clothes, and many groused about having to go into the pits on such a nice day. Then they straggled into the lamp cabin, where each received a locked safety lamp containing a freshly charged battery that would give light for ten hours. After filling their water cans, the men got onto the cable-operated rake, a series of coupled, low, wooden trolleys.

Laughing, joking, singing, they sprawled on the rake as it moved down the rails of the 12-foot-wide main slope into No. 2. This mine, leased by the Cumberland Railway and Coal Co., was one of the deepest coal mines in the world. It slanted, following a rich seam of bituminous coal, 14,600 feet into the earth, and reached, at its greatest vertical depth, 4340 feet below the surface.

As the rake descended, the temperature rose and the air grew humid. At the main slope, 7800 feet deep, the men transferred to a second rake. Groups swung off at the 13,000-, 13,400- and 13,800-foot "levels" (avenues leading to the face of coal), then walked about 1000 feet to the "wall"—where the seam of coal was being worked. Soon they were digging coal, breaking stubborn sections with compressed-air-driven chipper picks, and shoveling it into conveyor pans.

At 8 p.m. activity in the town, as in the mine, was normal. Mayor Ralph Gilroy was opening a town council meeting; church social groups were in action; a Wolf Cub meeting had just adjourned. Housewives had put the younger children to bed and were settling down to watch TV.

Five minutes later a violent "bump"—a kind of subterranean earthquake—ripped through No. 2. "Bumps" are associated with deep mining and generally attributed to the changing underground pressures resulting from man-made excavations. This one smashed along the working seam of coal from the 12,600 level down to the 13,800 level. The pavements (mine floors) heaved toward the roofs, twisting steel rails like paper clips, pancaking steel coal cars, and shredding hardwood timbers that had been used to support the roofs. It shook every building in Springhill and registered on a university seismograph in Halifax, 70 miles away. When it stopped, it had killed 75 men and destroyed one of Canada's largest coal mines.

But, at several places, the bump had whimsically refrained from pushing the pavements to their limit, leaving sizeable pockets where men might possibly survive.

Solange Maddison, at home with her 14-year-old daughter, jumped from her chair. "My God!" she exclaimed. "It's a bump! And your father is down there." Mayor Gilroy and the five councilmen at Town Hall broke for the door. Throughout the town, doors opened and adults and children were silhouetted in the light. Then they ran toward the mine.

George Calder, the mine manager, stepping into his kitchen when his house shook, dashed to the phone. "We don't know what's happened," said the surface foreman. "The telephones are out from the 7800 level on down." Calder, a miner himself for many years, rushed out of the house.

This was not Springhill's first disaster. In 1891 an explosion had killed 125 miners. Another killed 39 men in 1956. Since 1881, some 180 more men had been killed in small explosions, rock falls and bumps.

There had been no foreseeable reason to expect a big bump this October. True, in recent months No. 2 had been bumping in a small way every few weeks, tumbling coal off the face of the seam. But the mine had been laid out according to the most advanced mining knowledge and was regularly inspected by government experts.

Yet many miners worried. As Theodore Michniak, a veteran of the pits since 1919, said, "I had a feeling of dread every time I went down. That mine was

Since 1881, almost 350 Springhill miners
had died in "bumps," rock falls
and explosions. This had been
the temporary morgue in the Armory
in 1956 when an explosion killed 39 men.

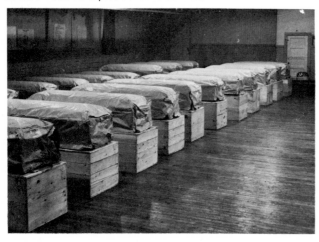

too deep." And whenever 22-year-old Larry Leadbetter, who had received his mining papers only the previous year, saw a mild bump shake coal off the seam, his mouth went dry and he found himself breathing heavily.

But these Springhill miners—mostly of Scottish, Irish, English and French descent—were strongly attached to their community and their work. Like their fathers, also miners, they were born and raised in Springhill, a sprawling hill town first settled in 1790, and they expected to stay there. Seven of ten owned their homes, had a car and TV. Though their work was dirty and dangerous, they felt it bound them together.

"On top," as Gorley Kempt put it, "I miss the camaraderie we have in the pits—no jealousies, no rank down there. We're dependent on each other, and in a crisis a man's first impulse is to help a buddy even if it means a 50-50 chance of getting hurt himself."

Just before that smashing, convulsive bump hit No. 2, Kempt had been walking up the "wall" near the junction of the 13,000 level to repair a coal-conveyor pan. "Suddenly the pavement seemed to explode," he said. "Everything flew with a terrible rushing of noise and wind."

At the same time, in the same area, Joe McDonald, gray-haired and older-looking than his 38 years—he'd been gassed in the 1956 explosion—was bent over, digging coal with a pick. "Suddenly the face of coal came toward me, and the floor jumped seven feet," he said. He came down with a coal pan on top of his legs. He groped for his light, tried to get up. His leg, broken in three places, buckled. Then he swung his lamp and saw a solid wall of coal and rock where seven men had been at work. He screamed.

Forty feet up the wall, Eldred Lowther was about to say something to Harold Brine when he was flung into the air, bounced off the roof and hurled against rocks amid choking coal dust. Ted Michniak was leaning on his shovel, waiting for a coal car. "Then I got pushed, and I was on my hands and knees. My shoulder and left side hurt. I heard a gurgling and put my hand to my ear. Blood was running out."

Hugh Guthro had his pick poised over his head when the bump gave him a tremendous boot in the pants, sending him skidding under the conveyor pans. Fred Hunter never heard a sound. He found himself spitting coal, trying to push a large rock off his legs and wondering how many men around him were still alive.

On the surface, manager George Calder's first action was to order the slopes of the mine cleared—which meant the coal cars had to be brought up and replaced with the passenger trolleys before rescuers could go down. Of hundreds who volunteered, Calder chose 20 men for the first rescue party, including seven mine, union and government officials.

The slope area was roped off to prevent disruption of the rescue activities. Just beyond stood a growing crowd of townspeople, some silent, some softly weeping. All Saints' Hospital went on standby. Harold Gordon, general manager of coal operations for Cumberland's parent firm, Dominion Steel and Coal Corp., was racing by car from Sydney, 264 miles away. "Draegermen" (miners specially trained for rescue work in concentrations of heavy gas) were driving from other Nova Scotia mines.

From other Nova Scotia towns
came specially-trained miners,
"draegermen" whose special skills
might help save some lives. Rescuers
worked on bellies and knees,
using sawed-off shovels and picks.
In heavy concentrations of gas,
because of the danger of sparks,
no steel equipment could be used.
There rescuers dug with their hands.

At 8:40 Calder and his crew rode down into No. 2, stopping to exchange words with dazed survivors climbing up the slope. They found the 13,000 and 13,400 levels blocked by methane, a gas released by coal. On the 13,800 level the gas was less dense, and the men moved in, picking their way for several hundred feet. Then they met a wall of debris, pavement, rails, machinery. With picks, shovels, crowbars and bare hands they fought through the rubble. Behind them, Dr. Arnold Burden, who had worked in the mines to earn his way through medical school, checked and tended the injured.

By 10 p.m. the cable-drawn trolleys had brought up all three-o'clock-shift men able to leave the mine, and had taken down some 100 local miners and draegermen. Three and a half hours after the bump the first rescue team broke through to 12 men trapped on the 13,800 level. At 1:35 a.m. another rescue team freed 11 more miners at the 13,400 level and, around 4 a.m., it released three others. Before Friday's rainy dawn 80 men had been rescued. Ninety-four others were dead or missing.

The search for survivors was brutal. Electrical equipment was forbidden lest it trigger a gas explosion. Men worked on their bellies and knees with sawed-off shovels and picks to hack out a yard-high, shoulder-wide passage.

Where gas was heavy, steel equipment had to be

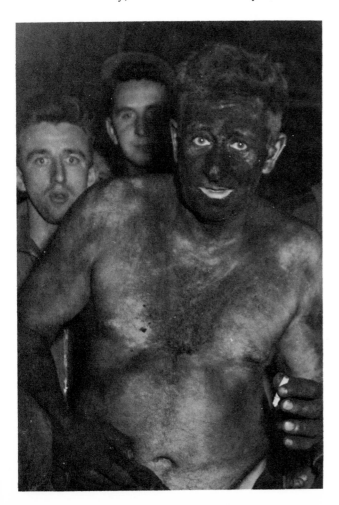

abandoned for fear of sparks. Here men worked with just their hands and sharpened pick handles. Loosened coal and rock they shoveled into buckets, which were passed from man to man out the tunnels. Sometimes rescuers broke into sobs from sheer exhaustion.

Progress was sometimes less than ten feet in eight hours. And though dangers of another bump (the pits continued to reverberate from time to time) or a tunnel collapse or a heavy concentration of gas continually threatened, nobody paid any attention. The job had to be done. Every trapped man had to be accounted for.

At noon Friday, with tears in his eyes, Harold Gordon announced there was little hope for the missing miners. But few people in the rain-drenched crowd accepted this as a signal to go home. They stood silently. In answer to inquiring looks from wives, Mayor Gilroy said, "We've got to pray."

By Sunday, three days after the bump, the mine officials privately accepted the deaths of all unaccounted-for miners. But Johnny Calder, head mechanic at the mine and brother of the manager, thought differently. "We're going to find men alive," he told his brother. "I know it."

In the homes of the missing miners feeling ranged from unalloyed despair to trembling hope. "By Monday," said Margaret Guthro, "I was sure Hughie wouldn't come out alive. I told our children he was dead. I made funeral arrangements, and cleared some of the furniture out of the living room to make space for the coffin."

On the other hand, Marguerite Kempt, who had a feeling Gorley was all right, kept the house lights burning through each night. "It didn't seem right," she said, "to turn them out when you were expecting somebody to come home."

Skittering between hope and hopelessness, Solange Maddison remembered the stories of mine accidents her father used to tell her, how one man was killed and the man standing next to him wasn't even scratched. "I kept wondering which one Bowsie had been."

Entombed nearly a mile below the earth's surface, Bowsie Maddison, whose lamp had been smashed off his helmet, had at first sat dazed and bewildered. Soon he heard young Larry Leadbetter, trapped in a cubicle of fallen rock, screaming, "Help me! My God, don't leave me!"

He saw Gorley Kempt crawl toward Leadbetter and direct his lamp through a two-foot aperture. "You hurt?" Kempt asked. Leadbetter said no. But he was frozen with fear. To shock him into controlling his panic Kempt said, "Then stay there," and began to crawl away. The ruse worked. Leadbetter scrambled out of his trap.

Ambulances stood by at the pithead,
ready to speed survivors to hospital.
And there *were* survivors.
On the morning of the seventh day,
rescuers broke through to 12 trapped men.

Then Bowsie discovered Caleb Rushton and Levi Milley nearby. Twenty yards below them Joe McDonald was yelling for help, and they crawled down to him. Moving as gingerly as possible, they dragged him 30 feet over the rubble to a safer spot. It took them an hour. The pain in Joe's leg was excruciating; the bones sounded like crunching glass when he moved the leg with his hands, and it had begun to turn black from internal bleeding. A few yards from him lay Ted Michniak, his dislocated shoulder and battered ribs flaring with pain. He bound his left arm to his body with his belt.

After an agonizing search of the living and the dead, the men found there were 12 survivors: Brine, Guthro, Holloway, Hunter, Kempt, Leadbetter, Lowther, McDonald, Maddison, Michniak, Milley and Rushton. They conferred on their next move. "I'll stay with McDonald," said Michniak. "He can't move. You boys take my lamp and try to find a way out. If you do, keep going, then send back help for us. Remember, there's gas in here. Keep low."

The ten men split into three groups to search for escape—up the wall, down the wall and out the level. El Lowther led Rushton and Harold Brine up the wall, scrambling over rubble tearing the skin off their hands and knees. After advancing 40 feet Lowther hit a pocket of gas, slumped as if clubbed. His mates dragged him back. Brine tried. He too was felled.

The other teams had no more success. Working on their knees and bellies, they tore a path around battered mining equipment, only to be blocked by fallen rocks.

By early Friday morning Kempt had the only lamp with any power. "We'll have to get batteries off dead men," he said to Lowther. They found a body. To reach the battery case hanging off the back of the man's belt, it was necessary to embrace him. "I can't do it," Lowther said. "He and I used to eat supper together every night down here."

"I'll do it," Kempt said. "I know he'd want us to." He cut loose the dead man's battery case and connected it to his own head lamp. He used the lamp sparingly.

Water was becoming a problem now. During the tension following the bump, the men had unthinkingly consumed most of the water left in their cans. They scraped around in the rubble, searching for dead miners' water cans. By Friday evening they had collected about two quarts of water and delegated Kempt to ration it out. Every four hours, by Rushton's luminous-dial watch, each man received approximately a half ounce, and each time the men took turns carrying a ration down to Joe McDonald and Ted Michniak—a 15-minute trip over sharp rubble.

Saturday evening Kempt's lamp flickered its last glow, and the men plunged into darkness. They sprawled silently, each sealed in his own thoughts. Lowther, frustration and fear digging deep into his mind, insisted that they *try* to get out. "Otherwise they'll find us only when they clean up—and that'll be too late."

"It's useless to dig," Kempt argued. "We have very little water, and we're getting weaker. We know they're trying to reach us. We'll just have to wait."

When Brine asked what they were going to do for water, Kempt replied, "We'll have to drink our urine." The group laughed—then realized it was no joke.

They were nearly a mile below ground. They had no food. They had enough water to wet their lips for only one more day. Death was all about them—they couldn't escape the odor of decaying flesh. And ahead lay the prospect of their own deaths, slow and terrible.

Caleb Rushton, one of the best singers in the Baptist choir, started humming. Milley said, "Let's have a song." Caleb began "The Stranger of Galilee": "And I felt I could love Him forever, so gracious and tender was He. . . ."

Before the hymn was finished the group was silently praying, and two men were trying to stifle sobs. "My grandfather was killed in this mine nearly 35 years ago," choked Leadbetter. "Now it's

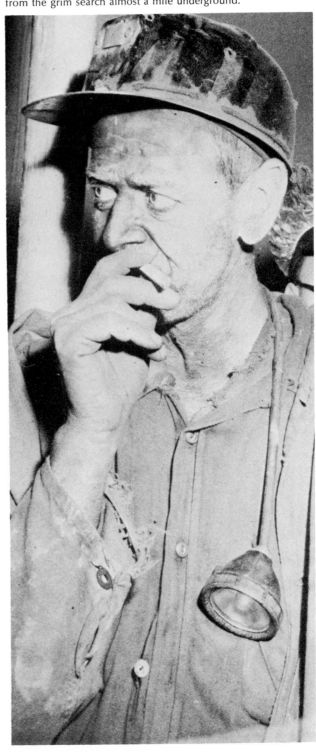

After the rescue of 12 men
trapped almost a week, seven more
were found—on the ninth day.
Among the seven was Maurice Ruddick,
shown here with his son Revere.

Hugh Guthro's wife had given up.
"I told our children Hughie was dead,"
Mrs. Guthro said. "I made funeral
arrangements and cleared some
of the furniture out of the living room
to make space for the coffin." Guthro
was one of the 12 men rescued
after close to a week in the mine.

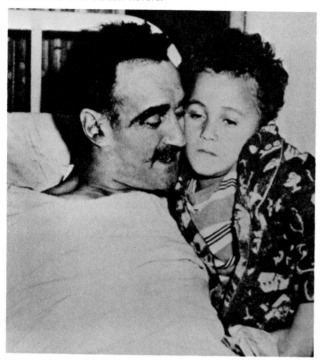

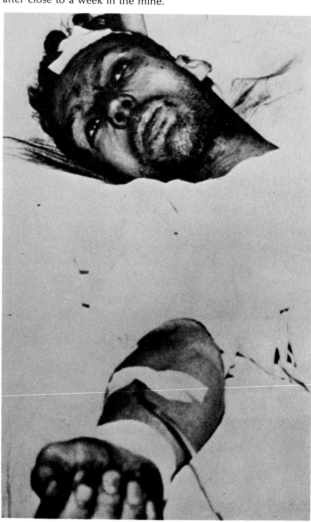

me. My two-year-old will never remember she had a father."

The others urged him to let go, and he wept until he relaxed. Then they reassured him: hundreds of their buddies were trying to reach them; escape was only a matter of time. This established a pattern. If compelled, each man felt free to break down temporarily; then he was bombarded with assurances. "Each of us got strength from the group," Kempt said.

Kempt had discovered a broken six-inch air pipe that jutted out of the debris 20 feet away. Now the men periodically crawled to it and pounded it 13 times to indicate life on the 13,000 level. It was a hated chore, for the open area around the pipe was very limited, and any movement of rock or coal could crush or seal a man off.

Sometimes during the lulls they heard tapping or grinding and their hearts jumped with hope. Or were they imagining the poundings and voices?

Once Rushton thought he heard a faint "hello" from up the wall. He nudged Brine. "Did you hear that?" The two men scrambled 150 feet toward the sound, then lay still, straining to hear it again. "Help!" Brine screamed over and over. When he was exhausted, Rushton took up the cry until his throat ached. No answer came.

On Sunday morning Rushton brought the dial of his watch close to his face. "It's going on seven," he said. "They'll be getting ready for church soon." The men began praying. Joe McDonald prayed almost continuously, using his fingers for a rosary. His leg, swollen to twice its normal size, was hemorrhaging, depriving his body of fluid and making him crave water more than the others.

Two feet away lay Michniak, his shoulder dislocation putting painful pressure on nerves. He and McDonald had tried to follow Kempt's laugh-provoking suggestion—that they drink their urine—but they couldn't keep it down. Finally they altered the taste, as did the others, by adding coal dust and bark from spruce and hemlock timbers. It worked.

Though neither his tomb-mates nor he realized it, Fred Hunter was the most seriously injured. A mild concussion had made him oblivious to the damage done by the rock that had smashed into his thigh. A clot had formed, cutting off circulation. This brought on gangrene. The men tried to relieve his pain with massage, but it didn't help, and he frequently let go with a scream.

Levi Milley seemed more susceptible than the others to the occasional drifts of methane. By Tuesday morning he was shaking his head, trying to erase a yellow glow before his eyes. Soon the others were beginning to see glows and flashes, too. "Look," said Joey Holloway, "it's almost bright in here."

Bowsie Maddison kept worrying whether he'd paid his last insurance premium and whether his wife, in case of his death, would be able to scrape by. Thirst had swollen his tongue. To escape the torment he started talking at random about anything that came into his head: dart throwing, deer hunting, the Montreal Canadiens. Soon all the men were talking as if they would leave on a hunting party the next hour.

Lowther got to thinking about his family, about playing baseball with his ten-year-old son, Bobby. The boy showed promise as a pitcher, and he hoped his wife, Goldie, would encourage him to practice. Absent-mindedly he turned to Caleb Rushton and said, "Now look here, Goldie. . . ."

"What do you want me to do—put my arms around you?" exclaimed Rushton.

Tears in his eyes, Harold Gordon of Dosco had publicly announced there was little hope for the missing miners.

Lowther mumbled self-consciously and tried to doze off. But whenever it grew especially hot or quiet, he worried about gas: it could kill one of them, and the others would have no way of knowing.

"Look," said Lowther, "we can't just lie here and die like rats. Somebody ought to bang on that air pipe."

Kempt and Brine crawled over the rubble and lay with their heads near the pipe. Suddenly Kempt put his ear against the opening. "I think I hear noises," he said. "Like pipes being disconnected." He took a deep breath and with all his power shouted, "Hello!"

"Hello," came a voice. And again, "Hello."

Kempt lay stunned. He felt hot tears on his lips. Brine laughed and cried simultaneously. "Wake up, boys!" he yelled. "Wake up! They're coming to get us!"

On the 13,000 level, rescuers had been making slow progress through the debris, so manager George Calder had decided to dig a parallel tunnel through the solid coal instead. As the miners pushed through the coal, an air pipe had to be advanced with them. They had progressed 700 feet when a rescuer's pick struck a disrupted six-inch air line (73 feet away at the other end of the bent but intact pipe, lay Kempt and Brine). Calder immediately called in ventilation engineer Blair Phillips. "Sample the air from that pipe," he said. "If it's good, we can use it for our supply."

Phillips had just recorked his air-sample bottle, and was backing out to analyze its contents when Kempt's shout stopped him. He was both shocked and thrilled.

More hello's were exchanged; then Kempt croaked, "There are 12 of us." He rattled off their names. "For God's sake come and get us!"

"We'll get you," answered Phillips.

Kempt crawled back to the group, hugged the weeping Rushton. When he returned to the pipe Lowther shouted after him. "Gorley, tell 'em we need water."

At six o'clock that Wednesday evening, six days after the big bump, the copper tubing slid down the pipe and hit Kempt's hand. Water poured through.

"Caleb, say grace for us," said one of the men.

Rushton held his water can and said, "Oh, Lord, we thank you for the pipe and the blessed water."

Coffee followed the water. Then the men settled down to await the breakthrough. "Every minute seemed like a day," Guthro said later.

Before dozing off Kempt thought a final prayer: "We're close now, so close. *Please* don't let go with a bump."

At 2:25 Thursday morning, the rescuers chopped their way through the last foot of coal and crawled to the men. Dr. Burden quickly examined each man, told him to protect his eyes from the surface light by pulling up a blanket, and saw him to a wire-mesh stretcher. As tenderly as possible, the miners dragged the stretchers through the narrow tunnel and put them on the trolleys. As they approached the surface one of the men asked, "What's the noise up there?"

"Those are people cheering you."

"That's good," he said. "I thought it was bill collectors waiting for us."

Johnny Calder now felt an inspired certainty that they would find other survivors. A crew of 30 began crashing on up the wall to the 12,600 level. In 48 hours they tunneled nearly 300 feet, and at 4 a.m. Saturday one of the lead diggers crawled back to report excitedly that they could see a man—"and he's alive!"

The diggers worked savagely to break through the rubble and broken timbers, shoring up their own passageway as they went, to reach the unconscious but still breathing victim, who was quickly rushed to the surface. And within a half hour they had pushed on through to a zone that was less heavily bumped. "What did I tell you!" exclaimed Calder as their lamps focused on six dozing men.

And Springhill buried more of her coal-miner sons. Seventy-five had been killed this time, almost twice as many as in 1956 but fewer than in the disaster of 1891, when 125 had died. Springhill wept again, comforted again by the sympathy of admiring people the world over.

At 9:15 that Saturday morning, after eight and a half days in the mine, the six men reached the surface to the cheers of hundreds jammed around the mine entrance. Said Mayor Gilroy, "It was as if those six men belonged to every family."

He sounded the sentiment felt round the world. Springhill's ordeal had brought some 40,000 telegrams and letters, and nearly two million dollars in contributions. The money came in pennies from children, a $100,000 check from a corporation, a liberal donation from Pope John XXIII. It was raised by college dormitories, square-dance clubs, professional wrestlers, church and concert groups, a race track, newspapers.

To the nearly 400 men who risked their lives to free the trapped miners went the medal of the Royal Canadian Humane Association, the first time the award had been made to a group. To the same men went also a special gold medal from the Carnegie Hero Fund Commission, the second instance of a group award by the Commission. (The other went to the heroes at the sinking of the *Titanic* in 1912.)

The bump left a great hurt in Springhill—but it also left great lessons. It taught the 7000 townspeople that faith and determination can turn men thought dead into living, laughing human beings, and that in time of suffering the world is filled with brothers. To the world the lesson of Springhill was expressed by Prime Minister John Diefenbaker: "Courage paid off."

THE
FAR
FRONTIER

Northern people have always stood
for courage and unconquerability.
They have the muscle,
the wholesomeness of life,
the strength of will.

Donald A. Smith (Lord Strathcona), 1915

The Man Who Refused to Die

For 58 days, in temperatures as low as 60 below zero and almost
without food, bush pilot Bob Gauchie fought back—longer by far than
any other man has ever survived, stranded in the northern winter

By Lawrence Elliott

Technology has devised a whole spectrum of ingenious communications and navigational aids for men who work in the sky. Yet, on a bitter-cold day in February 1967, every one of them failed bush pilot Robert Gauchie, leaving him with only his own human resources to pit against the overpowering violence of the Canadian subarctic.

Gauchie was 39 years old, a solidly built native of the far north. With his wife, Frances, and three daughters he lived in Fort Smith, in the Northwest Territories. In ten years he had logged 6000 hours of the toughest flying there is—hauling freight, fire fighters, trappers, whoever wants to go anywhere in that wild and empty land.

At 10 a.m. February 2, having left a group of government inspectors at the village of Cambridge Bay, just inside the Arctic Circle, Gauchie took off alone in his single-engine Beaver. The temperature had gone to 60 degrees below zero the day before, and he had to use a firepot to preheat the frozen-solid engine. He hoped to make Yellowknife, 525 miles to the south, by 3:30, and Fort Smith the next day.

Shortly after noon, he encountered a driving snowstorm. About to set an instrument course, he found that neither his turn-and-bank indicator nor the artificial horizon was working. Quickly he descended to 200 feet, and in the enveloping whiteness he flew by sight over the treeless, windswept barren lands. Finally, he spotted a stretch of blue ice and clattered down to wait out the storm, his skis rattling on the rough lake ice.

Arctic blasts of 50 below zero shook the aircraft. In the icy metal cabin, Gauchie climbed into a sleeping bag and pulled three others over him. He wore mukluks, three pairs of heavy socks, two sweaters and a fur parka. And still he shivered uncontrollably through the long afternoon and night.

When the sun rose on a clear and frosty morning, Gauchie preheated the engine and was soon flying south again. Then his compass failed. The weather worsened, with tiny ice crystals in the air threatening to turn into deadly whiteout, the milky ice fog that obscures land and horizon. He was running low on fuel. Gauchie began radioing what he thought to be his position, asking anyone to "come in." But there was only the crackle of static in his earphones. Finally, a Royal Canadian Air Force Albatross out of Yellowknife responded weakly: "I read you. Suggest you land and activate your SARAH so we can home in."

SARAH, a Search And Rescue transmitter with a self-contained battery, and CPI, a Crash Position Indicator, have led rescue planes to many a lost pilot. Gauchie had both devices.

"We'll have you out in a couple of hours," the Albatross said. That was the last human voice Gauchie would hear for 58 days.

Just south of the treeline, he found a narrow lake sheltered by a scraggly tree growth along its shoreline, and set down there. For a moment he sat, listening to the whipping rush of the wind. Then he depressed the switch on the SARAH. Nothing happened. Stunned, he pushed it again and again. Nothing. And it was the same with the CPI switch.

Bracing himself, he climbed out on the icy skin of the fuselage—lightheaded in the intense cold—and crept to the wingtip, to break the glass on the CPI. Still nothing; no hum, no buzz—only the endless racing of the wind. Unable to believe that both emergency radio beacons were inoperable, Gauchie got his tool kit and, crouched down on his heels while feet and toes grew numb, he worked for three hours—until dark—trying to activate them. But they remained mute.

Back in the cabin, he tried broadcasting again—over both the high-frequency and the very-high-frequency transmitters—"Mayday! Mayday! This is CF-IOB from Cambridge Bay to Yellowknife. Do you read?" There was no response. It was incredible: everything he relied on—navigational instruments and every piece of radio equipment on board—had failed.

He checked through the survival kit. There were a few packages of dried food, a pound of cube sugar, chocolate—enough to last 10 or 12 days if he was careful. He had bought 80 pounds of arctic char for his wife on one of his stops, but the fish were raw and frozen stiff. He found flares, a rifle, five packages of wooden matches and an ax.

Gauchie crawled into the sleeping bags. Toward morning he fell into a fitful sleep.

Next morning, the temperature gauge read 54 below zero. Clouds of loose snow billowed across the lonely lake. Gauchie judged that the Beaver was 400 yards from the near shore: a plane passing overhead ought to have a good chance to see it. But would there be a plane? He was off the main air routes, and the primary search area, based on his flight plan, would be about 100 miles southeast.

He drained some of the remaining gasoline into the plumber's pot he used for preheating the engine. He placed it under the battery, lighted a fire, then tried the radio again. "Mayday. Mayday . . ." There was no response.

It occurred to him that if he could chop a small tree and prop up the trailing antenna with it, he might improve his reception just enough to bring in a signal. He trudged toward shore and came back to the plane breathless and weak, but dragging a sapling. This he stuck in the snow some 50 feet behind the tail. The antenna, which was supposed to crank out of its reel on top of the fuselage, wouldn't budge. He spent the rest of the day prying the wire free, inch by inch, until it was long enough to wind around the sapling. But the radio gave only the same echoing, voiceless hum. Totally spent, he ate a sugar cube and went to sleep.

The next two days were hardly more hopeful. Gauchie used the rest of his gasoline trying to keep the battery alive—melting ice to make soup at the same time—but by the third day even the fruitless hum from the radio had faded. Once, when the wind went down, he walked out on the lake and tramped out an SOS in the snow, each letter 150 feet tall. But in half an hour the surface had drifted smooth.

That night, Gauchie felt a tingling numbness in his feet. He took off his mukluks and socks—and sagged back in horror. Three toes on his left foot and two on the right were dead black. He gagged at the stench, remembering instantly the hours he'd spent hunkered down working on the radio beacons, meanwhile cutting the circulation to his feet. He knew that if gangrene started up from the frost-bitten toes, he could be dead by morning.

The RCAF began organizing the search for Robert Gauchie just a few hours after he was overdue at Yellowknife. A two-motor Albatross took off at first light on February 3, retracing his anticipated flight path, but found nothing. Next day, a second Albatross and a DC-3 were assigned to the mission. And because, in crisis, all of the vast Northwest is like a single small town, a veritable squadron of private aircraft joined in.

In Fort Smith, each time the telephone rang, Frances Gauchie said a prayer that it might be news of her husband's rescue. A pretty woman with a hopeful outlook, she had great faith in her husband's skill and resourcefulness. But she needed all her nerve as day after day passed with no sign of promise.

After 12 days of the most intense effort, the RCAF was ready to give up. In a land that is huge and empty beyond belief, the searchers had painstak-

Arctic char, a delicacy down south, helped keep Bob Gauchie alive. He'd bought it to take home to his wife.

ingly swept 292,000 square miles. To some, the silence of Gauchie's SARAH and CPI indicated a crash so hard as to shatter both, which meant little hope for the fragile human aboard. Temperatures had plunged again to a record 60 below, and there had been fierce storms. All agreed that no one could survive for long in this harshest of winters. Still, when Gauchie's wife pleaded for a few more days of effort, the searchmaster agreed.

The official search was called off February 17. But the people of the Northwest Territories refused to give up. They collected money to pay a few bush pilots to continue the search. The little planes, hampered by terrible blizzards, logged another 100 hours. But by March 1, when Gauchie had gone unreported for 26 days, the last hope of finding him alive was abandoned. Reluctantly, Frances spoke to her priest about a memorial service, though she could not yet bring herself to name a date.

Bob Gauchie knew, almost to the day, when the main rescue effort would end. He had flown many such sad missions himself, looking for a single dark speck in the endless white wilderness.

His frostbitten toes hurt, and he knew that the pain would worsen when they started thawing. Still, they had not yet turned gangrenous. He unwrapped and inspected them each day, and kept the ax handy. He would try to amputate them at the first sign of blood poisoning.

The cold never let up, and Gauchie spent most of his time in the sleeping bags. The metal skin of the plane was no real protection against the cold, but it did shield him from the wind, which shook the little Beaver and sometimes threatened to send it skating across the lake. Though Gauchie ate only an ounce or two of his emergency rations each day, his supply was half gone by the eighth day, and almost completely gone by February 16.

Somewhere he found a ballpoint pen, and tore a page from his logbook to begin a diary, in case he was not found alive. The severe cold had frozen the ink, and the pen refused to work. But on the 15th day, when the weather warmed, the pen made a fitful line on the paper. Writing with mitts on, Gauchie began his diary—really a long letter to his wife and children:

I am sorry, Mickey, that I could not attend your first teen birthday, but I was sure thinking of you. Patti, I'm sure you will make a wonderful nurse. Lynda, your mom will need your help now, as she has a lot of responsibility placed upon her. And now, my darling Fran, if this is the final gun I want to tell you that you were the greatest event in my life.

The weather stayed mild for several days, but Gauchie knew that the cold was not over. His toes had become a gruesome sight, splitting and festering. The pain grew steadily more intense.

He remembered seasoned bush pilots who had violated the basic laws of survival by wandering away from a downed plane, and been lost. Now, alone in the limitless landscape, he knew how a man could let himself be deluded into thinking that just waiting was useless, that he had to *do* something, strike out for somewhere. But, with a kind of fury at his fate, he fought off such fantasies. And, every day or so, he forced himself to down a bit of the frozen char.

On February 20 his loneliness was suddenly broken by a pack of wolves on the lake. There were more than a dozen of them, and they circled the Beaver without fear, tugging playfully at the trailing antenna. Later, they staked out the lake in a great half-circle, and Gauchie guessed that they might be waiting for caribou. He readied his rifle—raw meat couldn't be any worse than raw char—but though a few caribou appeared at the far end of the lake, they came no closer. They and the wolves soon disappeared.

On the afternoon of February 28, hope flared dizzyingly. Just past 4:30, in the red twilight, the rising, falling sound of the wind slowly turned into the steady drone of an airplane engine. Incredulous, Gauchie listened for an instant, then bolted out of the sleeping bags, snatched up the flare gun and tumbled into the snow. Less than 2000 feet above him was a red Beaver. Trembling, Gauchie fired a flare straight up, watched it burst into pale color in the sun's glare. The Beaver continued on its inexorable course. He fired a second flare, but it was already too late. The burst went off well behind the unwavering little aircraft. Gauchie stood there as it disappeared.

Torturing himself with what might have been, he didn't sleep all that night. Next day, he gathered his waning strength and forced himself out on the lake, once again trudging out SOS and HELP signals. And once again the wind obliterated them.

"My God," exclaimed Glen Stevens, "Bob Gauchie's alive!" Stevens (left) and Ronald Sheardown spotted Gauchie, landed, taxied to him. He stood with a suitcase, "like a man waiting for a bus," said Sheardown.

On March 5 his toes thawed. The pain maddened him, racked his whole body, and for eight hours he drifted in and out of delirium. At least once he had the bindings off and the ax ready, then fell back exhausted and finally slept. His spirits slumped to lowest ebb:

Terrible cold week. Not much time for rescue now. I hope I can make peace with God. I love you girls. Pen won't write. Please pray for me.

He had used the last of the emergency rations, and the sugar as well. Now, all he had left was a bare shred of hope. This he clung to, ferociously, knowing that when *that* was gone, he would be, too.

On March 12, toward evening, two planes flew over the lake within an hour of each other, but neither noticed the flares that Gauchie frantically fired aloft.

On March 16 he wrote:

For my meal today I licked the inside of an onion-soup bag. That's living, isn't it!

He began reciting the simple prayers of his boyhood, the only ones he knew. On March 28, the 54th day, he wrote in the diary:

I know now I must be found within a week if I am to survive. I forced myself to eat some fish so I may have some strength return. Well, honey, at least you'll know that I tried to come back to you.

On March 30, the thermometer crept up to zero, and Gauchie's inexhaustible spirits rose again. It occurred to him that, if he could drain only a bit of hydraulic fluid from the plane's landing gear, he might be able to improvise a wick and cook bits of fish over the fire. With near-frozen fingers he coaxed a little fluid from the line, found some gauze for a wick, and lighted it. It worked! He held a fish over the small flame, watching the edges soften and brown. Then the whole length of the gauze ignited, fire flaring, and Gauchie had to put it out. But he had some warm food.

On April 1, at a little past 6 p.m., Gauchie was crawling into the sleeping bags when the now-familiar and maddeningly hopeful sound came again: the wind's high-pitched whine deepening into the steady drone of an aircraft engine.

He threw back the covers and fumbled with the door latch. The plane—a red turboprop Beaver—was right overhead. He fired the flare gun, all breath caught in his throat. The Beaver flew straight on. Gauchie felt the will seep out of him, but then he looked up again and saw that the angle of the Beaver had changed. It was growing larger. It was turning back!

Bush pilot Ronald Sheardown and copilot Glen Stevens were to have left Yellowknife for a mining camp near Coppermine at 2:30 that afternoon, but mechanical difficulties delayed them until after 4 p.m. So it was that, near sunset, they were over Samandré Lake when Stevens happened to catch a reflection of the sinking sun on what might have been glass. It was only the briefest flash, and it vanished even as he stared at it.

"Did you see anything?" he asked Sheardown.

Sheardown hadn't, and for another minute he held his red turboprop on course. Then something—he will never know what—made him put the plane into a steep turn and drop to 2000 feet. And in the next moment both men saw a dark figure moving out from an aircraft that was barely visible in the snow. Two flares lighted the lowering sky beside them.

With his wife and daughters, Gauchie reads accounts of his rescue. After recovery he trained as a helicopter pilot and went back to work in Fort Smith, N.W.T.

"That's Bob Gauchie!" Stevens cried out in utter astonishment. "My God, Gauchie's alive!"

It was the sheerest chance. The low-hanging arctic sun, which never rose high enough to reveal the downed Beaver itself, was, at 6:10 p.m., at precisely the right angle to flash off its windshield just as Sheardown and Stevens flew by. Had they left Yellowknife ten minutes sooner, they would have seen nothing.

The turboprop circled the lake, landed, then taxied toward the ghostly figure. Sheardown recalls, "He stood there with that blue suitcase, like a man waiting for a bus."

Bob Gauchie was a man who had just thanked his God. Ahead of him lay long hospitalization, during which he would lose all five frostbitten toes, then weeks of treatment. But he was alive! After an incredible 58 days—longer by far than any other man known to be missing in the northern winter had ever survived—he was alive. Now, in the moment of rescue, with the same determination that had so long sustained him, he drew himself tall and began limping toward the turboprop—a haggard creature with shaggy hair, one foot wrapped in dirty canvas, and a bearded, emaciated face lighted by a shining grin.

"Hello," Gauchie said. "Do you have room for a passenger?"

Gauchie spent 2½ months in hospital, six more months recuperating. Then he took a three-month course, qualified as a helicopter pilot and set himself up in this new line of work in Fort Smith. The Beaver which was his home for 58 days was flown out soon after the rescue. In November 1967 it crashed after takeoff in a storm near Little Dahl Lake, N.W.T., killing the pilot and his four passengers.

Wilderness Mother

On a flood-swollen river in the Rockies
two humans witness wildlife drama

By Mary E. Matheson

The Sunwapta was flooding. John and I both welcomed the excitement for it was happenings of this kind—a storm, a forest fire, a river in flood—that alone broke the monotony of our existence. We were the sole occupants of a valley in the Rockies, 50 miles from Jasper, Alta.

In the afternoon, when we found the Sunwapta was rising six inches an hour, we knew we were in for a real flood. After supper, without waiting to wash the dishes, we hurried to the riverbank.

The water, yellow and thick, roared past us. Uprooted trees rushed by, like great broken battleships, toward the falls and canyon below. From that canyon they would emerge torn to matchwood.

John pointed across the river. A cow moose and her calf had come out of the bush and were standing on the steep bank directly across from us. Both looked back, as if they feared pursuit; possibly a cougar had been after the young one. The calf was all legs, not more than three days old.

The cow moose paid us no attention. For a minute she seemed to be studying the current. Then she leaped from the bank into the yellow flood and struck out for our side, with never a backward glance toward her calf. It was but a second or two before the baby moose plunged in too and disappeared from our sight, completely submerged. When it came up, it had been swept several yards downstream. It set out gamely to follow its mother, but for every foot of headway it made it was carried four times as far toward the falls. Only its mother could help it now— but the cow moose, ignoring her calf, was continuing straight across the river.

"You brute—you wicked, cruel mother!" I cried. (John told me afterward.)

Although a powerful swimmer, the cow had to battle against the current to come almost squarely across the river. She reached the bank a little below where we stood and—still without looking to see what had become of her baby—crashed headlong into the forest.

John and I started to run along the curving river-bank. We had no hope that we could save the calf, but we simply had to keep that little dark head in sight. It was bobbing up and down like a forlorn cork. Trees were missing it by a hairsbreadth. Sometimes it was sucked under by the current, to emerge farther downstream. Always, however, it continued to make some headway toward our bank; it had passed midstream when John and I had to take a path through the woods where brush made the bank impassable.

We reached the river again at what ordinarily was a quiet pool of backwater. Now there was a great current sweeping around within the curving bank. As we reached its edge, we spotted the baby moose—it was being carried into that maelstrom, to be whirled around and swept out again into the stream.

Then we stopped dead, for out of the bush down the bend from us crashed the cow moose. She stopped as if to gauge the speed and course of the current, then hurled herself down the bank and out into the river. Finally, with perfect timing, she turned about to face the shore and braced herself against the current, just as the calf, still swimming, was swept against her flank.

Quickly the mother changed her position ever so slightly, so that the pressure of the current, if it should sweep the calf away, would carry it closer to the bank. There she stood, waiting till her little one ceased to struggle and discovered that it was now in shallow water and could find a footing. Both then moved toward the bank, slowly and carefully, the mother still buttressing the calf against the thrust of the current. Soon the calf was only knee-deep in water. It wanted to stop there and rest, but the mother—now that she had overcome one hazard— no longer was contemptuous of our presence. She nosed her baby up the bank, and mother and calf disappeared in the woods.

Slowly John turned. Then—"What are you crying about?" But his voice wasn't very steady, and I knew I didn't have to answer.

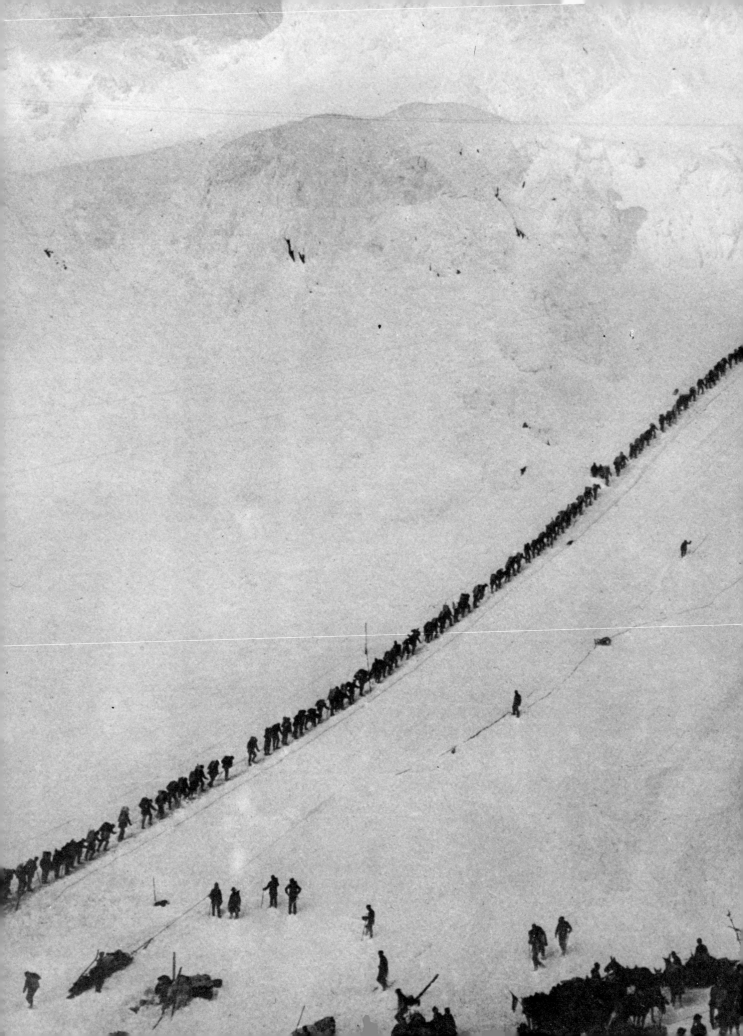

Klondike Stampede

His last silver dollar flipped tails and
George Carmack went *downstream*—to fishing
that was worse than ever, and gold that sent
thousands of men slogging over the
Chilkoot Pass on the Trail of '98

By Jo Chamberlin

Early one morning in May 1896, "Siwash" George
Carmack sat gloomily in front of a trading post in
the far Canadian Northwest with his Indian squaw,
Kate, and two Indian friends, Skookum Jim and
Tagish Charley. Broke again after 11 years seeking
gold, he would have to do what he had done before
in such straits—catch salmon to dry and sell. He
flipped his last silver dollar to decide whether he
should set his nets up the Yukon River or downstream.

The coin fell tails and Carmack went downstream
to a tributary, the Klondike. The salmon were few
and Carmack, disgusted, decided to try prospecting
again. Bob Henderson, a miner, suggested he try his
luck in a certain valley. On August 17, the party
stopped beside Rabbit Creek. While Carmack dozed,
Skookum Jim, to pass the time, filled his pan with
gravel and washed it out. As the muddy water
cleared, Jim's eyes popped wide. In the coarse gravel,
pinhead nodules, black and heavy. Gold and plenty
of it!

Skookum Jim yelled; Carmack and Charley came
running. They panned other spots. They had struck
it rich! The excited men staked out claims and hurried off to record them. Henderson was forgotten.
Carmack blew into the saloon at Forty Mile, drank
and babbled of his luck. When his listeners were
skeptical, he thrust a fistful of gold under their
noses. They stampeded. Sourdoughs struck out for
the new diggings without waiting to get proper
clothes or equipment. Drunken men were thrown
into boats and hauled along by their friends. Claims
were staked out far above and below Carmack's.
Within a few weeks, the Yukon was afire with
excitement.

For a year, the outside world had no inkling of
the news. On June 16, 1897, a steamer from Alaska
docked at San Francisco. Down the gangplank
clumped bearded men in worn and dirty clothes.
But they staggered under burdens of gold, stuffed in
old coffee pots, jam jars, paper bundles and moosehide pokes—$750,000 worth. Next day another ship

Blizzards often hid the 3600-foot peak
of Chilkoot Pass. This photograph
was made in a storm on
Chilkoot summit in 1898.

brought miners with $800,000 to Seattle. Newspapers screamed the story of the richest strike in history; untold wealth in the Klondike, millions still to be had.

Times were hard in '97, jobs few. A hundred thousand people started for the strike. The farmer left his plow, the bankrupt fled his creditors, the factory hand laid down his tools. Alaskan steamers were jammed with college professors, bankers, lawyers, doctors, gamblers, "con" men and loose women. Warned to wait till the following spring lest they arrive too late to prepare for the deadly winter, the gold seekers paid no heed.

The Klondike River is in Canada, just east of the Yukon-Alaska border. The favored route was by steamer to Skagway or Dyea in southernmost Alaska, on foot over the Chilkoot mountain pass into Canada, by scow through a series of lakes and streams to the Yukon River and down it 500 miles to the gold fields.

Chilkoot Pass, 3600 feet high, often hidden in fog or blizzard, was hard work even for toughened Indians; to office-bred gold rushers it became a trail of terror. It was lined with the sick and beaten—also with thieves and sharks, male and female. It was treacherous. At Sheep Camp, just below timber line, 70 men were buried alive in one April avalanche.

Each man's equipment ran from 800 to 1500 pounds, so that he had to toil up the steps hewn in the ice of the steep, boulder-strewn canyon trail again and again. Unless he hired Indians to help, it

usually took a man four weeks to get his goods to the top.

The long string of toiling men, thousands of them, looked from below like ants at work. They struggled and rested, struggled and rested. The pace was that of the weakest. You could not hurry. Neither could you rest except when others did, without losing your place in line. Arctic winds and rains whipped through thin tenderfoot clothes, chilling and killing.

There was confusion, squalor, death. Men quarreled with their partners, dividing their goods bitterly—even to sawing boards in half. Money was worth less than resourcefulness and courage. Sharing a few beans, lending a blanket, or a pipeful of tobacco—these things made men brothers.

To conquer Chilkoot was something to be proud of—but it was not the end of the ordeal. Down on the other side of the pass, men felled trees and sawed them into planks for crude scows—several weeks' work. They pushed the scows on log rollers from lake to lake, eventually reaching the swift-running, terrifying upper Yukon. In Miles Canyon, a narrow chute of racing water between high rock walls, many were drowned. More died amid the flying mane of spray in White Horse Rapids. Rude crosses, tin cans, blazed trees marked the graves of broken bodies and broken hopes. Of those who started only one in four got through to Dawson City. Sixteen weeks on the trail was accounted pretty good time.

There never was a boom town like Dawson. Where once had been the lone shack of trader Joe Ladue, a town of 20,000 sprang up in two years. Scows and flatboats packed the waterfront; tents, log cabins and shanties lined muddy streets thronged with howling Malemute dogs and bearded men. Saloons and dance halls ran 24 hours a day. It was wild, mad, wide open.

Fresh food was unobtainable and many a newcomer's teeth fell out from winter scurvy. Milk from the one cow was $30 a gallon. Butter was $3 a pound. Flour went up to as high as $120 for a 50-

Goldseekers carried what they could on their backs. For some greenhorns the gold rush was a trail of terror.

pound sack. Eggs were $1 each, if you could get them. A restaurant featured oyster stew at $15—when it had the oysters. A meal of bread, bacon and beans was $5 to $10. Doughnuts and coffee cost $1.25; a piece of pie, 75 cents.

Life centered in the saloons. Conspicuous on the bar were scales for weighing gold dust. One porter gathered enough gold from spittoons and floor sawdust to buy a good mining claim.

What gold roulette and faro in the back room didn't get, the dance-hall girls did. Champagne cost $60; the bottles were refilled with soda water and sugar and sold to drunks who wouldn't know the difference. The girls, modishly gowned, danced with sourdoughs in moccasins or heavy boots at $1 for three minutes, to the "professor's" banging on the piano. As most of the miners hadn't bathed in months and couldn't really dance, the girls earned their money.

Tex Rickard ran one joint. Chief competitor was "Swiftwater Bill" Gates, who had struck it rich on Claim No. 13. Swiftwater, a former dishwasher, strutted Dawson in a Prince Albert, a stiff hat and lots of diamonds. He offered a girl her weight in gold to marry him. She took the $30,000—but didn't marry him. To win this same girl, who was fond of

Dawson City was the daddy of all boom towns. It barely existed in 1897 (below). But under the midnight sun of June 21, 1899, lay a wild, wide-open, 24-hours-a-day city centered on the saloons.

eggs but not of him, Swiftwater cornered the egg supply at a cost of $2300. He talked of importing 200 schoolmarms from Boston to be offered to lonely miners as wives at $5000 each. In the fall of '98, a crowd actually waited at the dock when the prospective wives were supposed to arrive on the Yukon steamer *May West!* Two Englishmen arrived in Dawson with expensive bicycles, though there was no place to ride. Another Britisher arrived flat broke, but sold his supply of marmalade for enough to stake him six months. A restaurant proprietor announced that "a perfectly preserved mastodon had been found in the Arctic ice." He would serve mastodon steaks at $10 each. He really served beef. It was a town joke.

As more wives came in, a demand for reform arose. Eventually the better element won, and the red-light district was moved to the city limits—a few blocks away.

Names now familiar dotted the roster at Dawson City. Young Robert W. Service was there, a clerk in the Canadian Bank of Commerce. Rex Beach lived in a cabin below Dawson prospecting and cutting wood for river steamers. A fellow named Jack London came too late to make his fortune and spent a winter arguing socialism.

Some claims sold for fabulous sums, but proved to be no good. Others that yielded fortunes went for

a drink of whisky, or a live pig. Gold worth $400,000 was taken from one claim 90 by 300 feet. A "forgotten fraction" 13 feet wide yielded $20,000. There were claims where gold ran $1000 to the pan. At best, it wasn't all profit. It took a lot of labor at $15 a day to cut wood for fires to thaw the thick layer of frozen muck above the gravel that might or might not yield gold.

Any claim vacant 60 days was open for new filing. A Mountie would be on hand at midnight to see that new claimants staked it out properly. Then it would go to the man who got to a recorder first. Two dog-team drivers raced from abandoned claim No. 40 and tumbled inside the recorder's office, unable to gasp a word. The recorder, Solomon-like, divided the claim between them. It proved worthless.

Dawson in its 1899 heyday had a
population of 20,000. But that year
thousands left to hunt gold at
Cape Nome in Alaska.
Dawson was left with 2000.

By September '98, 17,000 claims had been recorded and precious few yielded fortunes. Disheartened men took jobs shoveling, or cutting wood. Latecomers hung around Dawson for a while, then sold their goods and started home. The high prices collapsed. In 1899, news of rich gold finds on the beach at Cape Nome, 800 miles west, drew thousands away from Dawson. Almost as swiftly as it had grown, it collapsed to a town of 2000.

What became of the Klondike sourdoughs?

Siwash George Carmack, who for 15 years had fought blizzards and gone hungry without being ill for a single day, died of pneumonia in a Vancouver hospital. Bob Henderson, whose tip to Carmack started it all, never struck it rich. He was given a government job, died poor. Swiftwater Bill Gates had matrimonial troubles and, after dodging the law for years, was killed in a miners' camp in Peru.

Some who never really panned gold did best. Rex Beach made a fortune with his novels. Robert W. Service lived prosperously from such ballads as *The Shooting of Dan McGrew*.

The Klondike gold rush had permanent effects. It gave decisive impetus to Vancouver, Portland and Seattle. It led to the opening of Alaska. Many defeated prospectors, caught by the spell of the north, stayed on to fish, trap, trade. Alaska and the Yukon began to pay rich dividends in other things as well as gold.

He Created Dan McGrew and Cremated Sam McGee

By Wallace Reyburn

Robert W. Service found his own gold in the Yukon, in his own way. The bank clerk who wrote *The Shooting of Dan McGrew* wrested literary fame and good hard cash from his days in the Klondike—and went on writing the rest of his life. His goal: to complete 1000 poems "if the Lord of Scribes will spare me to finish the task." He *was* spared and he *did* score his 1000.

After leaving Canada's North, Service lived quiet-ly in the South of France, with no fondness for pub-licity.

He wrote virtually until his death in 1958, aged 84. His two volumes of collected verse contain more than 1700 pages. But his fame rests mainly on the ballads he wrote down North.

The Shooting of Dan McGrew is one of them. It starts, "A bunch of the boys were whooping it up in the Malamute saloon," and goes on to describe how "a miner fresh from the creeks, dog-dirty and loaded for bear," had an encounter with Dangerous Dan McGrew and how "the lady that's known as Lou" stole Dan's worldly wealth when he got the worst of the shooting match.

Service spent the early part of his life in Glasgow. At six he wrote his first poem, in the form of a grace in which the mealtakers called upon God to bless the scones "Aunt Jeannie makes" and spare them all from stomachaches. At school he found he had a talent for storytelling and the other boys would crowd around while he told yarns, foreshadowing the fact that most of the Service poems that are famous today tell a story, often as farfetched as he confesses his schoolboy tales were.

By the time he was in his late teens he was work-ing in a bank and writing verse in every spare moment. When he was 20 he left Scotland for Canada, and spent several years drifting around be-fore reverting to his old job of bank clerk, first in Victoria, then in Whitehorse and finally in Dawson.

Had he stayed in Scotland, it is doubtful whether his verse would have brought him fame and finan-cial reward, because one of the main things that sells Service is his subject matter—the rough, tough life in the Yukon. His verse is so successful in capturing the spirit of the pioneer days that some of his ad-mirers still find it difficult to believe that it was as a very English-looking bank teller that Service spent most of his life here, not as a grizzly prospector.

The Dan McGrew ballad was written after a 20-minute stroll in the woods. Service had been asked to write something suitable for a recitation at a church social. He took a walk one evening after work: the poem took shape in his mind and he wrote it down when he got home. However, it was considered too red-blooded for the church affair. Other poems were dashed off with equal facility and when Service had written about 30 he decided to have them printed for distribution among his friends. He sent them to a publisher with a check for $100. A few weeks later back came the check—and a contract, for the publisher thought they were worth more than private distribution.

That was in 1907, and the sale of that book of verse and nine others left him free of financial worries.

Service was never particular where he got names for his characters. The heroine of his novel about the Gold Rush, *The Trail of '98*, got her name of Berna from the label of a brand of condensed milk that Service used in the Yukon. For his early poems Service chose names from the ledgers of the Whitehorse bank. He wrote a now-famous poem about a man from the Southern States of America who could never get used to the cold of the Yukon and eventually died from it. His partner found that taking the body back to civilization was too much of a burden, so when he came upon a wrecked lake boat he lit a fire in the boiler. "The flames just soared, and the furnace roared—such a blaze you seldom see. And I burrowed a hole in the glowing coal and I stuffed in Sam McGee." When he looked in to see how the cremation was coming along, Sam was sitting up with a smile on his face and remarked that it was the first time he'd been warm since coming to the Yukon.

The name Sam McGee had been taken from the ledgers and soon after publication of the poem Mr. McGee, taking a very poor view of the whole thing, withdrew all his money from the bank. Until the day he died, his life was made miserable by all and

Scots-born Robert Service wrote more than 1000 poems before his death at the age of 84.

sundry asking him: "Is it warm enough for you?"

Service was always careful to describe himself as a writer of verse or a rhymster, never as a poet. These rhymes gain new popularity as each new generation discovers him. *Songs of a Sourdough,* his first book, has sold millions of copies in English and North American editions. No other living English versifier—or poet—approaches anywhere near the number of copies sold or the income of Service. He was able to retire before he was 40, and his accumulated wealth was in the six-figure class for many years.

Since saying good-by in 1912 to Dawson, where the cabin he lived in is now a tourist attraction, Service spent his life in France. Handsomely gray-haired, he was proud of his erect figure and said he kept fit by eating copious quantities of potatoes (22,000 a year, he claimed) and chewing every mouthful 30 times.

At Monte Carlo, any flutter Service had at the gambling tables was limited to using his secret system to win enough money to pay for his lunch, then he stopped.

The Good Samaritan of Labrador

On cold, forbidding "Starvation Coast," Sir Wilfred Grenfell
gave the world a warm and memorable example of Christian love

By David MacDonald

At North West River, on Canada's rugged Labrador coast, an urgent radio message crackled in from a remote northern outport: a pregnant Eskimo girl was bleeding internally, her life ebbing away. Within minutes, a red float-plane took off on a race against death.

For two hours, while the pilot bucked heavy arctic head winds, the young English nurse beside him stared down at the bleak, brooding wilderness that early explorers damned as "the land God gave to Cain." Then the plane banked between jagged peaks, still snowcapped in summer, and settled onto Kaipokok Bay. A fishing boat brought the girl out from a huddle of huts. Pale and writhing with pain, she was lifted into the aircraft, which quickly took off again. After giving her a sedative, the nurse radioed North West River and described her plight to a Canadian doctor.

"We'll be ready," he replied. An hour and a half later—just in time—the patient was wheeled into the operating room of a Grenfell Mission hospital, where blood transfusions and major surgery saved her life.

For thousands of others in Labrador and northern Newfoundland, the world-famous Grenfell Mission has been the difference between life and death —and a lasting monument to the legendary Labrador doctor, Wilfred Thomason Grenfell.

Grenfell was 27 when he sailed from England to Labrador as medical missionary to the Newfoundlanders who fished there in summer. He didn't plan to stay long. But because he found such sickness on "Starvation Coast"—a 1000-mile stretch of subarctic tundra, where 5000 Eskimos, Indians and whites lived in grinding poverty—he devoted the rest of his life to its forgotten people. Slight and shaggy, with sparkling eyes and a face that grew lined and leathery from exposure, he spent 42 years making rounds by dog-sled, ship and snowshoe. Grenfell went wherever he was needed, treating the sick in sod-covered hovels, skin tents and igloos, operating in lantern-lit cabins.

Grenfell earned renown as "the Good Samaritan of Labrador" and founded the Mission—which grew to have four hospitals, 14 nursing stations and a staff of 400 to carry on his tradition of service. To millions, much to his own amusement, he was a glamorous figure—the hardy little doctor who wore Eskimo furs and slept on the trail at 30 below with his dogs. When he got lost one night in the wilds of New York City, newspapers relished the way he found his bearings—from the North Star.

Few people anywhere have done more to illuminate the meaning of brotherly love. The son of an Anglican clergyman, educated at Marlborough and Oxford, Wilfred Grenfell entered medical school at 18. Two years later, in 1885, he wandered into a revival meeting held by Moody and Sankey, the famous U. S. evangelists. "When I left," he wrote later, "it was with a determination either to make religion a real effort to do what I thought Christ would do in my place as a doctor, or frankly abandon it."

After his graduation, Dr. Grenfell joined the church-sponsored Royal National Mission to Deep-Sea Fishermen, whose motto was "Heal the Sick and Preach the Word." For five years he ministered to fishing fleets from Iceland to the Bay of Biscay.

Then, in 1892, he crossed the Atlantic in the small hospital ship *Albert* to look into conditions among some 25,000 men, women and children who sailed to Labrador each spring in a thousand Newfoundland fishing schooners. On his first day there, the *Albert* eased through a maze of icebergs into Domino Run. As ships ran up welcome flags, salty skippers rowed over to greet Grenfell, whose Oxford accent and candy-stripe blazer seemed grandly out of place.

That night he was called ashore to a dank shanty where a man lay dying of pneumonia and tuberculosis while his wife and six ragged children looked on, helpless. "I could only pray for him," Grenfell said later, "when what he needed was a hospital and a trained nurse."

TO THE MEMORY OF
THREE NOBLE DOGS.
Moody.
Watch.
Spy.
WHOSE LIVES WERE GIVEN
FOR MINE ON THE ICE.
April 21st 1908.
Wilfred Grenfell,
St. Anthony.

Grenfell (below) "begged" to make his dream of a chain of hospitals come true. CPR tycoon Donald Smith, soon to be Lord Strathcona, donated a hospital ship.

Adrift on an ice pan, Grenfell killed and skinned his three dogs and used their bloody fur to keep him warm while he awaited rescue. To Moody, Watch and Spy, he said his thanks with a plaque at St. Anthony, Nfld.

The Grenfell orphanage and boarding school at St. Anthony in 1910.

"Liveyere" youngsters learn carpentry at the St. Anthony school in this 1906 photograph.

Within two months he learned the harsh facts of life and death among Labrador's year-round inhabitants: the inland Indians, the Eskimos of the north and the wretched white "Liveyeres" (from "live here") who had clung to the coast for a century. In a land offering little food but fish and berries, scurvy and rickets were rife. TB killed one adult in three; one of three infants died within a year. And for a population that grew to 30,000 in summer, there wasn't one doctor. Before leaving that fall Grenfell stopped again at Domino Run. The man he'd visited there was dead, his family destitute. He gave them food, clothing and a promise: "I'll be back."

In St. John's, capital of Newfoundland, Grenfell roused citizens with harrowing tales: of a crippled child whose only dress was her father's cut-down trouser leg; of a Liveyere who'd killed his three youngest children and himself so that his wife and two eldest might have food enough to survive until spring. He told them he wanted to open two cottage hospitals on Starvation Coast. They donated the buildings, and a winter of lecturing in England brought gifts of medical supplies, clothing and money.

When he returned in 1893, he had two other doctors and two nurses in tow. They opened a 16-bed summer hospital at Battle Harbour, and another hospital 200 miles up the coast. Then Grenfell sailed to the far North, where no doctor had gone before.

Everywhere he met age-old superstitions. Both whites and Eskimos treated diphtheria by tying split herring around the victim's neck. Fishermen concocted weird potions by boiling pulley-block scrapings in water, and women tried to cure diseases of children's eyes by blowing sugar into them. Gradually they came to accept Grenfell's strange medicine. For he seemed like a miracle worker: simple cataract operations made the blind see again; after ten minutes of surgery on an ingrown toenail the lame could walk erect. He delivered babies, yanked teeth, broke and reset crooked legs, treated everything from chickenpox to cancer.

That summer, when the three doctors helped 2500 patients, Grenfell began dreaming of a chain of hospitals and nursing stations to serve the coast all year. So he went "begging." In Montreal he met Lord Strathcona, then Sir Donald Smith, a Canadian railroad tycoon who'd once worked in Labrador, and talked him into donating a sturdy hospital ship. Then Grenfell made a speaking tour across Canada, collecting cash and new followers. Slowly, his dream began to come true. In 1899, after winter closed his two Labrador hospitals, he crossed over to St. Anthony in northern Newfoundland. Isolated, beset by hunger and disease, it was Labrador all over again. There, at his urging, villagers cut wood and built a roomy hospital that became his Mission's permanent headquarters.

"When someone needs help," he often said, "nothing else counts." More than once he risked his life. On Easter Sunday of 1908, two men brought word that a boy was gravely ill at Brent Island. They wanted to rest their sled-dogs, then take Grenfell back with them. But he wouldn't wait. Fearing the boy might die, he set off alone. While short-cutting across frozen Hare Bay, his Eskimo *komatik* sank through rotted ice. Half paralyzed by the frigid water, he managed to cut his huskies free, then swam to a small ice pan.

To stay alive, Grenfell killed and skinned three dogs, wrapping their bloody fur around him. At night, drifting out to sea, he made a windbreak of the carcasses and curled up beside his biggest dog to sleep. Next day, with the legs of the dead animals bound together into a grotesque flagstaff, he waved his shirt at the fading shore.

Luckily, he was seen by a fisherman who'd climbed a cliff with a telescope to look for seals. When rescuers finally reached him, Grenfell's hands and feet were frozen. Yet his first words were, "I'm sorry to put you to all this bother."

A year later, aboard a transatlantic liner, Grenfell

Aghast at the suffering among
Labrador's Eskimos, Indians
and whites, Grenfell devoted
his life to improving their lot.
"The doctor," they called
him, and after he'd been
knighted, "Sir Wilf."

Scurvy and rickets were
commonplace along "Starvation
Coast," which offered little
food but fish and berries.

Grenfell loved and admired the
hardy "Liveyere" people. This
man, despite the loss of a hand,
could do the work of two
ordinary men, said the doctor.

Before Grenfell began his work,
one Labrador child in three
died within a year. Soon young
lives were being saved in
Grenfell's hospitals and nursing
stations along the bleak coast.

met Anne MacClanahan, a beautiful American socialite who had once turned down an invitation to hear him speak because she imagined he'd be "too dull." Before the ship docked in New York, they were engaged. Married in Chicago, they went north to St. Anthony, where Grenfell's young bride quickly busied herself with Mission projects.

And there were many. For Grenfell couldn't confine himself to medicine and religion. "How can one preach the gospel of love to hungry people by sermons?" he asked.

The chief cause of sickness in Labrador was malnutrition, induced by the poverty of that hard land, worsened by the fact that fishermen and trappers seldom earned cash. Instead, local traders gave them credit, only to claim their catches later at cut rates.

To fight such feudal exploitation, Grenfell rounded up furs, sold them on the outside market—at three times Labrador's going rate—and returned every cent to the trappers. In Red Bay, he helped 17 fishermen start a coöperative store. They bought their first supplies with money that Grenfell lent, shipped their catch to market in a schooner he provided. Before long, Red Bay was debt-free. In all, Grenfell launched ten co-ops. Most of them flourished; when one failed, he hocked one of his boats for $12,000 to pay its bills.

Another reason for Labrador's poverty, Grenfell felt, was ignorance. The few schools were all strictly sectarian. While some settlements had none, others had four—Catholic, Methodist, Anglican and Salvation Army—competing against each other. Unable to convince missionaries that they should unite their energies, he recruited teachers from the United States and started his own schools, open to all.

He brought five orphans back from Labrador and found an anonymous donor to build a children's home—the first of four—at St. Anthony. He started "cottage industries"—mainly handcrafts—so that Labrador would not be entirely dependent on fish and furs. U. S. and Canadian women sent him silk stockings and old dresses to be turned into hooked rugs—and money. He set up a dozen centers to distribute cast-off clothing, and opened two more hospitals.

To support his work, admirers in the United States, Canada, England and Ireland formed the International Grenfell Association in 1912. Their best fund-raiser was Grenfell himself, whose speaking tours pulled in huge crowds and hundreds of thousands of dollars. Wealthy men gave him X-ray machines, Yale and Princeton students financed two orphanages and schoolchildren sent their dimes to help.

"Dr. Grenfell has a genius for generating sympathy," a friend said. "He can wring tears from people's pocketbooks." Once, on a train to Boston, he noticed a woman wearing a huge diamond ring and boldly asked its cost. Grenfell introduced himself to the indignant woman and told her of his work. "What a waste to wear an expensive ornament like that," he added, "when there are so many hungry children in Labrador." The woman removed her ring and offered it to him.

"No one can eat a diamond," he said. "But I *will* accept its value in money." He got it—$2500.

Dr. Grenfell explained his dedication simply: "I've always believed that the Good Samaritan went across the road to the wounded man just because he *wanted* to." Many others followed his lead. Dr. Harry Paddon left England for Labrador after hearing a speech by Grenfell. His son, also a doctor, eventually served there too. Charles Curtis, a brilliant young surgeon from Boston, joined the Mission in 1915 and gave it the remaining 48 years of his life. Grenfell nurses often stayed alone on the coast for months, coping with problems that would have fazed many a doctor. Once a delirious Liveyere fisherman ripped his stomach open with a knife. With a priest serving as anesthetist and directions wired from the nearest doctor—Mission posts were linked by telegraph—a Grenfell nurse performed a complex operation and saved his life.

The regular Mission staff was aided by hundreds

of volunteers. Dentists and debutantes, businessmen and college students, they rolled bandages, dug ditches, taught school, crewed hospital ships, christened babies—hundreds called Wilfred—and did dozens of menial chores.

Most heartening of all, the Mission generated self-help. Because of the schools Grenfell opened and a special education fund his wife set up, the children of illiterate fishermen and trappers found wider horizons. Many studied on Grenfell scholarships, then came back as teachers, nurses, ministers —leaders among their own people.

In fact, when the Mission put up a new 80-bed hospital at St. Anthony in 1927, the project was directed by one of Grenfell's first Labrador orphans, who had studied engineering in New York. Built of reinforced concrete, the hospital was as up-to-date as any in North America. For Grenfell, remembering when there weren't a dozen bottles of iodine on the entire coast, its opening day was the proudest of his life.

A highlight of the day was a surprise announcement from Buckingham Palace: King George V was to knight the doctor. "I only pray," he said, "that this tag to my name won't be a barrier between me and my friends on the coast." It never was. Labrador people worshiped him.

Despite illness, Grenfell went on making speeches and writing books—more than 20 in all—to raise money for his Mission. In 1937, at 72, he had to retire as its superintendent. "I'm getting too old to drive dog-teams," he said sadly.

The next year his wife died, and Grenfell made his last trip to St. Anthony, to bury her ashes. Though the occasion was solemn, hundreds cheered when "the doctor" stepped ashore. In command of a hospital ship once more, he crossed over to Labrador to make his final rounds. There he found more than 20 doctors and nurses carrying on his work. The scourges of the coast—TB, infant mortality, malnutrition—were sharply reduced. Now the sick had proper care, there were homes for the homeless and help for the crippled and the blind.

The day he sailed away for the last time, all 600 residents of St. Anthony turned out to say good-by. A year later, at his home by Lake Champlain, he lay down for a nap before supper one night and never wakened. He died wearing the same old Oxford blazer he'd worn at Domino Run in 1892, on his first day in Labrador. In that cold land, Grenfell had given the world a warm, unforgettable example of Christian love.

Longest Main Street in the World

Come drive the Alaska Highway—1523 miles of adventure,
salted with small-town camaraderie

By Lawrence Elliott

Driving north on the Alaska Highway my wife and
I stopped at a roadhouse to get gas. The proprietor
chatted about the condition of the road, asked how
the Peace River wheat crop looked to us, then said,
"Mind dropping a case of engine oil at the next
Texaco station? I hear he's running short."

"Be glad to," I said. "Where's the Texaco place?"

"Just up the road, on your right. About 670
miles."

All along the 1523-mile length of the Alaska
Highway, from Mile 0 at Dawson Creek in British
Columbia to the end of the line at Fairbanks, Alaska, lodgekeepers and highway-maintenance crews
are linked by this same small-town sense of help-
fulness. Truckers, bus drivers, touring school-
teachers, rotating army families—all are apt to be
pressed into service as couriers on this longest and
most rugged Main Street in the world. A name and
milepost number are all the address that is needed to
speed a message—or a side of moose meat—to its
destination "just up the road."

For all Highway dwellers are neighbors, drawn
together by the loneliness of the empty land. They
will travel 500 miles to one another's parties, making a once-a-year visit sustain a community spirit
that cannot be broken by the winding miles or the
solitude of blizzard-driven winters.

Though only 400 miles of the Highway are paved
—the Alaskan section and the 84-mile stretch out of
Dawson Creek—its full length has been traversed
by hikers, motorcyclists, a Ferris wheel, a 150-trailer
caravan, and all manner of cars from Model T's
to Cadillacs. It is North America's adventure road
and all but 300 miles of it lies in Canada. It carries
you up around the continent's mightiest mountains,
across great river systems—the Yukon, Peace and
Liard—and past an astonishing array of wildlife.
A black bear throws up his arms like an embar-
rassed jaywalker and dives for the shoulder of the
road. A 1500-pound moose dawdles along in front
of you, in no rush to make room for human trespassers on what he has come to regard as a private

North America's "adventure road"
had its primitive beginning
during World War II.
Narrow wooden bridges
spanned turbulent rivers, and
bulldozers (opposite) fought
bush, muskeg and mud. Later
came huge steel bridges now
used by tourists exploring
this "last frontier."

path through his wilderness. Through your car window you can see valiant silver salmon choke a mile-wide river as they fight their way upstream to spawn and die.

Now there is change in the wind. A study recently completed for the Canadian government suggests that a paved Highway would result in great economic gain for the North country. Though not imminent—the costs would be staggering—a paving program is probably inevitable. When it comes, the adventure road will be buried under asphalt, and civilization will have caught up with another "last frontier."

Before the road was built, dreamers had been advocating a land route to Alaska for 50 years—and for 50 years "realists" had held that it couldn't be done. Then came Pearl Harbor. Because of the possibility of a naval blockade of the North Pacific ports, it was decided that the road *had* to be put through. A regiment of U.S. Army Engineers suddenly appeared at the tiny settlement of Dawson Creek, and another began toppling trees south of Big Delta, Alaska. A trapper, fresh in from the bush, took one look at all the soldiery and said, "What the hell's going on here? You'd think there was a war on!"

The soldiers were equally nonplused by their new environment. In the winter cold, bulldozer blades snapped. In summer, the ground turned to jelly, and muskeg swamps swallowed culverts, tractors and even mile-long sections of newly laid road. Mosquitoes were of such prodigious size that in one camp, so the story goes, the men shot them down with pistols.

Pushing north and south, the Engineers and Canadian construction workers crossed shifting moraine gravels, areas of permafrost, and rivers whose course could change by 200 yards during the lunch break. The builders did not, as once reported, follow the path of a drunken moose; the wild twists and turnings of the route were dictated by the need to get around mountains, bottomless bogs and mile-

high hills of ice. On October 23, 1942, the two work parties met at Mile 588, a place promptly christened Contact Creek. At a cost of nearly $100,000 a mile, some 16,000 Canadians and Americans had accomplished one of history's great engineering feats by punching the Alcan Military Highway through the wilderness in only eight months and 11 days.

Two years after the war's end, lodges and service stations were appearing almost every 50 miles along the road, now officially known as the Alaska Highway. Temporary bridges were replaced, the worst curves were straightened, and growing numbers of adventurous tourists were pounding along the gravel every day of the week, winter and summer. But many a man has learned—the hard way—that the Highway is still no parkway, and that prudence remains an essential traveling companion.

Every roadhouse has its favorite tale about the cheechakos (greenhorns). For 100 miles up and down the Prophet River they still slap their thighs when they tell about the tourist who came plunging downhill one black night, brakes screeching as he suddenly bounced aboard a ferry temporarily replacing a washed-out bridge. He was brought to a desperate halt only by the cable wires at the forward end of the craft. The crew waited until he had a grip on his shattered nerves—then told him that six nights out of seven they tied up on the *other* side of the river.

When the roadhouse people say, "So long, see you again," they mean it. Traveling the Highway becomes contagious. Alaskans, "liberated" by their land link to the south, now make the trip "Outside" regularly. And even cheechakos, once inspired by the road's rugged magnificence, are hard put to keep off it.

We first drove the Highway in 1961, reaching the last milepost weary and dust-laden and vowing never again. Two years later we were back, and again in 1965, this time with our children. And as surely as I write these words we will all be heading north once more—in a year, two years, sometime.

The adventure road is made for those of us who were born too late to sail uncharted oceans or blaze a trail through the wilderness. It richly rewards the urge to seek out the wonders beyond the next horizon.

It surprises you with a different face at every turning. Dawson Creek, a bustling community that was all but leveled when a dynamite warehouse blew up during construction days, is today the center of a burgeoning oil industry. The locals are now solid and staid, and saltily tolerant of tourists who clamber out at the main intersection to photograph the historic "Milepost 0" marker.

In the rich Peace River Valley, where there is land for the homesteading on every side, even a part-time farmer can grow 50 bushels of wheat to the acre, and the record is a staggering 83 (America's midwestern granary produces an average 25). Fort St. John sits on the far side of the river, caught between yesterday and tomorrow, many of its people still living in expanded versions of the huts and sheds thrown up when the Highway was building. On the other hand, the town boasts a nine-hole golf course and at least three of those absolutely essential Highway handmaidens, coin laundries.

Abruptly the pavement ends. Now the road becomes a lonely white thread winding through the green mat of the forest. A plume of brown dust follows your car, and a cloud of it engulfs you with every passing vehicle. Experienced hands drive with their headlights on in broadest daylight, and with a piece of bright-colored cloth tied to a fully extended radio antenna, the better to make their presence known in the dust storms thrown up whenever two cars meet.

I remember sneaking a sidewise look at my wife during our first trip, and noting with shock that the rich red color of her hair had faded and that her once-clear skin had the pallor of age. Twenty miles farther on, when I took off my sunglasses to wipe off an eighth-inch layer of powdered road, I realized what had happened: seeping silently through

Animals seen from the Highway show little fear— and frequently disdain— for human "trespassers."

"The loneliness of the empty land": the Highway swings bleakly across a river at Sheep Mountain, Mile 1060.

the locked car doors and tightly closed windows, the dust had not only aged us both but all but buried us. By the time we unpacked our car trunk at Fort Nelson, my electric razor—which had been protected by a zippered case wrapped in clothing inside a suitcase covered with a tarpaulin—was delicately coated with dust.

Because of the summer dust, many drivers prefer the winter road. Up to ten feet of snow has been packed hard and smooth, and the mosquitoes and the dust are gone. But there is no margin for error on the winter road, and it is no place for innocents abroad. A Highway engineer whose car skidded on a curve and flipped over calculated that he would be frozen to death in little more than an hour. Knowing that he couldn't afford to pin his hopes on another motorist happening along, he removed his tire chains, spun them up and around the electric wires overhead and short-circuited the line. At the relay station, the break was quickly pinpointed and a repair crew arrived at the spot in 45 minutes.

Beyond Fort Nelson the road veers to the west, climbing toward the snows that top the jagged Rockies. There is hardly a guardrail on the Highway. You may be driving along a high, straight section, the forests stretching interminably north and south, when suddenly, exactly 400 feet beyond a warning sign, the Highway wrenches away in a wild left turn. Ahead there is nothing: no road, no forest, only the blue sky and a thousand-foot drop to treetops below. If you haven't heeded the warning to slow down for the curve, you will not make it to Alaska.

Now the road crosses into the Yukon and swings toward Whitehorse. Through Whitehorse came the hordes who made the gold rush of 1898. Only a few struck it rich, although 100 million dollars in gold was panned from the fabled creeks by 1904. But Whitehorse prospered, and prospers now as the nerve center of the Highway. Like specters from some other world, the great white sternwheel steamers that once plied the Yukon River sit forever still on the bank.

Beyond Whitehorse, you will find no more than a handful of people in any one place—no towns, no communities, only a lodge or roadhouse every 30 or 40 miles. But in these places reside the soul and spirit of the Highway. Here are the valiant couples who pump gas, broil hamburgers and leave a light burning at night beside a cheery little note: "Take any room with the door open. Settle in the morning."

At Haines Junction you can, if you wish, leave the Highway and drive 159 miles south to Haines, and there catch an auto ferry homeward. For some years, Alaska's auto ferries, as large and luxurious as ocean liners, have offered summer service six days a week from Prince Rupert on the British Columbia coast to the towns and villages of southeastern Alaska, by way of the Inside Passage. In 1966 a new Canadian vessel inaugurated service between Vancouver and Prince Rupert so that visitors to Alaska can now make the entire trip by ferryliner one way and by car the other.

We didn't turn south at Haines Junction. We stayed on the Highway, driving up over the back-

The first of these signposts at Watson Lake in the Yukon was erected in 1942 by a homesick American soldier working on the Highway. Other G.I.'s did likewise; now tourists add to the colorful collection.

bone of the St. Elias Mountains, past Snag at Mile 1188 (where a North American record cold of 81 degrees below zero was once registered). Crossing into Alaska, we left the Highway at Tok and headed southwest toward Anchorage. Our 55-mile-an-hour speed on the unaccustomed blacktop seemed supersonic. Ahead was a great city with all its amenities—civilization! Then, barely ten miles from the soaring hotels, room service and chic restaurants, we stopped at a diner for coffee. On the next stool sat a thoroughly bemused bread deliveryman, his arm in a sling and his forehead freshly bandaged.

"I never had a chance," he was saying to the waitress. "The thing bounced right out on the road. The truck looks like an accordion."

"What thing?" I asked, "What did you hit?"

"Biggest damn bull moose you ever saw!"

The Amazing Crusoes of Lonesome Lake

The extraordinary story of Ralph Edwards, who wrested a home from the wilderness with little more than his bare hands. He mastered every adversity and won a rich way of life for himself and his family

By Leland Stowe

Throughout the 300-mile voyage from Vancouver one youthful passenger stared over the ship's shoreward rail as if he couldn't see enough of British Columbia's mountains. Otherwise, save perhaps for the reddish hair and his small size, five foot five, there was nothing about him to attract attention. No one could have conceived—on that August day in 1912—that this young man was bent upon pitting himself, alone, against a wilderness where no white man had ever lived.

Ralph Edwards had come from California to homestead a farm about which he had long dreamed. Landing now at the tiny village of Bella Coola, he set out into the interior. Forty miles of hard going brought him to Atnarko, whose half-dozen cabins marked the limit of permanent human habitations in this wilderness. Trapper Frank Ratcliff told him about a "real pretty" lake which lay over the mountains in the valley of the Atnarko River. So, with Ratcliff as his guide, Edwards set out on a resplendent October day to find, somewhere in the dense fastnesses, the site for his permanent home.

Two days later, after tramping and crawling through almost impenetrable terrain, they topped a crest and Ratcliff pointed northward where the Atnarko River spilled into a glittering, tranquil expanse of turquoise. Lonesome Lake lay between great escarpments of unbroken forest rising into the shoulders of a mighty mountain range.

Great flocks of ducks and geese circled in dizzy, clamorous flight over the lake. There must be fine fishing there, too. "And every kind of game you can think of," Frank assured him.

"We don't need to look any farther," said Ralph. This seemed like heaven on earth.

Who was this Ralph Edwards who, at 21, set himself to carve a farm out of primeval forest amid hardships such as few North Americans have confronted since pioneer days? At 17 he had been a hired hand on a California farm, working a 12-hour day, six days a week, to earn $35 a month. He heard there was free land in British Columbia.

For four years Ralph put all his waking hours into preparation for his great objective. He bought textbooks used by his employer's son at agricultural college and determined to master the same courses on his own. For four years he saved to accumulate his homestead stake. When he headed for Canada he was well prepared. And he had done it all—as he would do everything all his life—on his own.

In January 1913, British Columbia's land office granted Edwards a 160-acre pre-emption in the frozen wilds of the Atnarko valley. Almost anyone else would have waited until spring, but Ralph *couldn't* wait. In sub-zero weather he and Frank Ratcliff would "pack in" his initial supplies.

To reach the lake, they carried everything on their backs from the last spot where horses could travel in deep snow. They broke through undergrowth, across rockslides, up steep slopes along cliffslides, over almost impassable terrain. Again and again they struggled over this brutal obstacle course— Ralph later called it "The Ding-Blasted Trail"— each carrying 70 pounds on his back. They kept at it until they had 600 pounds on the lake shore.

Then they constructed a large sled, loaded the supplies and pulled it seven miles up the frozen lake.

As they made a final pause at the head of Lonesome Lake, a flock of great white birds broke into tumultuous flight. "Trumpeter swans," said Frank. "They winter here." To Ralph they seemed a good omen; they brought a sudden warmth into this still wilderness, and the promise of companionship.

That night, with the temperature ten below, they slept on balsam boughs. Next morning they started to build a cabin. Felling young cedars, they hewed them into logs, Frank showing Ralph how to notch them in. In three days they had the cabin up and roofed over.

On the fourth day Ratcliff returned to his trap line. Ralph began felling the colossal trees from which he proposed to wrest a farm single-handedly. The young homesteader had the merest smattering of the woodsman's art; yet, like a beaver gnawing a towering aspen, he hurled his five feet five against centuried Douglas Firs as tall as ten-story buildings and laid them low, a few more each day. He worked with the energy and purpose of a man whose toehold on existence is at stake. Bit by bit a heartening patch of blue opened high above him. Each day he counted another few square yards of newly-gained terrain. Each night he prepared his simple meal over an open fire.

All that first frigid, snowbound winter the young pioneer existed in loneliness greater than he had ever imagined. Each nightfall smothered his cabin with silence so suffocating that a sudden outburst of a pack of wolves was a relief. How to endure such solitude? Day after day Ralph worked himself into extreme fatigue, so that his evening hours were shortened by the need for sleep. He forced his mind each night upon tomorrow's quota of progress. Soon he learned that a routine of hard work is the surest means to vanquish loneliness.

By spring's late thaw Ralph had cleared a considerable rectangle near the forked stream he now called Home Creek. Using long poles for leverage, he pried out enough stumps to expose a small patch of fine dark loam. To keep out grizzly bears and deer, he surrounded his precious few square yards of earth with a high, strong fence. He planted his

"A man happy in heart and in great peace of mind"— Ralph Edwards of The Birches, in 1926.

Edwards' "quick-built" cabin
for that first winter of
1912-13 at Lonesome Lake.

first tiny garden: carrots, parsnips, beets, turnips. Then he went "out," to a summer job near Bella Coola. For years to come, summer work would finance seven or eight winter months of establishing his farm.

When he returned that autumn Ralph resumed his battle to whittle back the forest. Every day he learned new skills—by doing.

Rowing a clumsy raft down Lonesome Lake and back, for instance, was a backbreaking business. Even a primitive dugout canoe would be an improvement. What he recalled from reading *Robinson Crusoe*, he put to work. In a few days he had burned out a big cedar log and shaped it into a tolerably good canoe. It was cumbersome, but he got down the lake in it with much less sweat and effort than by raft.

By his third spring he had cleared several acres, and that autumn he began a permanent home, a three-room cabin for the family he hoped to have someday.

It took one full winter's work to fell the cedars, strip them into logs, split and hew them with painstaking care. But how to transport the big 12-foot logs to the cabin site? Here Ralph's inventiveness first came to light. "I must build a kind of trolley," he decided.

He cut and peeled slender alders, shaped them into a rough narrow-gauge track, pinned ties underneath with wooden pegs. To fashion crude wheels, he sawed three-inch pieces from well-rounded fir logs, then attached smooth birch surfacing for the rims.

Now bearings? Success or failure would hinge on having them, and he had neither metal nor forge. But he had noticed that wood partially burned becomes hard to cut. "I'll bet scorched birch would be tough enough for bearings," he said to himself.

He laboriously carved small pieces of birch into the desired shape, polished them fine and fitted them securely into place. Even under a heavy weight the bearings worked! With bear fat for grease, the rough

axles and wheels rolled well. He had only to build a strong framework for the car, and his trolley would be complete.

With it he now moved as many as nine 12-foot logs at a time across the 300 yards of clearing to the cabin site. For one small man, this was a tremendous victory, and it gave him courage and confidence for building the cabin.

Employing slanted poles and a rope pulley, Ralph got one end of each log bolstered into place, then the other. It was heavy work and excruciatingly slow, for he was forced to work exposed to freeze-up weather, through one sub-zero winter and then another. It took him two years to build his cabin—since each summer he worked "outside."

When he finished, Ralph had a solid structure with a 12-foot-square kitchen-living room, a 9-by-12 bedroom and a large room upstairs. He smoothed the cabin's interior walls until the cedar shone bright and clean. Then he hewed birch planks for flooring, thick and wide, leveling them with skill he would not have imagined possible three years earlier. Next he packed in windowpanes; by some near-miracle none of them broke.

After building and fitting in the windows, he installed homemade furniture—a table, a bench and two chairs—and built a front porch. He called his new home "The Birches."

Ralph Edwards learned by doing, and did well against great odds. He built well too: this wheelbarrow, for example, has no nails, no metal parts.

Trudy Edwards soaked braided cowhide and moosehide in bear grease to make belting and drive ropes for her father's sawmill. The mill was put together with wooden pegs; now bolts replace the main pegs.

Horses and cattle for The Birches come up Lonesome Lake on a raft. The first such seven-mile trip took four hours, with Edwards towing his stock behind a rowboat.

There remained the urgent task of expanding the clearing until it would provide, in gardens and pastures, the basis for a self-supporting farm. So again Ralph set about felling and burning trees on both sides of Home Creek, pushing his cleared ground down toward the river. By the spring of 1917, after five years, he had won from the wilds barely six acres. But these he had won permanently. It was well he had, for soon he would have to leave them.

When the United States entered World War I, he shut the door which had no lock, and set out on the 55-mile trek, by water and foot, to Bella Coola and thence back to the United States to enlist. Overseas with the 4th Division, he served from the battle of Château-Thierry to the occupation on the Rhine.

In September 1919, carrying 80 pounds of supplies on his back and a fine new rifle, Ralph Edwards hiked up the Bella Coola valley the 40 miles to Atnarko; next morning, he pushed on to Lonesome Lake. He found the overgrown trace of his old path and pushed eagerly through the forest to the clearing. There stood his cabin, snuggled among the huge white birches. Everything was as he had left it!

Ralph labored that autumn and into the spring with the energy of a man who had much lost time to make up, happy in heart and in great peace of mind. Thanks to money saved while a soldier, he now could speed development of his few acres. He bought a colt named Ginty, a stump-puller, a variety of tools, three steers and a heifer. Somehow he led each animal in turn safely over the Ding-Blasted Trail. But you couldn't get cattle up either side of Lonesome Lake on foot. Nor could they swim for seven miles. What to do?

Ralph built a large raft, then assigned to his 140-

Ralph Edwards mows hay in the fields he wrested from the wilderness. "We had a lot of peace here," he said.

pound frame a task which few six-foot athletes would relish. Hitching the heavily loaded raft to his rowboat, he pulled it seven miles up the lake! It took four hours.

Now The Birches, with a horse and cattle, had the makings of a farm, and before the deep snows came Ralph added a barn to his domain. The first big round against the wilderness had been won.

But his farm would progress faster if he didn't have to go "outside" to earn funds. Why not a trap line?

For the next 30 years trapping provided him with his only cash income. Although totaling but a few hundred dollars each season, it financed his winter supplies and farming equipment. He acquired a wagon one year, a mowing machine the next, a horse-drawn rake and other machinery bit by bit.

With these activities he continued his solitary existence on Lonesome Lake into its fourth postwar year. By that time he had learned the full meaning of the Biblical admonition, "It is not good that the man should be alone." Lonesome Lake had *almost* everything his heart desired. . . .

On a supply trip during the autumn of 1922 Ralph went on down the valley beyond Atnarko to the hamlet of Firvale, where settlers named Hober put him up overnight. His unassuming account of his wilderness experiences fascinated the Hobers; none more so than their slim chestnut-haired daughter of 18.

Ethel Hober had all the wholesome naturalness that came from a pioneer upbringing. She moved with the grace of one accustomed to the outdoors. Ralph sensed in her a maturity of mind much beyond her years.

How many young men have walked nearly 40

"Only our small clearing and buildings on the edge of the forest — they're the only changes." The windsock and roof of Edwards' airplane hangar are in the center of this photo.

miles—each way!—across frozen lakes and along cliffsides to court a girl? Regardless of sleet and snow, gales and frostbite, Ralph now found it somehow necessary to make more mail trips than ever. Even in good weather it was a strenuous two-day trek from upper Lonesome Lake to the Hobers'. But more than once, by pushing himself close to exhaustion, he did it in a single day.

That spring Ethel and her mother accepted Ralph's invitation to spend a week at The Birches. The farm itself, and especially the three-room cabin with its striking view, exceeded their expectations. When the guests left, the young couple were engaged.

After their wedding—at the Hobers' home on August 22, 1923—Ralph helped his bride into Ginty's saddle, mounted another horse he had bought, and they set out for Lonesome Lake. Ethel was to share all the hardships of the wilderness with the man she loved, laboring as he labored, exulting as he exulted, dreaming as he dreamed.

Together they harvested the crops. Together they got in the hay for cattle. Next came the need to fertilize the garden, for which nature provided chemicals in the sockeye salmon that swarmed up the Atnarko River every summer to spawn and die. Ralph and Ethel pitchforked one boatload of dead salmon after another. In the fall every daylight hour was occupied with preparations for winter.

With the coming of winter, Ralph's trap line compelled him to leave Ethel alone for days and nights at a time. Nothing was so difficult for Ralph as this—to trudge away with pack and rifle, turning for a last wave to that slender figure and knowing too well how the wilderness would engulf her.

The next September she went to Bella Coola's modest hospital for the birth of a son, Stanley Bruce. It was mid-November before the father dared expose mother and baby to the perilous trip home, but he could delay no longer; snow already covered the trails and freezing temperatures might drop to zero at any time. From slender maple saplings he wove a basket to carry the infant, papoose-fashion, on his back. The trip was an ordeal of five days and nights.

The baby so filled Ethel's days that the winter—and two more—sped swiftly by. Shortly before Stanley's third birthday a second son, Johnny, was born, and, some 18 months afterward, their daughter Trudy.

By now the ranch was producing almost everything needed for subsistence. There were a bull, a cow and her calf, and the garden yielded most essentials.

The food Ethel "put up" each year would leave most housewives aghast: 100 quarts of home-grown beef; most of the venison from two bucks; 50 quarts of sockeye salmon; 70 quarts of peas and 60 of tomatoes; 30 quarts each of string beans, beets, cauliflower and broccoli; 20 quarts each of corn and greens; 80 quarts of apples; 40 to 50 quarts each of strawberries, raspberries and gooseberries; and huge amounts of jams and marmalades!

For the few things they couldn't make themselves —sugar, salt, flour, kitchen utensils, nails, wire— they spent less than $200 a year. They spent perhaps $40 on store clothes. Whatever balance they could spare went for tools, and especially, for books. Anything else they built, invented or improvised.

By the fall of 1929 they had greater security and happier prospects than ever. But they would not remember October 1929 for this, nor for the Wall Street crash that shook the world outside. In that month their own world was shattered.

One afternoon, while digging potatoes, Edwards saw smoke billowing above his house. He broke into a desperate run. As he leaped over the creek he got a fleeting glimpse of Ethel, with six-month-old Trudy in her arms, shepherding the two boys into a nearby field. Sparks from the chimney had fired the cedar logs. In a few minutes their fortress against the northern winters was ashes.

A cruel irony prevented Ralph from saving any of its contents. Because of the grizzlies, they kept a supply of ammunition in the cabin at all times. Now the shells were popping like fireworks. Ralph couldn't go in.

Everything was destroyed—their supplies for the winter, their handmade furniture, almost every personal possession, their books, the rifles that were their source of food. The entire family's clothing was reduced to what they had on—and the three children had all been undressed when the fire broke out.

Stunned and heartbroken, Ralph and Ethel had only brief daylight before another below-freezing night. They rushed the children to Ralph's original 10-by-14-foot cabin on the upper edge of the clearing.

"We still have the cow for milk, thank God," Ralph told his wife. "Guess we'll have to kill the calf for food."

But what to do for cooking utensils? Poking in the hot ashes, he rescued a couple of badly twisted but usable frying pans. They ate a solemn supper that night.

At daybreak Ralph set out to obtain whatever necessities he might find in a trapper friend's unoccupied cabin down near the trail. From this 22-mile round trip he returned with two blankets, some old clothes, and priceless thread, needle and scissors. Ethel laid Johnny on a big sweater, spread his arms out and cut it down to size, making a "teddy bear" suit. Somehow, despite the difficult material, she fashioned similar apparel for Stanley and the baby.

Next day Ralph went down the lake again on the long trek for supplies—but with no money. When he recalls the reaction of Bella Coola, his voice breaks. Not only did storekeepers extend long-term credit, but friends contributed clothing and over $100 in cash—a good third of his annual income. Their generosity saved Lonesome Lake's pioneers from destitution. When he brought back this news, Ethel wept. That night, as before every meal, they bowed their heads. The words of grace Ethel murmured had never meant so much.

All that winter, they lived in the little earth-floored cabin with outside temperatures down to 30 below zero. It was cramped quarters for five. A double bunk, made of crosspoles and balsam branches, was the parents' bed. Opposite it was a bunk for the boys. There was but a three-foot passage between. Little Trudy slept in a basket beneath a rough drop table set against the cupboard. They had no cooking stove, only a patched-up fireplace assembled from remnants of the one at their destroyed home.

Ralph had partially completed a chicken house—12 by 20 feet—considerably larger than the cabin. He set about converting it into a temporary home. Before autumn they had an ample roof over their heads and a quantity of vegetables, fruit, canned salmon and meat. Their fenced-in fields stretched across the creek's twin forks. The clean land and the pastures, the forests and the mountains and the lake—all these were self-renewing and undefeatable. So was Ralph Edwards.

In every season he gloried in nature's secrets. Trudging through the snow along his trap line, he observed the imprints of other prowling creatures, the intriguing newspaper of the wilds. In a winter's trapping he might take 20 mink and as many marten, a few each of otter, beaver, fox, cougar and wolves, perhaps a wolverine or two and a lynx.

They were producing more homemade food and equipment than almost any other family on the continent, but still they needed to conserve their limited cash for essential projects.

What more could they make at home?

Shoes were expensive—why not make them? From government pamphlets Ralph learned to tan leather with boiled hemlock bark. At the ages of seven and five his sons assisted him. Then their father carved molds and devised from the home-tanned cowhide what he called "shoe packs"—pliable, practical footwear. For winter warmth he fashioned others of bearskin with the fur inside.

From shoes he proceeded to socks. "Why not spin

The family: Ralph and Ethel
Edwards as author Leland Stowe
knew them at Lonesome Lake,
and Stanley, John and Trudy
in a childhood pose
with the skins of two
timber wolves and a cougar.

our own wool and make our socks?" he suggested to
Ethel. He built a wheel of birch, then a treadle—
and they had a spinning wheel! Thereafter, Ethel
supplied their socks and sweaters.

Snowshoes being costly, Ralph fashioned them
from maple, bending the wood in a homemade
steam box. For the foot part he used cowhide; for
the toe and heel fillings, bearhide.

But if nature could often be made to serve man,
there was one place where almost nothing could be
done to alter her antagonism—that Ding-Blasted
Trail. Yet over this fiendish route Ralph managed
to bring a mowing machine, a farm rake, a hay
wagon and many other large implements.

He took each machine apart and discarded all
the wooden parts, since they were too bulky for the
narrow trail. Even though the horses carried only
the metal parts, several trips were often required for
one implement's essentials. Once he had the metal
parts at The Birches, he made all the wooden sections and pieces—by studying an illustration of the
machine or from memory. It took hours but it built

essential equipment and a great deal of character.

One day they heard there was a market for squirrel skins. Ethel had been proficient with a .22 rifle
from girlhood. "Whatever you get from squirrels is
yours," Ralph said. So Ethel sallied into the woods
as often as she could; she sometimes returned with
eight or ten squirrels, each shot through the ear or
eye—so as not to injure the hide. The pin money
she gained, at 50 cents a skin, was as much as $75
a year. It provided birthday and Christmas presents
for the children, and other modest extras. The
squirrel carcasses were not wasted. The ground
meat, mixed with grain and potatoes, made first-
class chicken feed.

Oddly enough, grinding this meat served as a
springboard for a series of mechanized improve-
ments, each a triumph of ingenuity.

After his customary resort to books, Ralph constructed a crude water wheel by the creek, hooked it
up with a pulley, and finished with a fairly satis-
factory small grinding mill. That sparked more
ambitious ideas.

Toting in kerosene for the lamps had long been an abomination. Why not get a generator, hitch it to the water wheel and provide the cabin with electric light?

Ralph built a large Pelton wheel employing a series of cups by which the rushing water would turn it. For cups, he cut 16-ounce evaporated-milk tins in half, split and twisted them into shape, then tacked them securely on the outer rim of the wheel. To add force to the creek's flow he constructed a ten-foot dam. To convey the water he prepared long tubes of hollow wood and inserted them in the dam so that many strong jets would strike the revolving wheel. Then he attached a pulley and belt from the wheel to the generator. The water jets spouted into the cups. The big wheel turned faster and faster. The belt spun. It worked! And there was electricity in the wilderness! The light from the single bulb in their cabin carried the promise of other mechanical revolutions to come.

For a sawmill Ralph needed a shaft that turned at 200 revolutions per minute. He installed a countershaft about a foot in diameter and got the right r.p.m. But his problem was still far from licked. The wheels turned for a while and then quit.

He had first linked the two drive wheels with manila rope. When the rope was dry it worked fine. It was impossible, however, to prevent the splashing water from soaking the rope, and then it tightened up until it stopped the machinery or broke.

"Why not try rawhide?" Ralph asked himself. He had never heard of such a device, but had used rawhide for all sorts of things. So he wove an eight-strand rawhide rope 160 feet long—to reach around the wheel, the pulleys and the countershaft. He softened the rawhide with bear grease, put it in place, started the wheel—and his sawmill was a going concern.

Since the nearest school was some days' journey away, Ralph and Ethel had to educate the children at home, at the end of tiring 12-hour days. Stanley, Johnny and Trudy were filled with curiosity, and their questions often stumped the parents. Ralph, who had only four years of grammar school, sent away for more books. The parents were soon educating themselves to keep up.

They also obtained from British Columbia's Department of Education correspondence courses for children in isolated districts. In this fashion the children "went to school." They wrote each assignment by post, and passed their mailed-in examinations grade by grade.

Ralph invented ways to make the lessons appealing. He had the youngsters apply mathematics to the farm, working out the number of board feet of lumber needed in the new barn or estimating how much horsepower would be necessary to lift a stump or given weight. He got books on mineralogy. He set up a homemade chemical laboratory. Few parents ever participated so extensively in their children's education.

Trudy, now ten, selected aviation as her first subject. From this she jumped to astronomy, then botany. Before long she was calling by its Latin name almost every tree, plant and flower in their wilderness world. A few years later Ronald H. Mackay of the Canadian Wildlife Service was to pronounce her knowledge of botany and zoology equivalent to a college degree in these subjects.

Were the children handicapped by missing a "formal" education? "They probably had a wider education than most youngsters," said Ralph. "They understood that if you want something you have to work to get it. They never expected the government, or anyone else, to provide it."

Ralph's own self-education thrived as he struggled to teach his children. At first his interests were confined by necessity to practical mechanics. But gradually he evolved into an example of how inestimably rewarding books can be. Once started on the trail of knowledge, he sought books with reverence and discrimination, and with rare intelligence used all they had to offer.

The library at Lonesome Lake came to consist of

A two-hour walk from Lonesome Lake is 1300-foot Hunlen Falls, one of the highest single-drop waterfalls in North America.

several hundred volumes. Among them, when I visited Lonesome Lake, I was not surprised to find books directly concerned with frontier problems. I scratched my head, however, as I read such titles as *Introduction to Cytology, Paleontology, Applied Entomology* and *Limnology.* Alongside several dozen volumes of the Modern Library nestled *The Psychology of Music.* Next to *Hundreds of Things a Girl Can Make* were such disparate works as *Asia's Lands and Peoples* and Thoreau's *Walden.* Most used of all was *Webster's Unabridged Dictionary.*

At 17, Stanley was anxious to do what his father had done at the same age—"paddle his own canoe." In another two years Johnny expressed a desire to do likewise. Ralph encouraged the boys and eventually both left for "outside." Stanley became an electrician, John a photographer. Trudy remained at Lonesome Lake and became her father's "right-hand man." It was she who took over responsibility for the trumpeter swans.

"I don't know which adopted which first," said Trudy, "but I suspect the swans adopted us."

Wherever the adoption was initiated, it is certain Ralph Edwards' decision to settle in the Atnarko valley led to a providential change in the fortunes of the great white birds. Noblest of North America's winged creatures, as well as one of its rarest species, *Cygnus buccinator* was then seriously threatened with extinction. Lonesome Lake was one of the few places on the continent where, from autumn's freeze-up to spring thaw, a flock of trumpeter swans—perhaps two dozen—could still be found.

It was not until 1925 that the Canadian Government heard of their presence in such an unlikely location. The chief Migratory Bird Officer for the Western Provinces, J. A. Munro, wrote asking for statistics on the flock. Thus the Edwardses acquired an exciting new avocation, and eventually Ralph became a part-time bird warden, feeding the swans every day. He was authorized to spend $25 on grain for feed—provided he packed it in himself over the Ding-Blasted Trail on his own time!

Mrs. Edwards feeds a deer
in the "back yard" at The Birches.

"Trudy's bridge" across the Atnarko River.
She was asked: "You mean you built this
bridge yourself?" Trudy, now Mrs. Jack
Turner, replied: "Certainly
not, I had the team (of horses)."

On this basis Ralph launched upon his contribution to the comeback of the vanishing *Cygnus buccinator*. For the entire family it soon became a lifetime mission. And, thanks to increasing supplies of Canadian Government grain, they saved their trumpeters.

Once the swans recognized the Edwardses as their providential providers, "they got the very human idea of making their wants known about dinnertime, 11 a.m." Thereafter the entire flock came winging up the lagoon punctually. Tooting in lusty harmony, they circled the cabin, sounding their own dinner bells in a melodious reminder. This ritual provided one of the happiest moments of the day, the one visit from neighbors which neither distance nor topography could restrict.

In 1943, at 13, Trudy became the swans' chief

administrator and closest human friend. Soon she was undoubtedly North America's outstanding female authority on *Cygnus buccinator*.

At 21, in her father's tradition, she looked around for "a really nice piece of wilderness to civilize." A mile and a half up the Atnarko River she found what she wanted—160 acres of rich bottomland thickly forested with cedars and firs rising to 120 feet. So she set out, by herself, to clear 80 acres of this homestead, a project so formidable that most males wouldn't have touched it with a ten-foot ax. But it was just about tough enough for an Edwards.

Trudy built a 30-foot bridge across the river, hewed out a road up the valley and erected a cabin to live in—alone, of course—while felling the forest giants. Next she built a barn that accommodated 14 cows in stanchions, with a loft large enough for 60 tons of hay. Finally she added an ample fenced-in yard (to keep out bears and moose) with a superbly hung swinging gate. And that autumn she slashed out her first acre where the birches were youngest, only up to 30 feet tall.

By February 1956, when I made a respectful inspection of her premises, Trudy had cleared a half-mile strip along the river, some 100 to 200 feet in width. The entire corridor—the only open space this stretch of the Atnarko has known since the Ice Age —was pock-marked with hundreds of stumps, many up to three feet thick.

"My next project," Trudy explained, "is to take Dad's stump-puller and extract them. After that I'll start on more trees. This cleared area is probably about ten acres. That leaves me only 70 acres to go."

When the first airplane skimmed low over Lonesome Lake's lagoon in the mid-'30's, its fleeting passage crystallized Ralph's most ardent dream into an obsession. Somehow they *must* get a seaplane. It was the only way to transport their increasing produce to market. But even a secondhand seaplane would cost $4000. Obviously, air transportation was something, as he admitted, "which we can hardly realize for a long time." For the next seven years all

Trudy Edwards feeds the Lonesome Lake trumpeter swans. Once there were only two dozen. The Edwards family has nursed the flock to almost 400.

he could do about it was to dream and scheme and save a few dollars. His chances of buying a plane were slim indeed.

And then the little frontiersman reached his most audacious decision. Except for the motor, he would *design and build his own seaplane!*

But to do so, he would have to educate himself in the entire field of aeronautics—from meteorology and engineering to aircraft designing and flying techniques. "We got books," he said, "but as soon as I started in on the engineering side of it, I found that my mathematics was not so good. So, in order to understand what I was reading, I had to get books on mathematics."

Beginning with Palmer & Bibb's *Practical Mathematics,* Ralph devoted years of evening studies to mastering everything from algebra to calculus. He found trigonometry "quite easy, and logarithms largely a matter of tables"; eventually he got a good working grasp of differential calculus. "But when I got into integral calculus," he confesses, "I found I was more or less stumped." Nevertheless, he reached the point where he was able to understand "what it was all about." Now he could pick up where he had hoped to begin.

Trudy, equally eager and impatient, "practically read over my shoulder." They were embarked together upon the great, long-term and crucial battle in which defeat—for them—was unthinkable. Together they read volume after volume of all phases of aircraft design and construction.

Trudy showed a quick grasp of aeronautic principles; but when engineering problems requiring advanced mathematics had to be tackled, Ralph had

to master these alone. One after another he worked
his way through such highly involved volumes as
Diehl's *Engineering Aerodynamics,* Wood's *Technical Aerodynamics* and *Aircraft Vibration and Flutter.*

"It was pretty tough," he said, "to solve problems
of flutter and vibration and lift, on your own."

All such calculations depended on the weight and
power of the engine his seaplane would have. Foreseeing this, Ralph had acquired—to his later great
good fortune—a reliable secondhand 85-horsepower
Continental engine. He could now figure out what
kind of body would best fit around it. Thus he was
ready to select the airfoil (the shape of the wings)
which would provide high lift capacity, "to rise
quickly above these mountains."

Bit by bit he forged ahead. In the meantime,

new associations had entered his life—thanks to the
trumpeter swans.

In 1949 the Canadian Wildlife Service, impressed
by the family's work with the great swans, authorized an experimental aerial delivery of barley for
winter feeding. In August pilot Johnny Hatch
set the first grain plane down on Lonesome Lake.

Ralph was delighted to talk airplanes with Johnny
and the other pilots who later flew in the grain. But
they brought a crushing disappointment.

"We know you can build your plane, Ralph,"
they told him, "but you can't use a home-built
aircraft until it has passed every test the Department
of Transport can think of. That's the law. If they
ever *did* clear it for flying, it would take two or
three years, or they might disqualify it altogether."

This, after ten years of plodding from algebra all

the way to an aeronautical design board! Said Ralph: "It set us to thinking seriously about buying a plane. We just couldn't afford to wait many more years to get into the air."

On a trip in with grain, Johnny Hatch informed him: "I've looked into the secondhand market a bit. If you shop around, I think you can find a seaplane within your reach." That was all father and daughter needed. Over the years of their aviation studies they had been slowly building their "plane fund": Ralph from his modest income from furs and an occasional sale of cattle; Trudy with most of the $100 or so a year she had recently been paid by the CWS for feeding the swans.

So they decided Trudy should go to a Vancouver flying school, win her pilot's license and buy a secondhand seaplane. She would go first because her father was now 62 and his age might be against him.

When Trudy arrived in Vancouver in 1953, she had been preparing herself for this moment for 13 years. In two weeks she had her pilot's license. She bought a secondhand 65-horsepower Taylorcraft, "checked out" in it and headed for home.

On July 8, Ralph Edwards heard a plane motor roaring up from the south. He spied a tiny blue-and-gold seaplane coming straight down the valley, skimming purposefully lower over the giant cedars' tops, coming down, down. . . .

"Here she comes!" he yelled to Ethel. They raced madly, choking with excitement, for the lagoon.

By the time they reached the shore Trudy was taxiing up . . . their pilot daughter . . . their seaplane . . . the tangible living realization of their dream. Suddenly the long years of holding fast to that dream, the years of saving, the years of isolated self-education in aeronautical science—all vanished in wondrous elation.

When he relives Trudy's homecoming, tears well into Ralph's eyes. For it is not possible to put into words the costs of an insuperable faith, nor the consummation of an immense desire, nor the meaning of the end of solitude for wilderness lives.

Next morning Trudy and her father took off from Lonesome Lake in their two-seater to drum up customers for their plane-to-market enterprise. Soaring up over Old Baldy Mountain's 8000-foot shoulder, they reached the summer camps on big Charlotte Lake—a two-day journey on foot—in less than 40 minutes. Soon Trudy was delivering their succulent produce, including fresh cream and homemade butter, to many isolated vacationists over the mountains.

Sometimes Trudy made three or four trips a day; sometimes she flew to Bella Coola with beef and garden produce. By mid-autumn she had delivered three tons of The Birches' flourishing yields, boosting their earnings to an unprecedented peak.

The following March Ralph went to Vancouver to get *his* pilot's license. When he presented himself for physical examination, the doctor surveyed the grizzled little frontiersman with undisguised skepticism. "Aren't you too old to fly?" It was the question Ralph had feared.

Imperturbably calm to all outward appearances, utterly the opposite inside, Ralph replied: "I'm 62. I understand a person can fly his own plane, no matter what his age, if he passes the flight tests." The medico was not at all convinced but consulted the Department of Transport by phone and grudgingly accepted their affirmative verdict.

After an examination, he burst out incredulously: "Why, you've got the blood pressure of a man of 26! You're in better condition than most men half your age."

Ralph threw himself into his pilot training with a youngster's *élan*. After 28 hours of instruction he embarked on solo flying. He was the oldest man in Canada ever to qualify for a pilot's license.

With *less than* 17 *solo-flying hours* in his logbook, he plunged into airlifting his farm's produce over the rugged mountains. Throughout the summer of 1954 it seemed there would always be a much greater demand for the produce than they could supply.

But then in October, just when their harvest was overflowing, the Taylorcraft's old engine conked out beyond repair. It could have been disastrous. But here Ralph's original determination to construct his own plane and his long years of aeronautical self-education paid off in a remarkable way.

"We'll have to replace the engine with the 85-horsepower Continental," he told Trudy. "Of course, it's heavier than the Taylorcraft engine. It will certainly require some pretty delicate readjustments."

That was putting it mildly. Few pilots would attempt such alterations, all demanding the skills of experienced mechanics with a wide assortment of spare parts at their disposal. But Ralph's equations indicated it could be done.

Using his knowledge of advanced mathematics, Ralph first calculated the effect the added engine weight would have on the seaplane's center of gravity. With Trudy as assistant mechanic, he groped through a jungle of wires, cables, dials and instruments. It took six weeks to make the structural alterations and get the engine installed.

But how would it act? The "85" had now been stored on the ranch through eight winters. Ralph had, however, treated it with the care he devoted to every someday-useful article. Keeping the engine up on supports and well oiled, he had turned it over several times every week—for eight years!

Now, at the very first flip, the motor caught. But would the Taylorcraft fly with this heavier engine?

Ralph taxied down the lagoon for a test flight which, under these circumstances, would have given most pilots concern. Then he turned on the power, and immediately the little seaplane picked up speed and was soon circling smoothly. Ralph's hard-won learning had saved the family from being "grounded" indefinitely.

Nevertheless, the plane's alterations had to be approved by the Department of Transport before it would grant a new certificate of air-worthiness. Ralph flew to Vancouver airport and presented his plane for inspection. The D.O.T. inspector shuddered at his improvisations, but he gave him the valued certificate.

One day the next summer, up the path to the cabin strode a tall young man. Where had he come from?

In a pleasingly courteous manner, the stranger explained he had "walked in over the mountains" on a vacation outing. He had heard that the Lonesome Lake region was beautiful. Would they mind if he stayed for a few days? He would gladly help with the chores, and he had his own equipment and sleeping bag.

Jack Turner lingered to discover the splendors of Lonesome Lake. Being enamored of nature—a civil engineer and surveyor who spent much of his time in British Columbia's least accessible regions—he found himself among kindred spirits. And the initial favorable impression he made was enhanced by the way he could handle an ax.

Before setting out on his strenuous return trek, Turner somewhat shyly asked whether he might visit again. The verdict was unanimous. The young man said he would write, and he kept his promise. His letters were addressed to Trudy.

During the longer second visit, Turner proved an expert surveyor. And whenever he calculated which project might best use an extra hand, it usually proved to be one on which Trudy was about to embark. So on most days, until his departure in late August, they went up the valley to her farm and worked together until dusk, slashing trees or extracting huge stumps.

And one day, at the end of a letter from Ralph Edwards, I read this sentence: "P.S. Jack Turner has persuaded Trudy to marry him, the wedding to be in the spring."

What is there in Ralph Edwards' philosophy that has enabled him to conquer obstacles such as few men ever face, and to do it on his own? What *were* the lessons of wilderness existence, I wondered.

"One of the most important," Ralph replied, "is

"One of the biggest wastes in the
world is in the unexploited
potentials of average human
beings"—Ralph Edwards

the immense satisfaction anyone feels in achieving a difficult goal, particularly if you've done your work to the best of your ability. We've learned a good deal from wild animals. Often I thought I was completely stumped. Have you ever watched a beaver at work? A beaver never lets anything stop him. We learned how any normal person by using his guts and intelligence can do a thing which looks almost impossible at first.

"For almost everything we've done around here we had to invent ways of doing it ourselves. But even though a man may not be trained for it, he can do a lot of things—if he *has* to. I have no more natural talent than many other people. What I *did* have was an awful lot of sheer necessity. One of the biggest wastes in the world is in the unexploited potentials of average human beings. Almost all of us, I think, are perfectly capable of doing many more things, entirely on our own, than we ever attempt.

"Finally, we have learned that if we deal fairly and squarely with everyone, things will work out in the end. I guess it amounts to faith—the idea that, if a person just keeps trying the best he can, he will come out all right. We didn't expect to achieve all the things we wanted at once; for many things we've had to wait and wait. We are still waiting for quite a few, working toward them as best we know how. But our life is getting better all the time."

Ralph's gaze swept out over his fields, past a great tree standing proud and solitary as if a symbol of his own wilderness life, and on up above the forest to the peak of Mt. Walker, gold in the lowering sun.

"I remember," he reflected, "exactly the way it all looked back in 1912 as I came over the mountains. The swans, the geese and ducks circling over the lagoon; the high peaks and the mountainsides green with firs and cedars; and the river; and the birches and willows and aspens all golden—and the life and beauty of this spot. Yet, as I look at it today, there's very little changed. Only our small clearing and buildings on the edge of the forest—they're the

only changes. Lonesome Lake is still unspoiled and wild. We've had a great deal of peace here."

With his ever-youthful smile, Ralph Edwards asked gently: "With all this, what more could we ask?"

After 53 years, Ralph Edwards' life at Lonesome Lake came to an end. He and Ethel sold the farm in 1965, to a California couple for whom it was the perfect place to retire.

"I flew my plane to many parts of northern B.C. and the Yukon," says Ralph, "looking for a new place to settle. I finally bought 3½ acres with a house and garden at Oona River, on Porcher Island near Prince Rupert. Then I got a gill-net boat so I could do commercial salmon fishing."

In July 1967, when he was 76, engine trouble forced him to land his plane on the Bella Coola River, at high water. "In trying to taxi to the aircraft float," Ralph says, "I had to turn downwind and was capsized. The current dragged the plane over the rocky bottom and damaged it beyond repair. So I am no longer flying."

Like themselves, Ralph and Ethel's children all live in British Columbia. Stanley, the elder son, is an electrician at the paper mill in Ocean Falls. John runs a fishing resort on Turner Lake. The Jack Turners live on Trudy's homestead. Their daughter Susan, like her mother before her, "goes to school" by correspondence. All around them are monuments to the original Crusoes of Lonesome Lake. One alone would be enough for most men: the flock of trumpeter swans the Turners still care for has grown to almost 400, a significant fraction of the entire North American population of these birds.

The Flying Judge from Yellowknife

John Howard Sissons — "The Man Who Listens," the Eskimos called him—
brought his own special brand of justice to their harsh land.
A report written in 1965, shortly before his retirement

By Lawrence Elliott

Judge and court travel by plane and dogsled
in a 1,300,000-square-mile judicial district.

Into the desolate arctic outpost of Rankin Inlet, on the west shore of Hudson Bay, flew a single-engine Otter airplane. As it skied to a halt, a door opened and out piled the entire superior court of Canada's Northwest Territories: the Honorable Mr. Justice John Howard Sissons, with his court clerk and court reporter, the Crown prosecutor and a police magistrate.

Judge Sissons had come 700 miles from his modern courtroom in Yellowknife to try the case of an Eskimo woman charged with murder and also with criminal negligence in the death of her daughter. Minutes after the plane landed, court was convened in a mining-company mess hall. A rickety table served as the bench, but the flag flew and Sissons, a bulky bear of a man, wore full judicial robes as he hunched forward to hear the facts in the matter of *Regina v. Kikkik*.

Three months before, in a little Eskimo encampment hard by the Arctic Circle, a hunter named Ootuk, maddened by hunger, had killed Kikkik's husband, then turned his rifle on her. But this tiny woman, grabbing a knife, had managed to kill him. Then she had taken her five children and set out for Padlei, 45 miles across the frozen land. She carried

the baby and pulled Nesha and Annacatha, the two next youngest, on a caribou hide.

On the sixth day of the journey, still not halfway to her destination, she could pull no more. She made a desperate decision: if any of them were to live, she would have to leave Nesha and Annacatha behind. She burrowed into a snowbank and put the two little girls there, carefully wrapped in the caribou hide. Then she gathered the other children and moved resolutely on. Late in the afternoon she was found by a Mounted Police patrol, but, by the time they reached the snowbank, Nesha had died.

When the lawyers were finished, Judge Sissons explained his concept of justice in the north country to the jury of four miners and two Eskimos: "This is an unforgiving land. We must consider not what is proper in the cities to the south, but what any reasonable and prudent person would do in this place and in these circumstances."

The jury returned a verdict of not guilty. Kikkik, it was clear, had killed in self-defense, and had achieved something of a miracle in saving four of her five children.

Late that same day the little plane was airborne again, continuing on a circuit that would take Sis-

161

Mr. Justice Sissons' rulings
proved to Canada's Eskimos
that justice is justice for all,
that native rights come first.

sons and his retinue to the far reaches of the world's largest and loneliest judicial district. It stretches from the 60th parallel to the North Pole, from the Yukon to the bleak eastern bluffs of Baffin Island—1,300,000 square miles of rock and bush and endless tundra. Seventy-two-year-old Jack Sissons has logged some 200,000 miles across this brutal land by plane and dogsled; and wherever he goes, he tempers the white man's law with an uncommon regard for the needs and traditions of the 32,000 people who battle the frozen north for life and livelihood.

The Eskimos call the big, pipe-smoking white man Ekoktoegee—The One Who Listens to Things. His precedent-setting decisions have firmly established the primacy of Eskimo native rights against the inroads of the white man and his made-in-Ottawa laws. Today in the Northwest Territories justice for all means exactly that. Sissons insists on a defense counsel in all cases, provided by the Crown if necessary. He has guaranteed the right of appeal all the way to the Supreme Court of Canada. But his most significant contribution is his very presence. The seal poacher at Cape Dorset, the Indian in trouble for stirring up a batch of home brew in Inuvik, the immigrant awaiting the citizenship oath in Resolute—all know that soon the judge will come flying out of the arctic mist, and justice will be done.

As a young man Jack Sissons left Ontario for the west. He taught school in frontier Alberta, worked in a lumber camp and, in 1921, earned his law degree from the University of Alberta.

Still farther west he pushed, hanging his shingle in the raw young towns of the wildly beautiful Peace River country, pioneering in courts just coming into existence. Not infrequently, he would drop everything to journey into the vast northland to defend—free—an Eskimo whose legal plight had won his sympathy.

Elected to Parliament in 1940, Sissons advocated building rail lines into the Peace River country to get the products of its soil out to market, to en-

The trial of Kikkik, described in this story.
Judge Sissons, seated, hears argument
from Prosecutor John Parker of Yellowknife.
Kikkik, in white, sits at the right.

courage settlement and industry. He argued for a highway that would pass through the Peace River country and link Alberta with the Great Slave Lake area of the Northwest Territories. His arguments helped both dreams become reality. Today the Peace River country is linked with both Edmonton and Vancouver by separate railway lines, and a car can drive by gravel road all the way from Yellowknife to Edmonton.

In 1955, Sissons, then judge of the district court in southern Alberta, was offered the bench of the newly constituted Territorial Court, headquarters Yellowknife. It was young man's country, rough and sparsely populated, and Sissons was already 63. But the challenge appealed to him, and he took it.

He was appalled by the state of justice in the Territories. Minor offenders were tried by local justices of the peace who knew little law. Those accused of major crimes sometimes languished in jail for years before a judge was flown in from "outside" to try their cases. So the new appointee loaded his court aboard the Otter and took off from Yellowknife on a 25,000-mile circuit that would give meaning to his deep conviction that every man has a right to a prompt trial among his own people. He has been doing it at least twice a year ever since.

A crusty, stubborn man, Sissons is often at odds with federal officials in Ottawa. Parliament and the bureaucrats—"the Wellington Street horse marines," he calls them—seem to him too often without knowledge of, or indifferent to, the north. He ignores rigidly held bureaucratic notions when he can, fights them when he has to.

For the Eskimos he has only compassion and

163

esteem. "Those who survive to wrest sustenance out of this land," he has said, "do so because they are harder than the worst the land can throw at them. They are magnificent."

The Eskimos respond with a profound respect for the judge's court. Understanding is sometimes another matter. The Eskimos' literal-mindedness can be a problem. "How can you say it was an accident?" asked Sissons of Antaluk the hunter, who had broken his rifle stock over John Sekoolia's head. "You hit him three separate times."

"Oh, hitting him was no accident," conceded Antaluk, finally understanding. "Breaking my rifle stock—*that* was the accident."

The judge is always alert for any dilution of native rights. In the case of *Regina v. Koonungnak,* he had to rule on the appeal of an Eskimo convicted of killing a musk-ox, an animal protected by Ter-

ritorial game laws. It looked at first to be an open-and-shut case, but a thorough reading of the trial record convinced Sissons otherwise.

One September morning a bull musk-ox had come lumbering up to Matthew Koonungnak's hunting camp. Koonungnak shot it dead, then trudged all the way to the tiny settlement of Baker Lake to notify the Mounties—and was summarily arrested. The local justice of the peace asked Koonungnak whether he understood the charge. Yes, he understood. Did he further understand the need for the law, to protect a creature which might otherwise disappear altogether? Yes, he understood. Finally, hopefully, the J.P. asked, "Well, then, if you see another musk-ox coming toward you, what will you do?"

"If he comes toward me," said Koonungnak, "I will kill him."

Down came the gavel. "Guilty as charged!" Koonungnak was fined $200.

Sissons quashed the conviction—with a typically blistering opinion. He noted, first of all, glaring flaws in the trial: the defendant had had no lawyer: he had been tried before a magistrate who was also the area game warden. Worst of all, his simple declaration that he had shot the musk-ox had been twisted into a guilty plea, "Guilty of what?" Sissons snorted. "This man was only trying to say that, in defense of his family, he had shot a dangerous animal, and that he would do so again in similar circumstances. Is that a crime?" As a parting shot, Sissons assessed court costs against the Crown.

No Sissons decision has had broader ramifications or aroused more controversy than one titled *Re Noah Estate*. Noah—designated E6-465 by the Department of Northern Affairs because, like most of his people, he had no last name—was a young DEW-line worker killed in a fire. He left his $25,000 insurance, plus savings of $1357, to his widow Igah and their baby daughter. Suddenly a government administrator noted that Noah and Igah had never been joined by a minister or justice of the peace. He decided that there had been no marriage and ruled that Noah's estate should go to his brothers and sisters.

Off to Broughton Island, 1450 miles northeast of Yellowknife, flew the Territorial Court, its judge fuming at a dictum that "capriciously bastardizes 11,000 Eskimos." Packed into an improvised courtroom were 200 of the late Noah's neighbors and friends. All day Sissons listened to testimony about native marriage customs, then returned to Yellowknife to write his historic decision.

"White Christendom does not have a monopoly on virtue. Eskimos have their own codes of morality and adhere very strictly to them." Though the north's vast distances often preclude religious ceremony, he sharply reminded Ottawa, an Eskimo marriage is solemnized by the lifetime pledge, "One husband, one wife." Because the couple will be living within a close-knit family group, the approval of all members—cousins, uncles, aunts, as well as parents—is required, and there is a waiting or engagement period. Noah and Igah had followed these rules.

Igah and her daughter were to have their bequests, Sissons ruled. In so doing he lifted a menacing shadow from the family life of a whole people.

Though accommodations on the circuit are often primitive—Judge Sissons has tried cases in kitchens, igloos and, once, in the cabin of a wrecked bush

Two Eskimo witnesses wait with an RCMP officer (foreground) to testify before Ekoktoegee.

plane—the dignity of the court has never been compromised. Every formality is observed.

The judge asks the members of each community to attend the sessions. Mounties are required to wear full-dress scarlet, and court is opened with the traditional, "Oyez! Oyez! Oyez! All persons having anything to do before our Lady the Queen's Justice, Justice of the Territorial Court of the Northwest Territories, draw near and give your attendance, and you shall be heard. God save the Queen!"

"The trappings are important," Sissons insists. "They demonstrate to the Eskimo that the brand of justice he is getting is no different than that in Toronto or Edmonton."

The Eskimo knows, too, that the One Who Listens to Things will go any distance to hear a case, and that the punishment he metes out is not revenge but the debt owed to those who have been wronged. In short, justice.

The Remarkable Eskimo Artists of Baffin Island

Out of the elemental struggle to survive has sprung a hauntingly
original folk art that has won acclaim in the "outside world"

By Lawrence Elliott

Thirteen hundred miles due north of Ottawa, beyond the farthest reaches of Hudson Bay, a scattering of tiny buildings clings to a high rise of rock. This is the settlement of Cape Dorset, on Baffin Island—a Canadian government outpost, trading center for a few hundred seminomadic Eskimos, and surely the most astonishing art colony in the world.

The artists can neither read nor write; yet here, where the arctic winds shriek and winter cold can kill in seconds, they have developed a hauntingly original folk art. Their pictures, sketched by the flickering light of a seal-oil lamp, have made the incredible leap from the bleak and lonely barrens to marbled galleries and salons on three continents. Their names—Tudlik, Niviaksiak, Kenojuak—are acclaimed in the rarefied realm of international art.

The Eskimo prints from Cape Dorset, first shown in 1959, excited the critics and captivated thousands. Museums rushed to buy examples for their collections, vied for the defaced stone blocks and sealskin stencils on which they were made. Prints meant to sell for $15 to $95 were soon being traded for as much as $1000.

The Eskimos were puzzled by all the excitement. They do not think of themselves as artists. They are hunters, as their fathers were, and the place of a *tituktowak* [print] in the Eskimo scheme of things is best indicated by the literal meaning of the word: small-marks-you-make-with-your-hand. Making a picture is something to while away the long hours when gales howl and even the mightiest hunters dare not leave camp. But when the winds are still again, a man must strike out across the tundra in search of walrus, seal, whale, bear.

For this is the land of the quick and the dead. The grim struggle to survive is all-important. The frozen ground yields nothing to appease a man's hunger, or clothe his body, or shelter his family. And yet the land is endlessly fascinating to the Eskimo.

"The *kaluna* [white man] sees only the harsh-

The goddess Nuliayuk, giver of sea life on which Eskimo survival used to depend, was carved in green Cape Dorset soapstone (left) by the artist Audla. The sculpture is seven inches high. The drawing, print and sculpture (right) by Joe Talirunili, of Povungnituk, shows the Eskimo artist's deep interest in people and things around him. On a 15-by-22-inch drawing, Talirunili recorded the names of the men in a seal boat. He made a black-and-white print (far right) from a stonecut of the drawing, then carved a 4½-inch-high sculpture (below) from gray soapstone.

ness and feels only the cold," says Tudlik. "But this is our home, and we can see its beauty."

They see, too, the essential mystery of life. Searching back into their dreams and fears and perplexities, they experience feelings not easy to talk about. So a hunter returns empty-handed—and draws a mischievous Talluliyak, the sea goddess who perversely lured the seals away from his harpoon. Another ponders the brilliant northern lights—and makes a picture of the gods playing catch in that other world, creating ghostly flashes as they throw seal skulls across the night sky.

Some of the pictures are direct, urgent. "To hunt the great bear," Niviaksiak once said, "you must *feel* like a bear." And his art shows the mammoth white beast poised for flight, or hunching low on an ice floe—stark portrayal of the quarry at bay.

Cape Dorset is one of the oldest settlements in North America. For 3000 years Eskimos have camped by its steep shore and fished its winding fjords. And for almost that long they have been revealing themselves in an art whose primitive purity has been undiluted by outside influence. With no tools but crude knives, they carved on odd bits of driftwood, antlers, ivory from a walrus tusk, the soft arctic soapstone exposed by an ebb tide—anything that came to hand. They had an almost eerie power of observation, the hunter's total familiarity with his world. They knew the lost look of an injured seal, and they wrested it from the lifeless stone. They knew the exuberance of the fisherman returning home with a full string, and they shaped it from a piece of ivory.

To this inscrutable land 20 years ago came a young Canadian artist, James Houston, for a season of painting the austerely beautiful arctic landscapes. The magic and mystery of the north took hold of him. He stayed two years—and when he finally did return south, it was only to wangle an assignment as an officer for the Department of Northern Affairs and to marry his fiancée. Then he returned with her to Cape Dorset.

Ellie Houston found three frame buildings and some tents housing a Hudson's Bay Co. store, a nurse, a teacher and ten Eskimo families. Some 300 other Eskimos, in three- and four-family groups, ranged across the 18,000-square-mile Foxe Peninsula, and once a year came to the village to trade white-fox skins for cartridges, fish nets and cloth.

Ellie loved the life almost from the beginning. She taught the women to bake bread, and Jim found time to paint glittering icebergs and the long scarlet sunrise.

The Eskimos had never known anyone like this soft-spoken picture-making *kaluna*. Saumik, they called him—the left-handed one. They were soon visiting the Houstons' hut, grinning as Jim and Ellie stumbled over an Eskimo word but secretly gratified at the couple's persistent efforts to learn.

One evening Kananginak, a distinguished hunter, brought a gift for Saumik—a small soapstone carving of a seal. Houston needed only one look to recognize its worth. "It was magnificent!" he says.

In halting Eskimo, Jim Houston asked if Kananginak could carve another seal. The hunter was puzzled. He had already made a seal. Why would he want to make another? A walrus, then? Ah, that was a challenge. Kananginak had never made a walrus. He went off to find some stone.

When the Eskimos learned that the carvings pleased Houston, they brought him more. Convinced that the world would respond to these unique expressions of a unique people, Houston prepared to take some south. First, though, he presented the villagers with a rifle. "It is for the carvings," he said. They stared at him, awestruck.

In Montreal and Toronto and Ottawa, wherever Houston showed the carvings, the reaction was: "Where can I buy one?" Encouraged by the Department of Northern Affairs, Houston made a marketing arrangement with the Canadian Handicrafts Guild, then returned north to convince unbelieving natives across the eastern arctic that there were people who would pay money for their

Artist Kenojuak, in the first
of this series of pictures
of Eskimo artists at work,
prepares a drawing to be made
into a print. Another Cape Dorset
artist (top right) makes ready
a stone block. Now the stone
is inked (lower left) and paper
(lower right) is placed
on the inked stone to make a print.

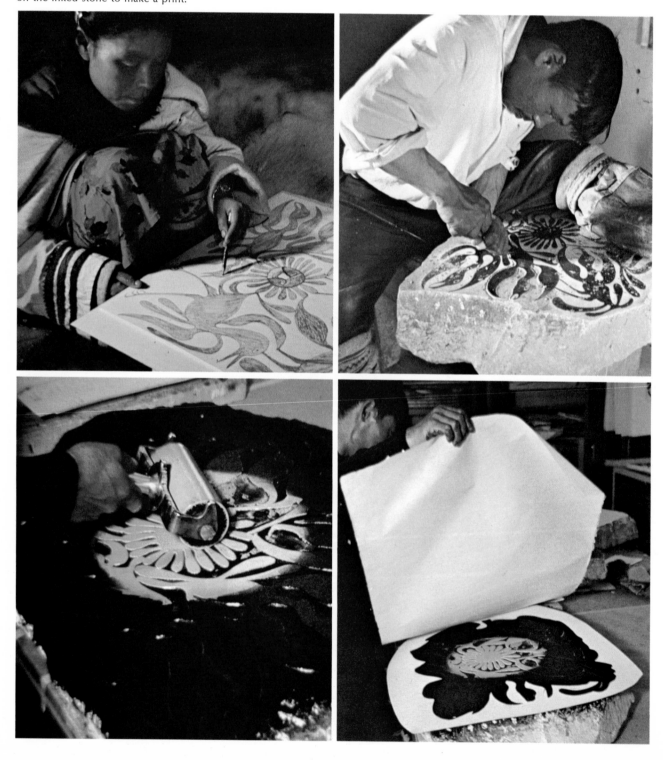

soapstone figures. For the first time the Eskimos had a source of income independent of the trapline.

One afternoon in 1957, Oshaweetuk, the carver, fingered a package of Jim Houston's cigarettes. "It must be tiresome for someone to paint this same picture on every package," he said. Trying to explain the process of printing, Houston took down one of Oshaweetuk's own delicately incised walrus tusks and lightly spread it with ink. Then he put a piece of paper over it and pressed gently until the picture on the tusk was faithfully transferred.

Oshaweetuk was entranced. "We could do that!" he cried—and instantly it occurred to Houston that the people of Cape Dorset could, indeed, be taught to adapt their artistry from stone to paper. Houston obtained leave from the Department and, drawing on his savings, flew to Japan. There, for four months, he studied with 72-year-old Unichi Hiratsuka, acknowledged master in a land where the printing craft had reached its peak. When he came back to Cape Dorset, an artistic revolution was in the making.

One decision was automatic: the basic art must remain the Eskimos' own, and the materials would be those they had always used. Hewn with a hand-ax, a block of stone was filed smooth and polished,

Hunting off the floe edge in winter,
this Eskimo has shot a seal in the water,
then retrieved it with a small boat.

An Eskimo father shows his son
how to use a telescope for sighting
caribou. In a polar bear hunt (below)
at Jones Sound, between Ellesmere Island
and Devon Island, sled dogs are released,
still in their harness, as soon as a bear
is sighted. They hold the bear
at bay until the Eskimo hunters
can move close enough to shoot.

Top: a female ptarmigan. Center: caribou
at Aberdeen Lake, in their annual migration
across the Barren Grounds west of Hudson Bay.
Bottom: the harp seal, common to the
Canadian Arctic, drifts down
the Labrador in winter. Seal pups
like this are born on the coastal ice.

When ice leaves Hudson Bay in summer,
walrus travel to *oogli*, places
where they haul themselves out of the water
to sun and frolic. The rocks of this *oogli*
are off Coats Island in northern Hudson Bay.

and on this surface the artist cut in low relief the forms and figures to be colored and gently rubbed off onto tissue-thin paper. All that winter the little heated *senlavik* [craft center] hummed with activity. Men and women brought their sketches, watched the newly taught printmakers re-create their art on paper.

The first small collection was exhibited at the Shakespeare Festival in Stratford, Ont. A few months later, when 1500 prints went on sale in Montreal, 600 were bought the first day, including copies for the Tate Gallery in London, the Museum of Fine Arts in Montreal and the Museum of Modern Art in New York. Dealers across Canada and the United States soon clamored for more.

But there would be no more until the following year's collection was ready. For, with Jim Houston's help, the people of Cape Dorset had formed a co-operative and made some important decisions. To avoid sacrificing the artists' ever-fresh individuality, only a limited number of designs, chosen and priced by an independent committee, would be printed. Of the 54 copies made before the stone was broken, 50 were to be sold and four kept as a permanent record in Ottawa and Cape Dorset. Each artist and printmaker would be paid for his work. The balance of the income (there was $20,000 that first year) was to be plowed back into the co-op.

The 1960 print collection earned more than $60,000 and the 4150 prints sold in 1961—the work of some 25 artists—brought over $80,000. In 1962 the co-op decided to finance and build its own store, then hired a *kaluna* to operate it—the first time in Canadian history that the traditional roles of Eskimo and white man had been reversed.

Though each family now has warm clothing and every hunter his own rifle, nothing is essentially different. The people must still move across the frozen tundra in search of the seal and the great bear, and their lives remain beset by the same hardships with which their ancestors lived and died. This, the old ones will tell you, is the way it must be.

But even the stern stoicism of the Eskimos was shaken by the death of Niviaksiak, perhaps the greatest of the Eskimo artists. His life and strange passing have become an arctic legend.

Often Niviaksiak would seclude himself on a small island to ponder the mysteries of life. Two years ago he grew obsessed with the great white bear. He knew it to be an inscrutable creature, its passions as deep and mysterious as man's own. For months he neither carved nor drew anything but the bear. Some said he probed too deeply, that there are things better left unknown.

Then on a still, cold morning in winter Niviaksiak led a hunting party to a camp 40 miles north of Cape Dorset where, one afternoon, they returned to find their canoe smashed. Niviaksiak and a companion followed fresh polar-bear tracks until, suddenly, they stood face to face with the great white creature. Niviaksiak threw his rifle to his shoulder, but he never fired. Instead, he cried out, "Ah, it is dark! I am falling." He dropped to the snow, and his companion fled.

Next day the hunters returned. Niviaksiak's body was untouched. The bear tracks ended abruptly, on precisely the spot where beast and hunter had faced each other for the last time.

The *kaluna* would search for medical clues to the

Carving in walrus bone, a fairly new technique
originating in the Rankin Inlet area, was
spurred by lack of soapstone there.
Eskimos saw that pieces of walrus bone
on the beaches resembled birds and animals.
Using files and drills, they quickly
and easily reshaped them as
Ugyuk did this 10½-inch-high sculpture.

Davidee (below), who lives at Lake Harbor, on Baffin Island, is "an incredibly competent man" to whom M. F. "Budd" Feheley of Toronto took these 18-inch walrus tusks. Through an interpreter, he told Davidee what he hoped might be made of the tusks. His only direction: "Be great."

Using needles and files, Davidee scratched his drawings into the ivory, then filled the delicate grooves with shoe polish. And two walrus tusks, in Davidee's hands, became exquisite works of art.

mystery, but the Eskimos know that Niviaksiak had, indeed, come too close to the great bear's secrets with his art and his pondering. He had been struck down by the spirits, and their earthly instrument had then vanished into thin air.

Eskimo art now is a fact of Canadian and international life. Several other Eskimo communities have followed in Cape Dorset's artistic footsteps. Canadian homes, stores, offices reflect the impact they've had. In Europe and the United States, major art galleries own their works.

The Cape Dorset colony is flourishing. At least 100 of its nearly 500 people are involved in some form of artistic activity—drawing, making prints, copper engravings or greenstone carvings. Canadian Arctic Pro-

ducers, a non-profit organization set up under auspices of the Coöperative Union of Canada, has applied the award-winning designs to textiles, calendars and Hasty Notes. Some of the best artists have their own art dealers. Yet in spite of worldwide attention, of modern conveniences such as electric lights and prefabricated houses, of visits by many outsiders, Dorset's art remains rooted in the animal and spirit world from which it sprang.

THE GOODLY LAND

Canada is bounded on the north by gold,
on the west by the East, on the east by history,
and on the south by friends.

Frances Shelley Wees, 1937

It is full of hope and promise.

Charles Dickens, 1842

The Land, Always the Land!

Bruce Hutchison takes stock of treasures to be found in the wilderness of the land he loves

My life forked many years ago when I purchased some acres of an old farm outside Victoria, B.C., and, 25 miles away, a cabin beside a mountain lake. In those days a poor man could easily buy real estate; but he could not truly own it by mere exchange of money and documents. Real ownership had to be established by his own labor, by the immersion, almost the premature burial, of his body in the earth.

Once I had driven my preliminary fence posts (some of them are still standing beneath tall trees planted at the same time), these upright shafts of pungent cedar, like exclamation points on a printed page, registered an irrevocable decision. And when I planted a garden, built more cabins beside the lake and cut my firewood of alder in the swamp, I realized I was beginning to master a second trade. But, as the heroine in the old melodrama of my young days used to confess, I was living a lie: my double life made for happiness but not for good journalism; on the other hand, I practiced enough journalism to prevent me from ever becoming a good farmer or woodsman. The jack of two trades was master of neither.

Now I am too old to care, and no man could have been luckier or happier in his surroundings, in half a dozen friendships (a high total as this world goes) and in wealth not measurable at the bank. My hoard includes, for instance, the unfailing income from the forest, the capital gains of massive woodpiles, the unearned increment of a vegetable garden enriched annually with manure from my neighbor's barnyard, the securities of spring blossom always at par, the gold-standard currency of dawn and sunset.

If the Department of National Revenue should happen to discover my real bank account, doubtless it would send me to jail. For I and all my countrymen have amassed more treasure than we deserve or can possibly spend—the first purple catkins dripping like wine from the March alders, the loon's eerie cry on the silent lake, the insect buzz in the parched

summer woods, the corn growing in the hot nights, the autumnal grin of pumpkin, squash and marrow, the drumbeat of winter rain, the moan of wind, the hiss of brush fires in the snow. All these are property enough for any man; but he cannot buy them with his checkbook, only with his hands and senses.

Riding in the high Rockies, far above timberline, I have seen things unsuspected by the traveler in train, automobile or airplane. Up there the air is clean, the type legible and printed boldly, in basic English; but you cannot read it until you have climbed slowly, day by day, and risked your neck on many a slippery ledge. And even when you have read that gigantic typography, you cannot reproduce it or convey its import to other men.

The message of the mountains is always confidential, cryptic and brief. Once, when fog, rain and snow had kept us in camp for two days, a narrow crack in the sky persuaded us to goad our unwilling horses along a shale slide to a ridge of rock where the clouds lay above, below and around us like wet concrete. Then, for half a minute or more, the wind struck from the west and almost blew us from our saddles. The sun bored through the concrete, the clouds were torn to fluttering rags of blue and

white, the valley of gilded autumn poplar at our feet was emptied instantly of mist. Sky, earth, mountain and forest, rock and tree, were convulsed like the colors in a child's kaleidoscope. The whole planet (how else can I say it?) turned into whirling, bubbling, molten substance as on the day of creation—a sight too dizzy for human eyes to look upon.

As suddenly as they had split, the clouds closed again, and we toiled blindly downward through them all day to pitch our camp in darkness. The Rockies had written their message and sealed the envelope. In all my later journeys I could never reopen it.

Nor could I appreciate the message until I had traveled in more distant lands. The barbered English meadows, the geometrical French fields, the tidy, upright Alpine farms taught me the essential difference separating the only two kinds of men, whatever their race or color—the outdoor men and the men of civilization, the trail men and the street men, forever separate.

In Europe the earth is domesticated and its owners with it. In America, outside our few urban strongholds, it is a wilderness which we may ravish but cannot tame; and some of us are not quite tamed yet, either, though we shall be in due time. A Canadian must see the old world before he comprehends the new. Invariably he will come home more Canadian than ever, and for myself, the return to my swamp and the whispered welcome of the forest seemed like release from a luxurious prison—a self-discovery worth all the cost and exasperation of foreign travel.

But the transatlantic cultural gulf has been closing fast; America is becoming civilized. It is a shaking fact, for example, that many children now growing up in Canada have never slept under canvas on hemlock boughs or hooked a trout on the end of a willow twig. The underprivileged generation of affluence, traveling by automobile, may get no closer to the land than a public roadside camp, with hot running water and firewood cut at tax-

"In the cities," writes Bruce Hutchison, "I
sometimes despair of the nation's future.
But one day in the outdoors, with outdoor men,
convinces me that the nation is safe."

payers' expense, and will go home in the pathetic belief that this is camping.

If I had any influence on national policy, the state would put all Canadian children in a real camp for at least a month every summer. It would be the best possible investment in health, sanity and true culture. I have always held that the nation is nourished in mind as well as body not mainly by the government, the school system or any man-made institution, but by the land and the people's dumb love of it. *There* is the true unifying force, more binding than Parliament, constitution and all the work of anxious bureaucrats who try to preserve the nation with statistics, slide rules and computers.

For this theory I have no proof, of course. Nevertheless, I could subpoena some impressive witnesses if the case were taken to court. They are obscure and nameless men seldom given to speech—dairy farmers on the cool evening porches of Ontario, wheat farmers on the hot Saskatchewan plain, loggers in a British Columbia bunkhouse, trappers in their winter cabins. Such men, Washington Irving wrote, might be rough, but they could never be vulgar. I have found also that they are rarely stupid or ignorant, for they have a direct knowledge of actual things, of weather, soil, growth, animals and the common creaturehood of all life.

Often, though speaking in monosyllables, they are more informative and interesting than educated men because they have mastered their natural environment by accepting it on its own terms and wearing it as comfortably as an old boot, while the city dweller is always in revolt against the synthetic environment of his own making, and his information is secondhand. He longs to escape, and commonly does so into a more expensive apartment, a cell more securely locked. The rustic needs no escape because he is not imprisoned.

In the cities, the businessmen's clubs and Ottawa's parliamentary corridors, I sometimes despair of the nation's future. But one day in the outdoors, with outdoor men, convinces me that the nation is safe. Surveyed from the saddle instead of the armchair, our democratic process looks vigorous enough to survive all the organized efforts to save it. I believe that no man can understand society until he has stood at a distance and seen the thing whole. No man can appreciate a cooked meal, civilization's first gift, until he has been long hungry, a warm bed until he has been cold, a lamp and an open door until he has been lost in the woods, a friend until he needs one, or a woman's love until he has felt the touch of loneliness. After much misery, and only then, his soul breaks out of the shadow and is riveted permanently to the substance.

There was small misery in my experience, but sufficient to give me a crumb of the substance, to tell me what better men had endured in this land. The land, always the land! And when you grow older, the land seems to grow richer and fairer, while the cities, swollen in size and power, diminish in your eyes. The westward traveler glances back to find the highest towers sinking below the prairie rim.

Such knowledge as we can find around us in the outdoors is not much; but, so far as it goes, it is reliable. We know that sap rises in the spring, buds open, leaves unfold and in autumn drop to rot and make the new soil on which all men live. Snow falls, frost splits the rock, and the mountains will slide perpetually until, as in its beginning, the earth is flat once more and lifeless. But for a little time the snow will melt again, a drop of moisture will ooze from some tiny crevice, hesitating between the eastern, western and northern watersheds, a brook will seek its ancient channel, and long after man

has gone the great rivers of Canada will move, unseen, to the three oceans.

This much we know on the outer fringes of truth—that our civilization is sick because man has separated himself from the earth, and that it will never be healed unless he rediscovers the flowing springs and green nutriments of his life. I have no doubt that the state will soon manage every aspect of society and solve all its exterior problems with neat blueprints and wise regulations; but the state's management will succeed only if, freeing man from insensate labor and society's cruel injustice, it gives him the chance to free himself from the state and find a different sort of labor, another test and a higher prize elsewhere. More and more the state abrogates our old inalienable rights, but it will certainly fail altogether if it abrogates our right to work, to suffer and to risk danger.

History's march is littered with the bones of rich nations and proud empires that lost their vital juices and collapsed before a handful of illiterate barbarians who still enjoyed work and welcomed danger. Without work, suffering and danger, there can be no satisfaction at the end. Without sharing, there can be no wealth. Without sacrifice for others, no rewards. Without self-discipline, no freedom.

These platitudes can be heard in any after-dinner speech, but they are quite true. Hence I foresee, and eagerly await, the day when man, fat with profit and bored with idleness, will rebel against enforced leisure, burst out of his upholstered jailhouse, walk barefoot on the earth and paint a picture, write a poem, or build a cabin with his own hands, refusing any pay. On a small but increasing scale he has begun to revolt already, as you can see every weekend in the city's exodus to the country. At the peak of the social revolution the signs of counterrevolution are encouraging. We must be patient. The full process will take time.

As Chaucer put it long ago, "The lyf so short, the craft so long to lerne." We have not learned it yet, but we are slowly learning.

Meet "Mr. Canada"

The story of John Fisher — folk historian,
radio personality, spark of Canadian pride and
the man behind that wonderful 100th anniversary
celebration we had in 1967

By Robert Collins

The applause swelled to a roar in Toronto's Royal York Hotel dining room as the outgoing executive director of the Canadian Tourist Association, the guest of honor, stood before 500 cheering admirers—clad in a gray prison uniform.

"John Fisher!" the chairman solemnly intoned, "we charge you with being an habitual and incorrigible *Canadian!*"

The chunky culprit beamed, guilty and glad of it. "Wherever I go," he replied in the resonant tones known to radio listeners across the country, "I'll *always* be selling Canada!"

With that, in May 1961, John Wiggins Fisher went to Ottawa, where he soon became Centennial Commissioner, boss of Canada's 100th birthday party.

For a man who wears maple leaf cuff links, 1967 was the climax of a long love affair with his home and native land. Since 1940, when he discovered the magic of Canada and of his own voice, John Fisher has shouted his nation's praises across the continent, hitting at "the strange Canadian disease of apology and nonsupport for things Canadian." At last he arrested the disease. In 1967 Canadians waved flags, had glorious fun in their own country, pointed with pride at their achievements—all largely because of "Mr. Canada."

Rousing such Centennial fervor seemed impossible when Fisher took on the job. ("Canadians," says Dan Wallace, head of the Canadian Government Travel Bureau, "consider it almost embarrassing to get excited about their country.") But Fisher was superbly equipped to be a national catalyst . For years he'd been a voice in the wilderness, a Canadian *proud* of his country. In wide-ranging travels from Ecum Secum, N.S., to Sandspit, B.C., Fisher has become an ambulating *Encyclopedia Canadiana*. He delights in knowing that there's a statue to a mule in the Rocky Mountains, for example, or in relating how a New Brunswick M.P. kept on orating when the Parliament Buildings caught fire in 1916, just to get his name into the Hansard records.

John Fisher's enthusiasm for his country has drawn some fire. "Mr. Fisher has earned himself a considerable reputation as a raconteur," the magazine *Forum* once observed. "But there is a thin dividing line between raconteur and windbag." Other critics call him a "professional Canadian."

"Sure, I'm Canadian, I make no apology for it," says Fisher. "But I don't *praise* Canada as much as I *prod* it. My object is simple: a strong country at home can make a better contribution abroad. We've got something here. Let's make more of it. It's a neglected story."

Fisher was destined to tell that story. He was born in Sackville, N.B., in 1912, one of five children of a prosperous stove manufacturer of Loyalist stock. An ancestor, Hon. Charles Fisher, was premier of New Brunswick and a Father of Confederation. His maternal grandfather, Cecil Wiggins, a fiery Anglican preacher, passed on his flair for oratory. From his father, an amateur poet, John inherited a taste for journalism and an insatiable curiosity. Sunday afternoons were lively talkfests at the Fisher home, with business and university people in for tea. Young John listened, learned, and constantly strove to improve himself. A skinny boy, he doggedly took body-building courses until he won the Maritime intercollegiate wrestling championship.

At Dalhousie University in Halifax he studied law and became a sharp debater. His budding Canadianism was nourished by the editorials of the great John Dafoe in the Winnipeg *Free Press*. Then, in 1933, Fisher met Prime Minister R. B. Bennett, who was visiting in Sackville, and added a new dimension to his Canadianism. "Young man," Bennett advised, "learn French!"

Fisher promptly enrolled in a summer school at Trois Pistoles, Que. The lectures were too advanced for him, so he wandered around town, listening, trying to learn. At the summer school's farewell dinner he delivered a speech in passable French.

After graduation from Dalhousie in 1937 Fisher worked briefly as a legal researcher for the Rowell-

One of the Centennial's most colorful features
was a cross-Canada canoe race along rivers
and lakes where *voyageurs* once paddled.

"Imbued with a sense of national unity
and destiny," John Fisher broadcast
simple stories with unfailing exuberance.
"Pride-builders," he called his
Sunday talks on "John Fisher Reports."

Sirois Commission on dominion-provincial relations, then switched to newspaper reporting in Saint John. One day he interviewed CBC talks supervisor Hugh Morrison. They hit it off immediately. "John was imbued with a sense of national unity and destiny," Morrison recalls. "I felt we had to get him on the air."

He asked Fisher to do a broadcast on the coöperative movement at Antigonish, N.S. It brought a flurry of letters and telegrams—Fisher's first taste of the power of national radio and his own voice. Turned down for military service in World War II because of a lung spot, he joined CBC Toronto, went west ("I felt the hunger of people for knowledge of their country"), and made a few talks on his return. They grew into a series which took the country by storm.

Fisher's simple broadcasts brimmed with exuberance for places, people and all things Canadian. He said Canada is a maple leaf, crisp and clean in autumn; it's the beaver minding his own business and working hard; it's the smell of boiling sap, burning brush, sweet hay, ripe grapes and fresh sawdust.

"Some of John's talks were like draught beer—when you blew off the foam there wasn't much

left," says Ernest Bushnell, then CBC program director. "But John was clearly sincere. He was a good missionary."

He won converts. Canadians had never heard anyone talk so glowingly about their country. Hundreds of thousands tuned to "John Fisher Reports" on Sunday nights and stood tall and proud amid the corn. "My talks weren't objective, they were always favorable," Fisher concedes. "But they were pride-builders. All I did was eavesdrop on people who had a stake in a community and tell a story the way they'd like to have it told."

He found stories everywhere. "Each part of Canada has its own flavor, its own personality," he insisted. He reported on the charms of B.C. ("Lassos and Lace"), Americans in Canada ("Sons of Sam"), and quaint Quebec City ("Christmas-Card Town"). A listener once told CBC president Davidson Dunton, "Last week he had me all set to move to British Columbia's Okanagan Valley, the *best* place in Canada. This week I find out the *very* best place is the Annapolis Valley of Nova Scotia!"

Fisher's praise had one main purpose: to arouse his countrymen to Canada's potential. One of his favorite lines of verse was from Sir Charles G. D. Roberts: "Awake, my country, the hour is great with change." And the country *did* stir under his prodding. Fisher's first series drew 27,000 requests for script copies. Letters began averaging 1500 a week.

Within five years Fisher logged 140,000 miles between speaking engagements. He spoke in factories, hockey rinks, schools and drill halls at fees up to $500 a night. He once attended a barbecue in Jasper, Alta., on condition that he'd get a plane ride to Edmonton the next day for his CBC broadcast. The small aircraft was late. As it bounced through turbulent air, Fisher tried typing his script on his knee. When he landed—13 minutes before broadcast time—he had written only some notes. Yet he walked into the studio on the dot and adlibbed for 15 minutes about the Rockies, tourism, Jasper—and his rough flight.

The big "sleeper" among Centennial attractions
was the Armed Forces Tattoo, a huge hit
wherever it played across the country.

Part of Fisher's charm, then as now, is his phenomenal memory. He loves people and history and can lard any speech with authentic local lore and first names of those in the audience. At a Centennial meeting in Ottawa, he introduced nearly 100 people without a slip. With the memory goes an ability to concentrate completely on the problem or person of the moment. "When people approach him, they get his *full* attention," says Jeann Beattie, a one-time assistant. "It's like a benediction—the warm smile, the gaze, the questions about their home-towns."

In 1956, when Fisher was getting 3500 speech

invitations a year from all over North America, he accepted a new challenge—the executive director-ship of the Canadian Tourist Association. In this capacity, he turned sharply critical: he chided Canada's "mental constipation" and "hemorrhage of brains" to the United States; deplored the lack of good restaurants and decent hotels at home. In five years he doubled the CTA membership and tripled its revenue.

Then one day Prime Minister John Diefenbaker summoned him to his private railway car in Toron-to. Would Fisher become his special assistant? "I was happy at CTA," Fisher recalls. But he had been boosting Canada's Centennial since 1949 and the Prime Minister indicated that he would later be made Centennial chief if he joined his team now.

As Diefenbaker's special assistant, Fisher was "a sort of glorified prime ministerial stage manager," in the words of one newspaper columnist. He paid particular attention to Diefenbaker's speeches. "I'd give him local stuff—names, tie-ins, people to mention, a little human touch." Diefenbaker kept his word and Fisher got the job he wanted.

The Centennial Commission was born late, and at the height of Canadian nationalism and provincialism. An air of disenchantment ran through the country. The Liberal minority government was so occupied with survival that Conservative-appointee Fisher didn't always get quick decisions. There were squabbles with his government bosses. There were staff problems (administration is not one of Fisher's greater talents). Above all, there was no precedent for planning a centennial.

"For once," says Fisher, "we couldn't run to the Americans for ideas. All they had in their centennial year was a fair in Philadelphia."

However, Fisher did what he always does superlatively: he traveled, glorified, goaded. Mostly he did this by opening eyes to local assets. "You're the world's leading nickel producer," he reminded Sudbury, Ont., so the city erected a huge reproduction of a five-cent piece. "Look at that old wharf down there," he'd cry on the West Coast. "It's history; clean it up, make it a tourist attraction." "Write a local history!" he urged others. "Write a regional cookbook!"

Everywhere, Fisher needled the nation. To a hotel association convention he said it was "time for lethargy to come to an end. Canadians must let their hair down." He told the Home and School associations that "Canada has been lounging on the psychiatrist's couch so long and so often we don't know how to get up." He urged a cleanup of parking lots ("they look like bomb sites") and highway approaches ("treeless wastelands of garish signs").

It began to pay off; people caught Mr. Canada's spirit and thousands of projects took shape at all levels. The Centennial train and caravans—roving repositories of Canadian history which Fisher envisioned as early as 1947—drew over eight million people. There was a traveling festival of the performing arts, a military tattoo, a British Columbia bath-mobile race (tubs powered by outboard motors), a prairie balloon race.

"Suddenly," Fisher says, "everyone latched onto the Centennial and had *fun*, which people said Canadians couldn't do."

Far more than the fun and games, Fisher prides Centennial for its deeper achievements, events often overshadowed by Expo but with long-term implications: an athletic awards program for all Canadian schoolchildren, an interfaith religious conference, a youth travel program which swapped groups of youngsters all over the country. "A centennial can't cure the ills of this country," says Fisher, "but it can put us into a mood in which the chances of solving our problems are greater."

In four years of Centennial campaigning, Fisher traveled 250,000 miles. Late in 1967, when the big party was almost over, he resigned his Ottawa post to accept yet another challenge—as publisher of Northwest Publications' two daily and five weekly newspapers in British Columbia.

But close friends aren't forgetting one further ambition that Mr. Canada expressed earlier in 1967. "I wish we could share our Centennial planning experience with other countries," he said. "As a start I'd go to the President of the United States and say, 'You'll soon be celebrating your second century. Here's what to do . . .'"

And if anyone knows what to do, on past performance, it's John Fisher.

The Men Before Columbus

Explorers have uncovered a Norse site in Newfoundland which carbon-14 tests date to about 1000 A.D. A Viking map indicates exploration of much of the North American coast about that time. Out of four years of study for his book, "Westviking—The Ancient Norse in Greenland and America," Farley Mowat reconstructs the Viking story

Dawn broke on the west coast of Iceland shortly after midnight. There was no true darkness, since it was spring, and the subarctic sun lingered below the horizon for only a few hours. The year was 981.

In a small, almost landlocked cove along Breida Fjord, a seafaring ship lay at anchor. It was a handsome, double-ended craft, graceful as a canoe though nearly 80 feet long. From its prow a short and heavyset Viking with pitiless eyes and an unkempt red beard searched the waters for unfriendly ships. "Nothing moves upon the fjord," he growled. "No clouds tell of storms to come. The course we steer will be straight and true."

So started the voyage of Erik Rauda—Erik the Red—who was to lead a handful of Icelandic Vikings westward across a wilderness of ocean to the unknown shores of North America.

Erik was not seeking new lands; he was fleeing Iceland, having been sentenced to three years' exile for starting a bloody feud, a sentence which under Icelandic law made him fair game for anyone to kill. Erik lived in a feuding time. His father had been outlawed from Norway for multiple murders. Erik himself had already been outlawed once, in 970, at about the age of 20, for butchering two neighbors. Now he had started a new feud which led to the death of several more men and to his own exile.

It was the usual thing for outlawed Icelandic Vikings to raid eastward to the coasts of Europe. Erik sailed westward, but his purpose was the same. He did not sail into the totally unknown. Even at that early date, the lands west of Iceland were not unexplored. People whom the Norse called *Westmanni*—Celts and Picts from Ireland and the Scottish Islands, whom the Norse had driven out of Iceland—had settled along Greenland's southwestern inlets, in country that they named *Irland Mikkla* (Greater Ireland). When Erik sailed out of Breida Fjord, therefore, he knew where he was going and what he expected to find—not new lands, but Westmanni settlements to plunder.

A tough crowd of about 20 men accompanied

This painting by Christian Krohg hangs
in The National Gallery in Oslo:
Leif Eriksson sights North America
in about 995 A.D. Fourteen years earlier,
his father, Erik the Red, had landed
on Baffin Island, the first European
to reach America. Leif made it to Trinity Bay
in Newfoundland—Vinland, he called
the country—and returned home a hero.

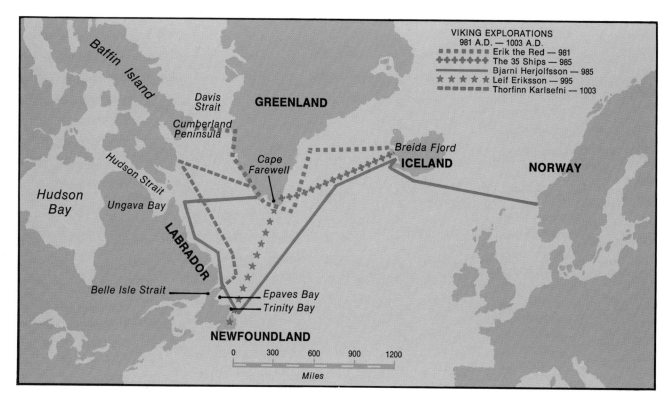

VIKING EXPLORATIONS
981 A.D. — 1003 A.D.
▪▪▪▪▪▪▪ Erik the Red — 981
✚✚✚✚✚✚✚ The 35 Ships — 985
——————— Bjarni Herjolfsson — 985
★ ★ ★ ★ Leif Eriksson — 995
▪ ▪ ▪ ▪ ▪ Thorfinn Karlsefni — 1003

Erik. Probably there were also slave women, since the Vikings were a notably lusty lot.

The crossing to Greenland was an easy matter. But the Westmanni whom Erik expected to find near the southwestern tip were gone; only their decaying sod houses remained. Erik waited out the long winter, then set out in the spring again in search of the vanished Westmanni.

Making use of the long subarctic days, Erik worked his way north along the west coast of Greenland until he reached a gigantic mountain standing with its feet in the sea some 500 miles north of what is now Cape Farewell. The mountain was a natural observation tower. From its summit the party could look a hundred miles north, along a rugged coast, with the great central ice field of Greenland glittering starkly behind it. Then one man glanced idly out to sea.

"Erik! Look west! Land!"

It so happens that Davis Strait is at its narrowest

(200 miles) between the highest peak in west Greenland (7300 feet) and the highest peak in Canada's Baffin Island (7100 feet). In summer, each of the two lands can be seen clearly from the other.

Erik now turned his ship westward. "To the north it is worthless country, all rocks and ice," he reasoned. "The Westmanni would be fools to go that way. But due west—I think we might find them and their cattle there."

He landed near the sea cliffs of the Cumberland Peninsula of Baffin Island. None knew it, but he and his crew had become the first Europeans in recorded history to reach a true part of North America. The date was 982—510 years before Columbus sighted *his* island in the Caribbean Sea.

The coast of Baffin Island was a disappointment. Chilled by the polar waters of the south-flowing Canadian Current, it was less hospitable than even the opposite coast of Greenland. There could be no Westmanni farmers here—no easy pickings for

An Icelandic map of the late 1500's, based on tales of early explorations, shows Norway at the upper right. From the British Isles (lower right), anticlockwise, are the Orkneys, Shetlands and Faeroes (and a mythical island called Frisland), Iceland, Greenland, Baffin Island (Helleland) and Labrador (Markland). "Promontorium Winlandiae" is remarkably like the great northernmost thrust of Newfoundland.

Viking raiders. After a summer of seals, polar bears, walruses and narwhals, Erik returned to Greenland to work out the remaining months of his exile. In the spring of 984, he rounded the south tip of Greenland bound for home, his weatherworn ship laden with ivory, furs, oil and hides—of fabulous value in Europe. He had a dream now: to build his own prosperous Viking settlement in south Greenland, over which he would rule as king.

Once home in Iceland, he set about lining up recruits for his kingdom. With a genius that any modern real-estate man might admire, he began calling his new country *Green*land. It was a brilliant piece of deception, and it soon had Icelanders clamoring to join the settlement voyage. Through the early months of the year 985, western Iceland was in turmoil. Men sold their farms and drove their livestock to the shores of Breida Fjord, where the colonization fleet was gathering. When June brought good sailing weather, 35 vessels crowded with cattle and with a thousand men, women and children set sail for the southern tip of Greenland.

Meanwhile, another event was in the making. It was to have as far-reaching consequences for Western man as any other single incident. In midsummer of 985, a single ship arrived at Iceland from Norway—a trading vessel skippered by Bjarni Herjolfsson, who, with his father Herjolf, owned a merchant-trading establishment in Iceland. Every second summer, Bjarni sailed to Norway with a cargo of homespun, walrus hides and ivory, seal oil, gyrfalcons and other Icelandic produce. He then spent the succeeding winter trading for ironware. The following summer, he'd sail back to Iceland. Now, coming home, he learned that his father had sailed with Erik to set up a trading post in Greenland, leaving instructions for his son to follow.

Pausing only to provision ship and take aboard the wives and children of his crew, Bjarni took off after the fleet. He had almost reached south Greenland when a polar nor'easter burst. For days his ship was at its mercy. The gale died, but the ship was then lost in fog. When the fog finally cleared, Bjarni saw land on the western horizon.

It was not Greenland. It was the eastern coast of the vast island we now call Newfoundland.

Bjarni sailed closer and found a rolling country covered with forest. But he did not linger along this new-found land. He did not even go ashore, for he was no explorer; he was a merchant-skipper whose job was to get his ship and passengers to their proper port as fast as possible. Sighting on the pole star, he sailed north, coasting part of Newfoundland and almost all of Labrador. Then, reaching the latitude of the Greenland settlement, he changed course and made his landfall not far from the cape where his father had already reestablished the family business.

It seems incredible that the news Bjarni brought should have roused only casual interest among the Vikings. His own reaction seems to have been embarrassment that he had got so far off course. The

Typical of Norse craft at the time
of the first voyages to America
is the Oseberg ship, built about 850 A.D.
and discovered in 1904
in a burial mound near Oslo Fjord.

rest of the Greenland colonists could hardly have cared less about another new land—they already had their hands full.

For the next decade the Greenlanders ignored the discovery, partly because Erik Rauda was not prepared to let anything interfere with his becoming a self-made king. But Greenland had a serious drawback: it lacked native timber. At the start, the settlers had got by with driftwood; but after a few years they had to begin importing wood all the way from Norway at tremendous expense.

About 995, Leif, the elder son of Erik, saw a way to profit from the shortage. He recalled that Bjarni had seen great forests in the land to the southwest. Quietly he made a deal whereby he and Bjarni would sail to that land and fetch a cargo of timber. After five days at sea, the two reached Newfoundland's Trinity Bay. They pitched camp ashore

and went to work. The vessel was loaded deep with birch and pine, and with dried wild grapes from the profusion of vines—whence the name that Leif gave the country, Vinland. Leif returned to Greenland a hero.

In 1003, a new face appeared on the scene. Thorfinn Karlsefni, an Icelandic merchant-trader, brought in two shiploads of colonists from Iceland. By now Erik's grip on his new kingdom was threatened by the rising power of his son Leif. To refurbish his personal reputation, Erik suggested to Thorfinn that his party and a group of Greenlanders make for Vinland and together settle the new land —in Erik's name.

Hammer of Thor, left, a ten-foot Norse signpost in the Arnaud River estuary in Canada's Ungava. Other recent Ungava finds include the ruins of a stone-and-turf longhouse 81 feet by 27, and this stone-lined box set in the longhouse floor. It is similar to Norse ember pits discovered in Greenland. A knife indicates its size.

Karlsefni led a flotilla of four ships west to Baffin Island, then south along the Labrador coast. The ships reached Belle Isle Strait in late summer, and a winter camp was made at Epaves Bay on the north tip of Newfoundland.

During the next three years the newcomers explored the general area, but they never succeeded in locating the Vinland of Trinity Bay. Instead, they began warring with Dorset Eskimos and Beothuk Indians, and the Vikings got the worst of it. In time, the survivors straggled back to Greenland.

As far as we know, this was the only attempt by the Norse to plant a settlement in North America. But, for the remaining five centuries of their history in Greenland, they continued to send ships to Labrador for timber and into Hudson Strait and Ungava Bay on hunting expeditions.

The knowledge gained by Erik and his contem-poraries about the western sea routes and the new lands was never lost. It spread throughout the European maritime community. Columbus must have absorbed it, because he made a voyage to Iceland before setting out into the Western Ocean. He probably wanted to find out all he could about the location of the new lands so he could set a course far enough south to miss them on his projected voyage to China and the Far East.

Columbus, of course, failed to miss these lands, and in 1492 he "discovered" America.

Unbeatable *Bluenose*

She was Canada's darling, a working schooner
with the sleek lines of a yacht,
and her racing feats brought the romantic days
of sail to a thrilling close

By David MacDonald

For most of the 40-mile race that brisk fall day in 1921, off Halifax, America's champion *Elsie* and Canada's new *Bluenose* had sifted along bow-to-bow, two graceful fishing schooners gliding over blue water on wings of white canvas.

But now as they swung into a long thresh to windward—sailing's moment of truth—an amazing thing occurred.

While the *Elsie* reeled in pounding seas, bucking a 27-knot blow, the *Bluenose* suddenly shot ahead. With spray flying from her sleek bhoulders and salty cries from her skipper—"Come on, you beautiful bitch!"—the black two-master heeled into the howling wind and left the *Elsie* in her foaming wake.

As she swept home, winner of the coveted International Fishermen's Cup, crowds on shore let out thunderous cheers that soon echoed across the seven seas. For *Bluenose* went on to become the most famous sailing ship of this century, so beloved at home that her image is still kept bright on all Canadian dimes.

All through the '20's and '30's—the last days of sail—the big clipper from Lunenburg, N.S., was acclaimed queen of the North Atlantic fishing fleets. Under crusty, hard-cussing Capt. Angus Walters, who stood barely five-six in his sou'wester, *Bluenose* beat the fastest schooners that U. S. and Canadian boatbuilders could send against her. For millions who followed her rousing Cup races, she provided a thrilling end to the romantic age of wooden ships and iron men.

To seafarers and landsmen alike, the *Bluenose* was a breathtaking sight. Even when she was at anchor with tall spars bare, the sweep of her bow and the lithe lines of her hull had the look of speed. And under full sail, with the wind singing in her rigging, there was no doubt of it. "When the skipper got her trimmed up right," recalls a former crewman, "she seemed to surge with sheer joy."

In Angus Walters' firm hands, the wood, rope and canvas of the *Bluenose* came to life in an uncanny way. At the helm, Walters always *talked* to his vessel—sometimes softly, more often in a raspy screech—and crewmen swore that she understood and obeyed him. "The *Bluenose* is nearly human," observed one. "And so's Cap'n Angie."

Indeed, though he was hot-tempered and tough, Walters had a tender, almost mystical feeling for his ship. "The *Bluenose*," he said once, "was like a part of me."

Both were products of a proud tradition. Angus Walters was born in 1881 in Lunenburg, a snug little German-settled port boasting the world's largest deep-water fishing fleet—150 windships that plied the stormy Banks of Newfoundland. There, over the years, spirited rivalry developed between the Lunenburgers and schoonermen from Gloucester, Mass. Each claimed to have the best boats, the finest sailors. Walters went to sea at 13 and by the time he became a full-fledged skipper, at 21, the friendly rivals had begun racing each other back from the Banks, with holds heavy and sails piled high, for the wild, freewheeling fun of it.

March 26, 1921: *Bluenose* is launched at Smith and Rhuland yard in Lunenburg.

The Yankee vessels usually came in first; Nova Scotian bankers were built more for capacity than speed. But only the crews knew or cared who won.

In 1920 all that changed. After an America's Cup yacht race was canceled because of a brisk 29.5-knot wind, the Halifax *Herald* decided to sponsor a series between boats of sterner stuff, the best of the U. S. and Canadian fishing fleets.

In the first contest that fall, Gloucester's *Esperanto* won with humiliating ease and took the new International Fishermen's Trophy back to "the Boston States." It was a crushing blow to Lunenburg's pride—too much for Angus Walters. That winter he stayed ashore, raising money to build a boat as fast as any Yankee clipper. While he sold 350 shares, at $100 apiece, an amateur marine architect from Halifax, William Roue, designed a deep-bellied, spoon-bowed working schooner with the trim lines of a racing yacht; 143 feet long, it carried 10,000 square feet of canvas.

At the shipyard Captain Walters fussed around like an expectant father. When the hull was framed, he found there was only five feet of fo'c'sle headroom. "My crew ain't midgets!" he snorted. So the bow was raised 18 inches, giving it more heft and a distinctly patrician hook.

On the gala March day she was launched and christened *Bluenose*—New England's nickname for all Nova Scotians—many old salts took one squint

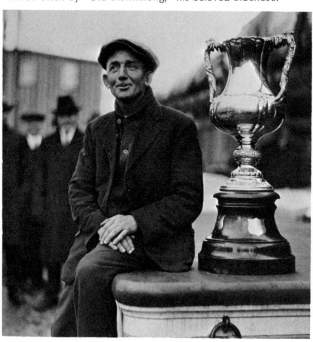

Capt. Angus Walters and the Fishermen's Trophy
won so often by "Old Stormalong," his beloved *Bluenose*.

In 1930, from Gloucester, Mass., came
a trim new challenger, *Gertrude L. Thebaud,*
captained by Newfoundland-born Ben Pine.

and shook their heads. "That bow's too big," they grumped. "She'll never go." But after her first sea run, Angus Walters brought in a different verdict. "By God," he said in his Lunenburg Dutch dialect, "she's a wery good wessel!"

Yet nobody dreamed *how* good—not until *Bluenose* trounced Gloucester's *Elsie* in '21 and took the championship she was never to lose. It was that great bow that really made the difference. For on decisive beats into the wind, when the *Elsie* shuddered under the impact of combers crashing down on her decks and tumbling aft, the high-swept *Bluenose* rode easily over the whitecaps.

After she'd won the Cup for Canada—and the nickname "Old Stormalong" for herself—the Fishermen's Cup races became front-page news. Seven schooners were launched in Canada, and five in the United States, in hopes of beating *Bluenose*. But in spite of tougher competition, the weatherly Lunenburg windjammer outsped all comers for the next nine years.

Then, in 1930, British tea magnate Sir Thomas

Lipton, who had tried long and vainly to win the America's Cup, proposed an unofficial best-of-three series between *Bluenose* and a trim new challenger, the *Gertrude L. Thebaud,* built by a syndicate of wealthy Bostonians. Her skipper was Ben Pine, a bluff, barrel-chested Gloucesterman whom Angus Walters had raced—and beaten—before.

Ill-fitting new sails hampered the *Bluenose* in the first race off Gloucester, and *Thebaud* won. The second heat began in a stiff nor'-easter. The *Bluenose* had leaped miles ahead—at a record 17 knots—when the race committee decided it was too rough to continue. Walters flew into a rage. "If you boys can't stand the gaff," he railed at the committee launch, "get the hell ashore so's me and Ben can settle this like *men!*" But it was no go.

In the final race, when *Bluenose* was leading handily again, Walters pulled a rare boner. Instead of keeping the *Thebaud* covered, he tacked away from her. Suddenly the wind shifted. While *Bluenose* was becalmed, the Yankee picked up a land breeze and slipped away to win the Lipton Trophy.

Thebaud, a heavy sail-carrier, leads *Bluenose* at the start of a race. The Gloucester schooner was the only challenger ever to defeat *Bluenose.* *Thebaud* was wrecked on a breakwater in Venezuela during a storm in 1948—two years after *Bluenose* struck a coral reef and sank off Haiti.

"They didn't beat *Bluenose,*" Walters insisted later. "They beat *me.*" He cared more about her reputation than his own.

But both were at stake the next year, when Ben Pine and the *Thebaud* entered the Fishermen's Cup race. For once, *Bluenose* was the underdog. At the starting line, as though she sensed it, Walters felt the big banker quiver. "The old girl's some eager," he called out.

And so she was. The *Bluenose* avenged her only defeat by trimming the *Thebaud* twice in a row—once by a full half-hour. Afterward, when their crews held a party, Walters gleefully ribbed his old foe. "It was awful lonesome out there, Ben," he chuckled. "Next time we'll wait for you."

Next time—the last—was seven years off. Meanwhile, the *Bluenose* earned good profits for her shareholders and crew on the cod-fishing Banks. Walters worked his men hard, himself even harder. It was a rough, risky life—a thousand Lunenburgers have perished at sea—but he loved it. When he was once introduced as "the famous racing skip-

per," he drew up sharply. "I'm a *fisherman,*" he said, "and damn proud of it."

Above all, he was proud of his great schooner. Canada showed her off at the 1933 Chicago World's Fair, and sent her to England in 1935 for the silver jubilee of George V. The "sailor king" was so taken with the *Bluenose* that he gave her skipper the mainsail from his own yacht. "He seems like a nice, ordinary fella," Walters told newsmen. "We chewed the rag quite a while."

Homeward bound, the *Bluenose* ran into an awesome storm. One night, lying under bare spars after four days of steady pounding, she was knocked over by a gigantic wave. As she lay on her side, tons of water pouring in, her horrified crew seemed doomed. But then, with a groan from deep inside her ribs, the old schooner slowly heaved herself up and stood erect—battered but unbeaten. "God only knows how she did it," Walters said later, "but she saved our lives."

Her own days, however, were numbered. As ugly, efficient diesel trawlers began crowding the Banks,

Bluenose, the most famous sailing ship of the century, outraces a rival on this 50-cent stamp issued in 1929. Her image is kept bright on Canadian dimes.

forcing even the *Bluenose* to take on engines in order to compete, the age of windships neared its close. In the summer of 1938, as if to symbolize the end of an era, the Fishermen's Cup was permanently awarded to *Bluenose*. But at Ben Pine's request, Walters agreed to race the *Gertrude L. Thebaud* once more, for old times' sake.

By then, after 17 years of hard work, fresh paint and new sails couldn't hide the fact that *Bluenose* was worn and weary. The first race, off Boston, proved it. The younger *Thebaud* stole an early three-minute lead and held it to the end. *Bluenose* sailed better the second time and won by 12 minutes. The next two races were split, *Thebaud* winning the latter when *Bluenose*'s backstay parted in a strong blow. Now the contest was tied, two-to-two.

In the final race, while thousands watched from shore and millions more listened on radio, Captain Walters outmaneuvered the *Thebaud* at the start, stole the wind from her sails and pushed his *Bluenose* out front. As the two tall schooners swooped around the course under clouds of canvas, *Bluenose* clung to her narrow lead. Suddenly, with victory in sight, her staysail halyard block gave way and the *Thebaud* came charging up. There was no time for repairs—only for hope. Angus Walters' high-pitched voice rose above the rush of wind and sea: "—Just *once more!*"

With that, creaky "Old Stormalong" nodded on the crest of a wave, caught a puff in her sails and surged across the finish line—winner by less than three minutes but still Queen of the North Atlantic.

When *Bluenose* returned in triumph to Lunen-burg, the whole town turned out to greet her with flags, bands and a parade. Standing on an oxcart, Angus Walters made a brief speech. "The wood that can beat the *Bluenose*," he said, "ain't been planted yet."

When Walters quit the sea in 1939 to open a dairy, he urged Nova Scotians to preserve the *Bluenose* as a monument to the great age of sail. But with war approaching, few were interested. A year later, when the proud champion faced the disgrace of a public auction, to pay $7200 still owed for her engines, Walters mortgaged his home and life insurance and bought out other shareholders to save her. "I had to," he said simply. "She never let *me* down."

But after *Bluenose* lay idle for two years, losing money, he finally had to sell her to a Caribbean freighting firm. The day she cleared Lunenburg for the last time, her lofty spars shorn and ugly housing over her deck, Captain Walters cast off her mooring with tears in his eyes. "I felt like someone in my family had died."

Four years later, in 1946, the *Bluenose* ran onto a coral reef off Haiti. There she sank, abandoned by her crew and far from home. In Lunenburg, the news stung Angus Walters. John Pardy, a former mate, simply sat down and cried. "Her passing is a national sorrow," commented the Halifax *Herald*, "the ignominy of her death, a national shame."

In 1963, however, a Nova Scotia brewery built *Bluenose II,* a full-scale replica costing $450,000, and invited the men who had sailed the original on a cruise. All hands agreed she was a fine vessel. But she didn't *feel* the same.

"There was only one *Bluenose*," Angus Walters told an old friend as they walked slowly home, past the harbor that was once a forest of masts. "And there'll never be another like her."

People of the Sea

Hardy Newfoundlanders have mixed feelings about
the changes that came with "jinin' Confederation"

By Farley Mowat

He was a wizened little man with a red-painted
ship's prow for a nose, pale blue eyes under a salt-
bleached brush of shaggy eyebrows, and not a tooth
in his head. Standing in the cuddy of a little motor-
boat, he was impaling chunks of frozen squid on
the hundreds of hooks in his four tubs of trawl gear.
Harvey Pink was a typical outport fisherman,
"pretty well up in years, but still right smart." A
Newfoundlander to the core.

He was 50 when Newfoundland "jined Confederation" in 1949. Now he is 70; and a mere 20
years has not turned him into a Canadian. For two
decades, in Newfoundland's history, is a mere
twinkling of an eye.

It is hard for Canadians to comprehend the an-
tiquity and tenacity of the human roots in this
rock-girt island in the broad maw of the St.
Lawrence Gulf. One day I was poking about in a
graveyard at Ship Cove (a small fishing village on
Conception Bay) when I came across a headstone
dated 1650. The name Dawes was still readable. The
discovery fascinated me and I had to share it with
someone, but the only person around was a vener-
able graybeard scything hay between the graves. I
called to him and pointed to the stone.

"Just think of that!" I said in awe. "Three hundred years ago a man named Dawes died here. I
wonder where he came from, and who he was." For
a moment the old man looked at me suspiciously, as
if he feared I was pulling his leg; but then he
realized that I was only another ignorant Main-
lander. "No need to wonder, me son. He were
Johnny Dawes, he were. Borned and died in Ship
Cove. Belonged here, like his pore old dad afore him.
Like me, ye might say . . . Uncle Jim Dawes is me
name, an' you cares to know."

And I remember when Howard Morry of Ferryland took me up to a Gaze—a lookout on a hill
above the wide gray waters of the Western Ocean—
to tell me how his great-great-great-great-grand-
mother used to go there to watch for the return of
her husband's sailing vessel after a long voyage to

the Azores and Portugal. That was in the early
1700's.

Howard is a fisherman of about 80, who looks
and acts about 40, and who knows the history of
Ferryland from its first use as a summer fishing
settlement around 1500 better than most of us know
the history of our newly built commuter suburbs.
As with most older Newfoundlanders, history means
something to him because he is, and knows he is, a
part of it.

"I'll tell ye how it is with us. There was no larnin'
in the outports until just a few years back. Most
people couldn't read nor write. But my, how they
could talk! As youngsters we used to sit by the hour
listening to the old people yarn. We heard stories
from 300 years ago that was just as fresh as yesterday. But 'tis all changing now. The history of this
island, kept alive inside our heads for a dozen
generations or more, is soon going to pass away now
that Confederation's come." Without knowing it,
Howard was reflecting the ambivalence that so
many Newfoundlanders feel about the changes that
came with joining Canada.

Discovered in 986 by Greenland Norse who made
an abortive settlement in the north part, Newfoundland began to take shape as a European entity in the
west as early as 1450, when Basque and Portuguese

Fishing huts cling to a rocky coast
at Pouch Cove, not far
from St. John's. History is full
of meaning for older
Newfoundlanders, says Farley Mowat,
because they are a part of it.

Fishing boats lie at anchor
near Port de Grave
in Newfoundland's Conception Bay.
More than 300 outports
have died in recent years.

whalers and fishers were regularly sailing to the Grand Banks and to the good harbors that ring the island. Until the 1700's it was illegal to settle in Newfoundland. Wealthy English fish merchants engineered such laws to prevent establishment of a native fishery in the "New Land."

But by 1510, runaways from fishing ships—the Masterless Men of tradition—had spread like a slow, silent tide into remote Newfoundland bays. They lived hard lives in a hard land, but they lived. There were 6000 miles of sea-roaring coasts to hide them, and here they built their little "tilts" of sod or logs, concealing themselves from strangers and passing ships, subsisting mainly on fish. By 1550 a large part of the Newfoundland coast was occupied and these early "Liveyeres" (people who "live here") slowly increased in numbers.

The odds against them were terrible. Starvation was the common lot through the first three centuries of Newfoundland's recent history; hunger filled most of the fourth. But new blood came in from Ireland, southern England and the Channel Islands, in the form of labor brought over by great merchant companies to man their fishing factories. These indentured men and women were practically slaves; many slipped quietly off to freedom in the secret little coves. The English outporters met French fishermen-settlers and Micmac Indians. Since all were equal before the sea, marriages took place freely across the lines of race and blood.

So the Newfoundlanders evolved into a unique people—a true "People of the Sea" who eventually ringed the island with more than 1300 outports, ranging in size from two or three families to 50.

They struggled for survival. In small open boats the men fished the year round, with time off for grueling voyages in schooners carrying salt cod to Europe and the West Indies. Every September at "settling-up time" the salt fish was carried to the merchant who bought it at his price—not for cash, but as payment against the endless debts of the fisherman and his family.

The merchant class of Newfoundland held the people in a deadly economic vise. Until as late as the 1950's in some outports, a man was born, grew up and died in debt to the local trader.

As the long centuries slipped by and a score of times Newfoundland became a battlefield, usually between French and English, the outporters often lost all they possessed and had to start again with nothing but their hands. During all those years nothing really changed: the poor stayed desperately poor, and the rich grew fabulously rich. St. John's, the only real town the island boasted, was the home of the great merchants—the "Water Street men." Even as late as 1950, St. John's claimed more millionaires per capita than any other city in North America!

But the majority of the people knew only grinding poverty. One outport man recalls the way it was: "In the '30's—the 'Hard Times,' we called it—the merchants would give out no more credit and the people had no money. Fish was a glut. Nobody would buy our fish. People all up and down the coasts were starving. Nobody will ever know how many children died, but a good many grown men starved to death. The government gave out the dole—six cents a day for a family and you took it 'in kind,' often rotten or weevily flour. My people were a little better off than most, and many's the time neighbors would come to our kitchen for a feed. I mind how they smelled. My mother told me: 'Son,' she says, 'that is the smell of poverty. Don't you forget it.'"

Hard times! Yes. But a Newfoundlander was used to hard times. He begat immense families, often 15 to 18 children, but it was rare for more than a few of them to reach maturity. When they were grown-up the sea would take its toll of the men—"Bridegrooms of the Sea," they called the drowned—while TB took a heavy toll of the women.

It was like that right up until Confederation. When union with Canada was mooted, the "Water Street men" fought bitterly to prevent it. They

Older Newfoundland men still go fishing in little boats, because they love the life.

wanted things to stay as they were. But they lost. One day in April of 1949, Newfoundland ceased to be the oldest European settlement in North America and became the youngest of the ten Canadian provinces. And an ancient mold was shattered, almost overnight—by the baby bonus!

The baby bonus accomplished in a few years what the merchants had been able to prevent for centuries. It brought cash, and therefore a measure of freedom to the people. Its effect was unbelievable. My neighbors in the outport of Burgeo, where I lived for some years, never tired of recalling what happened.

"Before my wife got her first bonus money," one of them told me, "nobody in our family had ever seen a five-dollar bill. If we saw five dollars in silver in a year—that was a lot. Everything we sold went to one merchant, and everything we bought had to come from him. He owned us, do you see?"

Here is how things now stand in this old island. Nobody starves to death anymore, not even children. Few people die for lack of medical services. For

Small boats of fishermen,
a big ship at pierside,
and the Newfoundland Hotel
on the horizon—the main elements
of most pictures of old St. John's.

the first time, every child can learn to read and write. Men who never had anything to lean on except their own strong muscles can now draw unemployment insurance, sick benefits, or relief assistance, while their wives gather in the baby-bonus checks. Old people, who used to survive (or try to) on a government pension of $120 a year, are now so relatively affluent that they hardly know what to do with their money. The population is exploding; not because more children are being born, but because a lot more of them are surviving.

It all looks very good indeed. And yet there is a shadow over the paradise created by Confederation. Having tasted the fruits of the Canadian way of life, more and more Newfoundlanders are turning their backs on the pitiless gray sea which made them what they were. The vast Newfoundland merchant marine—about 500 sailing vessels as late as 1939—has all but vanished. Employment in the fisheries has fallen sharply. Where once 50 men, working for starvation wages, could land a certain weight of fish, now four or five men, better paid and operating a modern dragger, do the same job.

As standards of living go up, the number of acceptable jobs at these new standards goes down. And so Newfoundland, once the world's greatest exporter of salt fish, is now exporting men and women as its major produce. They go because they must, and because the new generation will not accept the kind of life their fathers knew.

With the dignity of age,
weatherbeaten houses march
up a steep St. John's street
not far from the sea.

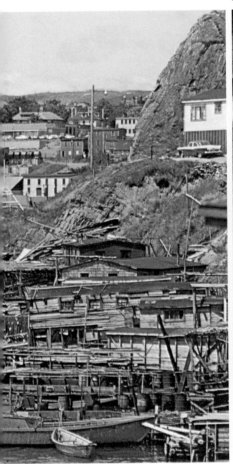

But more than their physical presence is being lost. The tough core of courage, resourcefulness, ability, endurance, personal pride that was a product of the evolution of the outport man and woman—the by-product of adversity—is disappearing in the interval between one generation and the next.

This is the terrible paradox of our times: as we make life easier, less demanding, so do we weaken the sustaining fabric of pride and strength which made us men in the first place.

In Burgeo, as in most of Newfoundland, the older men still go fishing in their little boats, although there is no longer any need for those of 60 to 70 to endure cold seas and cutting gales. They go because they love the life, not for the money that is in it. But they know they are the last of their kind—that their sons and grandsons will soon be gone from Heart's Ease, Pushthrough and all the other outports. They know that in recent years more than 300 outports have died, or been abandoned. They know that many young people will go to the mainland. But they have a feeling that these men of a new age will somehow be less than the men their fathers were. The sons and grandsons will be Canadians, but for men like Harvey Pink, the centennial celebrations on the mainland in 1967 had little meaning.

"Yiss, me darlin' man," he told me, "we's had our Cen-teen-ial, ye might say—t'ree or four hunnert year gone by . . ."

The *Draveurs*
Cowboys of the Forests

They are men such as our cities no longer produce — hardy, vivid French Canadians who herd logs by the thousand down the streams and rivers to the great paper mills

By Ira Wolfert

In the romances of Canada, Quebec's forest river-men, the *draveurs*, hold a place quite as legendary as that of the cowboys of the old West. Bearing names like Télesphore Sainte-Marie, Primat Boisvert, Dieudonné Tranchemontagne, these French Canadians are dark, rosy-cheeked, bright-eyed men whose job, in essence, is the same as that which cowboys did on the Western cattle trails, but with logs, not steers. They round up the "stock" on the riverbanks and brand each "head" in case it strays. Then they ride herd on the stock; driving the logs like so many head of cattle along the waterways to the mills, where they are made into paper to supply one of every six newspaper pages printed in the whole world.

Though truly strong men have all but vanished from our cities, they still abound in the Quebec woods, as I learned on my first day there. I was encumbered with a suitcase that, since its contents included a typewriter and books, weighed 70 pounds. Toting it was quite a chore as I clambered over the litter of a logged-over bush trail. A *draveur* offered to relieve me of it. For politeness' sake I hesitated, since he was shorter than I. Much to my relief, he insisted. A moment later he was pointing at a bird passing overhead—pointing with the hand that held my suitcase. I thought he was kidding me, but when I mentioned it he was as startled to see the suitcase as I was. He'd forgotten he was holding it.

I watched the *draveurs* work in a forest area which lies in the watershed drained by the St. Maurice River, midway between Montreal and Quebec City, beginning north of the belt of settled land and ending where the trees start scrubbing out into tundra. A small plane can fly across the area in an hour, yet these forests produce one third as much newsprint as the entire United States. Every year they draw out of these woods a ribbon of paper five feet wide and nine million miles long.

New logging techniques have made it economically feasible to range all over the forest and fell trees selectively, harvesting the woods rather than plundering them. The secret is the rivers—the Manouan and Mattawin and Mekinac, the Wabano and Wolf, Trenche, Vermillion, Little Shawinigan and Rivière aux Rats. They make a lacework of the forest as they wind down among the trees to the St. Maurice. And where the St. Maurice empties into the St. Lawrence at Trois Rivières, there lie most of the paper mills.

The *draveurs* have transformed these rivers into the equivalent of an automated railroad, whose main line is the St. Maurice. The locomotive power is the water, which, in the 250 miles from the top of the watershed to the bottom, falls 1380 feet. This gives it speeds up to 35 miles an hour. Along the rivers a great network of dams impounds the waters until freight is ready to be shipped. Behind each dam is a log corral. The *draveurs* have only to open a gate to start the freight on its way to the mills. This extraordinary railroad transports enough logs in a year to fill 100,000 freight cars.

The logging season used to last only six months and in the valley of the St. Maurice as many as 10,000 men were needed. Now it is a ten-month season, with a permanent, year-round force of 1350 lumberjacks swelling in fall and winter to 6500— a nation of villages complete with radio-telephones and TV aerials, hospitals, garages, smithies, firehouses.

The modern lumberjack uses machines which not only fell trees but also remove limbs and bark. Some even reduce a tree to wood chips right in the forest.

But some trees still are cut by hand and amid the growl of the big machines is heard the high whirring-burring of hand-held power saws called "partridges." Still heard too is the cry "*Attention!*"— French Canadian equivalent of "Timberrrr!" And a few horses still snort and puff in woods where once there were thousands, before the machines began their takeover.

The dramatic river drive is now confined largely to the main rivers. Trucks deliver pulpwood from the cutting areas to the riverbanks where, in the

Huge machines do more and more of the work each new logging season. Some fell trees and remove limbs and bark, others turn trees to wood chips right there in the forest.

cold, dry air the tumbling logs ring like bells. Higher and higher they pile, spreading back over the banks in colossal mounds.

Then suddenly, usually in the latter part of May, spring bursts in the forest. The cracking of the thawing ice is like cannon shots. The logs displace the water in the lakes and rivers and it comes flooding out over the banks to undermine the mounds there. So the "railroad" loads itself automatically.

Little streams turn into roaring giants. Deep in the forest you can put your ear against a tree trunk and hear thunder underground. It is the Windigo or Little Bostonnais, perhaps Creek George, rushing, pounding its bed like surf, shaking the earth. Closer to the river, the thunder moves up out of the earth to fill the air—a drumming and booming of water, a crashing and splashing of logs, all surging down out of the forest to the broad St. Maurice.

In about two weeks the spring floods subside. Then come the *draveurs*—a select group of 200 experts led by tall, frosty-looking George Hamilton,

who has been on the rivers since 1929. These are red-eyed days, sometimes 18 hours long. Breakfast is at six o'clock: bananas and cream, oatmeal, tea, hot breads, jams, jellies. Then comes steak, with beans and potatoes, and three to four eggs for each man. All this is blanketed down with flapjacks and salt pork. The *draveurs'* labor is so consuming they eat as much again at 11:30. Then at six o'clock supper they really pack it in.

Meals like that give the *draveurs* strength to battle the logs, which pitch and toss and jam and stampede in the water. They can be as ornery as the wildest range animals—as the rude crosses along the riverbanks prove. These mark where a *draveur* disappeared under the logs and nothing of him could be found. But when the logs reach the St. Maurice they're like cattle, slowing suddenly as they reach pasture and spread out to browse.

Seven big dams have transformed the St. Maurice into a series of giant ponds, whose current is so slack and so deep that it moves the surface of the water less than the wind does. Some of them are 40 miles long. The logs meander and drift in these ponds, now this way, now that, gathering together in scores and hundreds, finally in thousands.

Then suddenly, like a herd of cattle deciding to crowd on to new pasture, a common purpose comes into them and the logs begin to drift with the current down toward the dam. The wind usually dies at dusk in this valley, then picks up again a few hours after daybreak. If it's a contrary wind, the great drove of logs moves back slowly during the day. But, in the meantime, other logs are coming out of the tributaries to add their weight to the purpose, and in the still of the night, when the contrary wind dies, the logs move forward again with the current, always farther than they've moved back. Nothing stops the herd once its purpose has taken hold. They make eight to ten miles a day when the wind is favorable.

The *draveurs* herd them by means of booms—variations of the kind used to fence off harbors during World War II. Curtain booms keep the logs from going up the bays and inlets and becoming stranded there; wing booms guide them away from sand bars and islands; conducting booms nudge them to the side of the pond where the current is faster.

Behind each dam are holding booms to corral the logs until the way over the dam is open. It is when a corral is overcrowded that a stampede is likely to occur. A big storm lashing a close-packed herd makes the logs goad each other into a frenzy and jump the fence, or break it down. But when one corral becomes overcrowded, the *draveurs* have only to wait until the wind is blowing in the direction of a corral which isn't crowded, then open the gate. The excess stock moves over with the wind to the corral that has room for it.

At one time flotillas of tugs were employed to do all this work in the big ponds. A herd would be lassoed and hauled about as a raft. Then the *draveur* bosses pointed out that nature would do the job if allowed to. The companies thought it might be worth a try.

But it was a risky venture. The making of newsprint has become one of the most dazzling examples of modern technology. Almost any kind of wood can be used for paper, but the soft woods are preferred. Where hard woods sink in rivers, soft woods like spruce, balsam and jack pine float and can be transported cheaply. At the mills the wood is chewed to a pulp by large revolving grindstones, or cooked to a pulp in acid. The wood comes out of either process looking like a fluffy hot cereal. It is then fed to a

Sometimes dynamite must be used
to break logjams. Author Ira Wolfert
"felt the presence of happiness" in *draveurs*
when they "found something out of tune
with the river and set it right."

Like steers strayed from the herd,
wayward logs are rounded up
by *draveur* "cowboys" and driven back
into sometimes turbulent rivers
for the long journey to pulp and paper mills.

paper machine which converts it into paper by felting its fibers into a web, then stretching, drying and finishing them.

One of these machines, at Shawinigan, is 460 feet long. It makes paper 21 feet wide at the rate of 2500 feet a minute. Suction and heat are used to dry the pulp as it speeds along. It speeds so fast that the air screamed loud enough to deafen the mill workers until ways of muffling it were devised. Each hour, day and night, seven days a week, Canada's 151 newsprint machines turn out 1500 *miles* of 25-foot-wide paper. The machines are so expensive that their owners cannot afford to waste a day. How could notoriously capricious nature be trusted to keep pace with the voracious appetites of such monsters?

Finally, rising tugboat costs drove the companies to risk a trial. It was a day George Hamilton will remember as long as he lives. The big bosses came from as far away as Montreal to watch. From Rapide Blanc where they stood they could look up along a great pond for miles to where it bent out of sight. All the way there was nothing to see, just faceless water, with hardly a stir of wind. Only the light of the sun moved, idling on the pond's blank, motionless surface. Suddenly there was a gasp from the crowd, and Hamilton let the tension out of him in a sigh. There, wheeling grandly around the bend without a human hand to prod it, was the head of what proved to be a seven-mile herd of logs.

Since then, the companies have been content to retire their tugs and let nature do the work. She needs no fuel, no maintenance and never breaks down. Her so-called caprices are all part of her clockwork that men can profit from if they're willing to get in rhythm with it.

Of all the men who must dance to nature in the woods, it is the *draveurs* who must dance liveliest of all. For them it's a matter of life or death. I learned that one morning when the field telephone rang. The logs had jammed downriver. Twelve miles of logs were bearing down on the jam and would soon add their weight to the crush.

Six *draveurs* went out in a *"pointeur,"* a small boat sharp at both ends. One carried dynamite under his seat to break the jam. Four of the men were *rameurs,* two on each side with 11-foot poles. Braced in the stern, using a nine-foot paddle as a rudder, was the *derrière-de-barge*. Standing in the bow, facing straight ahead, was the chief of the crew, the *devant-de-barge*. He held an 11-foot pole poised like a lance, thrusting it now and then against a boulder to help the *derrière-de-barge* steer away from it.

They moved slowly at first. Then the current gulped them up with a *whoosh*. Even in the sun the river was panther-black. The *devant-de-barge* never took his gaze off the surface of the water. He directed the crew with hand signals, with swift, curt nods of his head to right or left. When he wanted extra effort extra fast, he cried, "Ho!" When he wanted maximum effort and wanted it maintained

215

Designs of logs and
log booms are part
of the face of Canada
in rivers from coast to coast.

he cried, "Ho! Ho! Ho!" Apparently this is the only human sound that can carry over the roar of a river in this mood.

They came to an island of stillness a mile and a half long—logs jammed into the bottom and piled up on each other so tightly that not a drop of water showed. The *devant-de-barge* let the boat go plunging down one side of this island, aiming for the narrow space of dead water he knew he would find at the lower end. Judging the moment precisely, he thrust his pole vertically into the current and pulled down with such violence that he levered the nose of the boat into jumping sideways two feet in a single bound. "Ho! Ho! Ho!" he cried in a tremendous voice, and the boat's ribs shuddered as the full force of the current drove into them.

The *rameurs* paddled for dear life. Slowly the *pointeur* was torn from the grip of the current and came to rest in the quiet water at the end of the island. It took only one man to hold it there. The five others swarmed out over the island with long-handled pikes. A jam like this could be caused by a single log wedged amid boulders. Sometimes this log is driven in so deep it has to be dynamited free, but just as often it comes free itself as soon as the others are pulled off its back.

The job is to locate and isolate this key log. The men worked at it by sticking their pikes into the logs on top of the island and pitching them one by one into the current. Now and then there was movement among the buried logs. Every eye would instantly turn to the *devant-de-barge*. He'd study a moment, then shake his head, and the men would go back to their swift, steady dismemberment.

Suddenly every pike on the island lifted. The *devant-de-barge* stood motionless, head raised. There had been a soft sound. The whole island seemed to exhale and hunker down deeper into the river. Had the current got in to nibble away a mere part of the jam, or was the key to all of it turning? Suddenly a low grunt came from the *devant-de-barge:* "Ho!"

The *draveurs* ran lightly over the logs, threw themselves pell-mell into the boat and began ramming their way through the now unfolding logs to shore.

Then, at the shore, I saw something unforgettable. From men who had bet their strength and skill against death, and won, you would expect exultation. But their victory only made these men feel at peace. The crew sat in the boat and stared quietly at the logs lumbering by. No word was said, but I felt the presence of happiness. Finding something out of tune with the river and setting it right seemed somehow to have set the men right with themselves.

In the old days the men used to come brawling out of the woods with a whole season's pay, often as much as $2000, in their pockets, a tag on their jackets bearing the address of their only "home," the employment office of a logging company. They'd give all their money to a saloon-keeper and tell him, "Carry me home when it's gone."

But today, with mechanized equipment, a stream of amenities and necessities—movies, doctors, fresh food—flows through the camps all year round. They have parking lots for men who bring their cars in order to be able to week-end with their families.

At night the camps take on the look of placid French villages. The little cluster of huts is surrounded by a million years of nearly unbroken silence. Wolves can be heard howling, bears rummaging. But television is going on inside the huts. On the camp street, men gather in knots around the blacksmith's forge to talk, or around a mouth organ that sooner or later will strike up *"M'en revenant de la jolie Rochelle."*

For even though most of the men who sing so yearningly of the beautiful city of La Rochelle have never been there and have no intention of going, the old French songs persist. It is part of the men's respect for their very great heritage.

216

Man of Laughter

A warm and intimate word portrait of Canada's most
famous humorist, by a man who studied under him at McGill

By Leslie Roberts

The first time I saw Stephen Leacock at close quarters he came swinging into a classroom in Moyse Hall, the serenely ugly old Arts Building of McGill University in Montreal. The room was packed with undergraduates like me who had come with huge curiosity to listen to their first lecture on political science by a man whose humorous writing had rocked the English-speaking world with laughter, but who was a campus character for very different reasons.

Leacock enjoyed a reputation for eccentricity and for an impish individualism that expressed itself in blunt speech on every subject. Naturally we looked him over carefully.

What we saw was a shock of graying hair crowning a rugged face that wore a friendly smile, emphasized by crinkles of mirth about the eyes. I remember thinking, "He could use a haircut." His necktie had slipped its moorings, and his tweedy suit looked slept-in. Across his vest his watch chain had come apart in the middle and had been put together with a safety pin. The effect was of a man who gave no thought to his appearance. But his manner was far too buoyant to suggest the absentminded professor.

His apparel was topped by one of those loose, black gowns professors wore in those days. Leacock's had been acquired about the time he received his Ph.D. from the University of Chicago in 1903. Even though the garment was showing signs of wear in 1914, it was still one of the essential properties of his playacting. At least a dozen times during every lecture it would slip off his shoulders and seize him by the crook of his elbows. Without pause in the flow of talk and motion—he was a walking lecturer—a great shrug of the shoulders would hoist the gown partway into place.

Leacock was tremendously proud of his Ph.D., but it was inescapably in character that he must spoof it. "The meaning of this degree," he quipped in a lecture, "is that the recipient has been examined for the last time in his life and pronounced full. After this, no new ideas can be imparted to him."

English-born Stephen Leacock graduated from the University of Toronto in 1891 and taught modern languages for two years at Upper Canada College before going to McGill as a political science lecturer.

In similar vein, after returning from a holiday abroad he told his class, "I was sitting quietly in my cabin when a steward knocked and, after making sure I am called Doctor, asked if I would come and look at the stewardess' knee. I was off like a shot, but another fellow got there ahead of me. He was a Doctor of Divinity."

What came through to me, even in the first lecture, was Leacock's warmth and humanness. I knew I was listening to a man who loved young people and was determined to give them as much wisdom as he could. His teaching methods were unconventional. He couldn't resist the temptation to explore bypaths. In discussing the days of Queen Victoria, he mentioned Disraeli, and this set him off to talk about the man rather than the prime minister—his way of living, his quick mind, his dilettantism, his great love affair with his wife. The digression lifted the great statesman into a framework of his own and, when Leacock returned to the main line of his subject, the

The "Canadian Mark Twain,"
a world-famous humorist and lecturer
and author of 56 books—and
a fascinating and beloved old man.

listener understood, in a way no textbook could inform him, how such a man could bring off the coup which gave Britain control of the Suez Canal and made the Empire impregnable for decades to come.

His classroom methods were often the target of men who taught by the book. To those who complained that he was too unorthodox, Leacock retorted scornfully, "Economics isn't a rule-book business. Any theory which fails to recognize human aspirations is pure nonsense. People aren't statistics. Hell's bells! They're alive!" His critics, who related all teaching to exams, could never understand that by his methods he was fulfilling the purpose for which any university exists: he was teaching his students to think. "College," he once said, "is to teach the mind, not the thumb."

The humorous writing which brought him international fame and five times the income his job paid was an avocation which, to quote him, "played hell" with his workday and his sleep. But there is where his heart lay. "I would sooner have written *Alice in Wonderland* than the whole *Encyclopaedia Britannica*," he once remarked.

A direct line of laughter runs from Mark Twain through Leacock to such successors as Robert Benchley. The cord which ties them together is the feeling each had of the ridiculous nature of many of life's little complexities and of their own professed inability to cope with them. Critics and scholars have written that the essence of this brand of humor is its lack of malice. My own opinion is that many of the situations at which Leacock poked fun actually infuriated him. He simply set out to slay them with the light rapier of ridicule, instead of the heavy cudgels of wrath.

Teaching, writing and long hours of good talk were still not enough for this man of remarkable nervous energy. He plunged intermittently into Canadian politics with boiling enthusiasm. He could have had cabinet posts in two Conservative ministries, but he turned them down. "I can't picture myself as a professional stuffed shirt," he used to say to his cronies, "or as being in agreement with my prime minister for four consecutive years." What he meant was that he would allow nothing to sever him from teaching.

His students all knew vaguely that Leacock was a devoted husband and father, but on the campus he lived for them. And because he loved his profession, it was in his nature to deride it affectionately. "A teacher has more time to think than a businessman," he once told a business audience, "or, better still, time to stop thinking altogether for months." Again, on being appointed to head his department at McGill, he could not resist remarking wryly that he had "now reached an eminence so high that the emolument places me distinctly above policemen, postmen and streetcar conductors, and I am even able to mingle with poorer businessmen on terms of something like equality."

Leacock was every student's friend. He liked undergraduate talk and company. To the student with a serious financial problem he was the softest touch

Leacock's now-famous summer home at Brewery Bay, on Lake Couchiching, near Orillia, Ont. The town, the model for Leacock's Mariposa, bought the house and its library in 1957 and converted them into a Leacock Museum.

on the campus. He was the only senior faculty member I ever saw around the Students' Union on any but official occasions. He dropped in as casually as any sophomore, usually in search of a game of billiards, a favorite pastime, which, he always maintained, "stimulates conversation."

Indirectly this was my own introduction to a firm friendship with Stephen Leacock. His favorite opponent was a convivial campus character named William Ewart Gladstone Murray, later chairman of the Canadian Broadcasting Corporation. By some preposterous device of their own invention, this happy-go-lucky pair became involved in a billiard match for 20,000 points, which was still in progress when Stephen died in 1944. The score then stood 18,975 for the retired professor and 16,793 for his ex-student. The marathon had been staged at various times in Montreal, Toronto, New York, Vancouver, London, Birmingham, Biarritz and Monte Carlo.

Once, after a long absence from Montreal, I ran into Murray as he was heading for the University Club to see Leacock. I went along, and kept going back. Leacock soon became a combination of friend and critic-of-manuscripts. At times when my economic problems were severe the telephone was likely to ring and a voice from an advertising agency would say, "Dr. Leacock suggested you might be willing to write a brochure for a client of ours." Any attempt to thank Stephen would be waved aside with a quip: "I hope you had the good sense to put a high price on your talents. The trick with these advertising fellows is to find out how much money they have—and don't take a cent more!"

He would push everything aside to help a former student, or any young person fighting his way up the steep ladder of the lively arts. He wrote a book for one young woman illustrator to fit drawings she had already made, thereby turning normal publishing processes upside down.

Leacock was probably the first Canadian to qualify as a "pro-American British imperialist." A colleague,

Leacock never changed. Leslie Roberts'
description of the young lecturer at McGill
fits *this* Leacock of three decades later:
"What we saw was a shock of graying hair
crowning a rugged face that wore a friendly smile,
emphasized by crinkles of mirth about the eyes.
I remember thinking, 'He could use a haircut.'
His necktie had slipped its moorings."

Prof. John Culliton, said of him, " Long before Winston Churchill, Leacock was saving the Empire every Monday, Wednesday and Friday at 3 p.m. in Room 20." He was also ahead of his time in prodding Americans and Britons toward greater friendship and understanding.

His feeling for both sides of the Atlantic came naturally. He was born on the Isle of Wight in 1869, and emigrated to Canada as a six-year-old. On his retirement from McGill, influential English friends urged him to return to live in the land of his birth. He refused, saying, "I'd hate to be so far away from the United States. It's second nature, part of our lives, to be near them. Every Sunday morning we read the New York funny papers. All week we hear about politics in Alabama and Louisiana, and whether they caught the bandits who stole the vault of the National Bank—well, you know American news. There's no other like it."

In the eight years of his retirement, Stephen produced the work he believed most likely to endure. It was far removed from the kind of wit which had made him famous. He described his history, *Montreal: Seaport and City*, as "the best job I've done." Unlike most historical works it bubbles with the author's laughter. In his foreword, after thanking two former colleagues for checking the manuscript, he added that any errors which remained obviously must be theirs. "Acknowledging these debts," he concluded, "I also feel that I owe a good deal of this book to my own industry and effort."

Midway through World War II, I asked Stephen if he would write a foreword for a book I had written on the Canadian Navy and its gallant role in convoy escort. He agreed. Sometime later he handed me more than 20,000 words, in which he had told the whole fascinating background story of Canada's life-long relationship to the sea. His research was staggering to a reporter who had simply described events and engagements to which he had been an eyewitness.

"I got interested," he said. "If you don't like it, throw it away and I'll write something shorter."

Not a word was changed. To my joy, the book appeared under our joint by-lines. Soon after, throat cancer took Stephen from the thousands of Old McGillers who loved him.

Leacock loved human beings for their little vanities and pretensions—and laughed at his own. The fictional town of Mariposa of his famous "Sunshine Sketches" is obviously Orillia, Ont., where Leacock built a summer home and developed a farm, which, he said, "used to lose a few dollars a year, but by dint of hard work and modernization, I have contrived to turn that into a loss of thousands." The citizens of Orillia had little difficulty in self-identification when the book reached town, but they soon realized that Leacock had ribbed his own idiosyncrasies more sharply than he had pinpointed theirs. Today's Orillians speak of him with the awe given to any community's adopted son, though it was he who adopted Mariposa-Orillia.

Stephen Leacock was so honestly simple that to many men he seemed to be a mass of complexities. To the world he remains the man of laughter. His greatest achievement, however, was that he taught thousands of young men and women to want to know. By example he proved one simple fact to all of us who attended his classes, certainly to that numerous crew who came to enjoy his friendship—that the right of outspoken dissent is the free man's most precious heritage. Such men do not often pass this way.

How We Kept Mother's Day
By Stephen Leacock

One year our family decided to have a special celebration of Mother's Day, as a token of appreciation for all the sacrifices Mother had made for us. After breakfast we had arranged, as a surprise, to hire a car and take her for a beautiful drive in the country. Mother was rarely able to have a treat like that, because she was busy in the house nearly all the time.

Leacock declined two opportunities
to be a cabinet minister. "I can't
picture myself," he said,
"as a professional stuffed shirt."

But on the very morning of the day, we changed the plan a little, because it occurred to Father that it would be even better to take Mother fishing. As the car was hired and paid for, we might as well use it to drive up into the hills where the streams are. As Father said, if you just go out driving, you have a sense of aimlessness, but if you are going to fish, there is a definite purpose that heightens the enjoyment.

So we all felt it would be nicer for Mother to have a definite purpose; and anyway, Father had just got a new rod the day before, which he said Mother could use if she wanted to; only Mother said she would much rather watch him fish than try to fish herself.

So we got her to make up a sandwich lunch in case we got hungry, though of course we were to come home again to a big festive dinner.

Well, when the car came to the door, it turned out that there wasn't as much room in it as we had supposed, because we hadn't reckoned on Father's fishing gear and the lunch, and it was plain that we couldn't all get in.

Father said not to mind him, that he could just as well stay home and put in the time working in the garden. He said that we were not to let the fact that he had not had a real holiday for three years stand in our way; he wanted us to go right ahead and have a big day and not to mind him.

But of course we all felt it would never do to let Father stay home, especially as we knew he would make trouble if he did. The two girls, Anna and Mary, would have stayed and got dinner, only it seemed such a pity to, on a lovely day like this, since they had their new hats. But they said Mother had only to say the word and they'd gladly stay home and work. Will and I would have dropped out, but we wouldn't have been any use in getting the dinner.

So in the end it was decided Mother would stay home and just have a lovely restful day around the house, and get the dinner. Also it turned out to be just a bit raw out-of-doors, and Father said he would never forgive himself if he dragged Mother round the country and let her take a severe cold. He said it was our duty to let Mother get all the rest and quiet she could, after all she had done for all of us, and that young people seldom realize how much quiet means to people who are getting old. He could still stand the racket, but he was glad to shelter Mother from it.

Well, we had the loveliest day up among the hills, and Father caught such big specimens that he felt sure Mother couldn't have landed them anyway, if she had been fishing for them. Will and I fished, too, and the two girls met some young men friends along the stream, and so we all had a splendid time.

It was quite late when we got back, but Mother had guessed we would be late, so she had kept back the dinner to have it hot for us.

We sat down to a big roast turkey. Mother had to get up and down a good bit during the meal, fetching things, but at the end Father noticed it and said she simply mustn't do it, that he wanted her to spare herself, and he got up and fetched the walnuts from the sideboard himself.

The dinner was great fun, and when it was over all of us wanted to help clear the things up and wash the dishes, only Mother said that she would really much rather do it, and so we let her, because we wanted to humor her.

It was late when it was all over, and when we kissed Mother before going to bed, she said it had been the most wonderful day in her life, and I think there were tears in her eyes.

Unforgettable Ma Murray

She couldn't write a hang — just "told" things
— but this newspaperwoman became a sort of national resource

By Georgina M. Keddell

"Your father rolled back the map of western Canada, and I stood on it," my mother used to say. But that wasn't quite true. Mother could never just *stand* anywhere. She boiled and bubbled with life. As her newspapering husband pursued the frontier—and his grand dream of a populated and prosperous Canadian Northwest—Mother zestfully contended with the details: managing the family, and scrounging copy and enough advertising to feed the cranky machinery of the latest Murray weekly.

Dad never stopped until he had strung a dozen newspapers across the 650 miles of wilderness between Vancouver and Fort Nelson in the northernmost reaches of British Columbia. Mother hasn't stopped yet. At an age when most people are quietly contemplating the past, she is still busy editorially assaulting profiteers and prime ministers, poor roads and rich Easterners. Now she is "Ma" Murray, a sort of national resource, and her salty little Bridge River-Lillooet *News* ("This week's circulation is 1796 and every bloody one of 'em paid for!") is quoted across Canada.

To this day I can close my eyes and feel again the rumbling vibrations that filled our house every Thursday, when the old Cranston press rolled from early morning until dusk. Mother was everywhere, reading the wet sheets, affixing subscribers' addresses with homemade flour paste—and regularly scribbling them sassy little notes: "If you can't pay in cash bring in a chicken. We got to eat too."

She was never constrained by the fact that her formal education had ended with the third grade. Once, responding to a letter of complaint that she couldn't punctuate to save herself, she printed two solid inches of periods, commas and semicolons, and invited folks to help themselves. Her prose was pure pyrotechnics, but it was impossible to misunderstand. When a water shortage threatened Fort St. John, she pithily wrote: "Only flush for No. 2, curtail bathing to the Saturday-night tub, go back to the old washrag, which could always move a lot of B.O. if applied often enough." That Thursday night you could hear the gasps of astonishment all the way to Dawson Creek. But Fort St. John saved 65,000 gallons of water next day, and every day after, and the crisis was over.

Born to poor Irish immigrant parents on a farm in Windy Ridge, Kan., Margaret Lally grew up both shrewdly practical and extravagantly romantic. Working in a saddlery in Kansas City, she took to stuffing notes in with the saddles bound for Alberta ranch country, soon was mooning over photos of broad-shouldered Canadian cowboys. Then, of course, she had to go see for herself. She went, and became, not a rich rancher's lady, but the Girl Friday on a struggling Vancouver weekly.

There, the girl from Windy Ridge would listen wide-eyed as her boss, George Matheson Murray, told how someday men would build a road through British Columbia to Alaska, opening all the great land to settlement. Here in the West lay Canada's future! After a bit, she would gently remind the tall, dreamy young man that it was payday and he'd best go out and collect some advertising accounts if the staff was to be paid. Once she went off to Calgary for a few days and returned to find him waiting at the railroad station. He hadn't realized how much he depended on her and her good sense and good cheer, he said, and, by God, they'd better be married right away!

No two people could have been less alike: he the genteelly reared Ontarian whose flights of rhetoric were flawlessly wrought and who would tip a waiter with his last two dollars; she the uninhibited Irish-Catholic girl from the plains who hoarded nickels and freely confessed that she couldn't write a hang —she just "told" things. But their partnership lasted nearly half a century, and produced, besides my brother Dan and me, a vision and drive that helped transform British Columbia.

Journalism and politics signposted every twist and turn in our lives. We lived in a succession of houses, all of which seemed improvised, and on occasion, between newspapers, we lived more or less off the

George Edward Murray hears some straight talk
from the most compelling and most listened-to
of all the Murrays, his grandma.

land. Then Father decided that no one was really pushing for development of British Columbia's hinterland. As of that moment, he announced dramatically, he was a candidate for the legislature.

While Father eloquently declaimed the need for railroad expansion, for improved mining trails and construction of a highway to Alaska, Mother trumpeted the virtues of the candidate. Once, unable to gain the attention of an unruly saloon crowd, she paid the bartender a dollar to lock the doors, pounded a beer glass on the bar and yelled, "Now you're going to listen to what I have to say about this man Murray or we'll by God stay here all night!"

Enough people listened so that Dad was elected. The first thing Mother did was to tearfully embrace the new member of the Legislative Assembly of British Columbia. The second was to tell him that, since we were going to be living in Lillooet, we might as well start a newspaper there.

She found a house that looked ready to slip into the Fraser River before dinnertime. The editorial office was a creaky upstairs bedroom with a hole sawed in the floor so copy could be lowered directly to the press. Dan and I were the first staff members, although Mother soon commenced teaching strays to set type for our nearly exhausted press, a relic of the Klondike gold rush.

There was never a shortage of lively news. Even a printing of the hotel registry attracted avid readers; one year the paper figured in seven divorce actions, and *that* service was discontinued. Then there were gold strikes, violently contested elections and a sulphuric battle over the gold camp's ladies of the night.

But suddenly the world was at war, and the highway to Alaska that Father had advocated in vain for so long became a military necessity. Some 400 miles north, near the tiny Peace River town of Fort St. John, soldiers began bulldozing a path toward Alaska.

While supposedly attending a Women's Institute convention in Regina, Mother slipped away and headed for Fort St. John by train, truck, ferry and foot. Her readers deserved a firsthand report on this road that was going to affect all their lives, she reasoned, and George would want to know all about the look of the changing land. After all, it was *his* road!

Back home, Mother's enthusiasm came pouring out before she had so much as taken off her raccoon coat. "George, that country is everything you said! It's the future, and that highway is turning it into today!" So the newspapering Murrays moved north again, and one day in 1943 they stood together poring proudly over the first issue of the *Alaska Highway News*.

Those were rough and sometimes bloody days, and Ye Ed, as Mother took to calling herself, saw that they were faithfully reflected in her stories. Thus her account of a domestic tragedy: "She had unknowing used airplane gas for cleaning clothes in the kitchen. She was blown out the side of the house leaving quite a good-sized hole in the wall." An automobile accident: "The passenger had her forehead de-fleshed and will need silver plates to make her arms work again. The driver is still unconscious after 30 hours and is a general mess."

When the highway and the war were both finished, Fort St. John settled down to make a community of a raw frontier settlement. Naturally, Mother led the way. For a starter, there was the matter of the town's broken-board sidewalks. For months she had been charging the town council with the need for a major reconstruction, to no avail.

Ma Murray and husband George kick up their heels at their daughter Georgina's wedding reception—which coincided with their own wedding anniversary. "Mother dug up an old evening dress," said Georgina, "somebody gave her a dozen carnations, and she was the 'bride' of the evening, as I wore just a suit."

Then, walking to the *News* office one afternoon, she stepped on a loose board which sprang up and knocked her galley-west. Clutching the offending board, she marched directly into a meeting of the council and declared, "Gentlemen, I'm here to get new sidewalks. It's either that or"—she brandished the broken board—"the first one of you I reach is going to get hell!" The appropriation was voted forthwith.

Ye Ed was even more irked by the seeming indifference of the provincial government in far-off Victoria. "They don't know we're alive up here," she once wrote. "And if we don't make them take some notice, we won't be!" Then she hit on the idea of a straw poll, asking her readers how they felt about seceding from British Columbia and joining the province of Alberta. Most of the answers were affirmative, and Victoria couldn't help noticing *that*. Soon construction was started on the Hart Highway, first land link between Vancouver and the Peace River Valley.

Father went to Ottawa as a Member of Parliament in 1949, and soon after, with Mother proclaiming the virtues of the Peace River country in print and him prompting federal interest in homesteaders and oil exploration, the country filled up and prospered. Today the Peace is spread with rich, fertile farms, and every major oil company in the world has shared in its underlying wealth.

In 1958, Father and Mother decided that the time had come to retire. The Lillooet paper was sold, and Dan and I took over the *Alaska Highway News*. The retirement lasted just three months. From Vancouver, Mother wrote: "Did you ever get up at 6 a.m. and then try doing nothing all day? It's being the ruination of me. There's no sap flowing inside."

And so, now well into their 70's, they happily bought back the Bridge River-Lillooet *News*. This time, though, their unalloyed joy in work and each other would not last long. On August 19, 1961, Father died of cancer and was laid to rest in the cemetery at Fort St. John, in the heart of the land whose bright future he had glimpsed and fought for.

Dan and I worried about Mother. She couldn't cry or in any way let loose the turmoil of emotion in her heart. In September, she flew to Ontario to see Dad's family, then on to Montana to deliver a speech. All the way home she thought about what she must remember to tell the family about the trip.

Then the stage came clattering into Lillooet, and she ran up the rickety stairs of home, dropped her bag and called out, "George, wait till I tell you what happened in . . ."

She was undone by the sound of her voice and the answering, echoing silence. She saw his hat on the hall tree where it had hung since that last trip home from the hospital, and she knew at last that she would never again share the latest news with him. She clutched the hat to her breast and made it to her bedroom before the tears started.

Now Mother is in her 80's, and her sole concession to the years is a homemade scooter in which

No quiet old-lady contemplation of the past for Ma Murray. Well on in her 80's, she still speaks her active mind each week in her Bridge River-Lillooet *News*.

she rests an ulcerated leg while scurrying from typewriter to press. She has met the dignitaries of the nation, appeared on television, and still regularly prompts a nervous quaking in Victoria with her editorial blasts.

She addressed the Lillooet high-school graduating class: "Remember this, kids. Nobody owes you a thing. You have had 12 years of living, loving and learning which have cost your parents and the taxpayers a lot of dough. Now grab every minute as if it were your last, for it's a damshur if you don't accomplish for yourselves, no one else will."

She once told me, "I want to leave a good rollicking feeling when I go. I'm going to put it in my will that there's a couple of hundred dollars for a good wake, enough whisky for everybody to get a skinful." Then that Kansas practicality took over. "Of course," she said, "I'm going to expect the neighbors to supply the sandwiches."

For the Love of *Maman*

Two stories by Robert Fontaine about his boyhood
in Ottawa, the "Happy Time" which lives on as a book,
a play, a movie, a Broadway musical

Robert Fontaine
died in 1965, aged 57.

When *Maman* was stricken with rheumatism and had to go to bed for a time, I insisted I stay home from school and be a nurse to her. When I was sick or had a twisted ankle from skating, *Maman* had always been ready with kisses and medicine. Now that she was ill, it was my turn to care for her.

I sat mostly in the parlor, reading. Now and then I ran to the kitchen and prepared hot soup. Often I fixed the pillows behind her weary head and told her incredible tales of daring, always featuring myself as the modest hero.

I was sad, of course, at *Maman*'s rheumatism, but I was happy I had grown up enough to be of help. I told myself, with fierce clenchings of my fists, that there was nothing in the world I would not dare to make her well again.

Alas, one day I learned that when we love we often estimate too highly the strength for fine deeds this love will bring us.

"*Bibi!*" my mother called in a weak voice that always made my heart seem to crack a little. "Will you do something for me?"

"*Mais oui, Maman,* anything!"

"It is something hard for a little boy to do. Perhaps you will be shy."

"*Pas moi!* I am not any more a little boy. Besides, I wish you to be well again and to laugh and sing and make pies."

My mother smiled and drew me to her, muttering as the exertion pained her arms.

"All my nightgowns are stained with liniment. Maybe I am foolish, but I think I would feel much better if I had a nice new clean nightgown."

I began to blush already.

"Will you go," she continued, "to Poulin's and buy one you like? You can put it on Papa's bill."

I backed slowly away and sat down, worried and silent. "*Maman,*" I said at length, "I would be very, very nervous to go into a women's store and buy a nightgown. I would be afraid that someone from the school would see me. *Maman,* I will do anything . . . but, please . . . not to buy a nightgown in the big ladies' store." My mother sighed and leaned back, shutting her eyes.

"All right," she said. "Never mind, *bibi.*"

I went slowly back to the parlor and tried to read, but it was impossible. I was very unhappy and ashamed.

"*Maman* is sick," I spoke to myself. "You who are always telling her how brave you are, you are as weak as soup."

I took a deep breath, then got my cap and went into my mother's room. "I am going to play ball," I told her. "I will be back soon."

I walked past M. Poulin's store once and peeked in at the mysterious pink and white articles. Then, looking up and down the street like a crook in a movie serial, I walked in, my knees knocking. All around me were women's pants and shirts and stockings, and other strange objects I had never seen before.

"Can I do something for you?" asked a pretty girl at the counter.

"I wish," I said in a whisper, ". . . my mother, who is sick, wishes . . ."

231

I took hold of the counter with my small hands and thought hard of dear *Maman*. It gave me strength.

"I wish a nightgown," I explained rapidly. "For my mother. To wear in bed. She has the inflammatory rheumatism. A pretty nightgown."

The clerk drew a gown from a large box and held it out, full length, against herself.

"Do you like this?"

Name of a name, I thought, does she have to wave it around like a flag?

I blushed and glanced down the aisle. *Sacre!* A Mrs. Framingham whom I knew was approaching with her little boy. I went quickly behind the counter, crouching down beside the astonished clerk. The Framinghams passed by without noticing me, and I came out of hiding.

"What's the matter?" the girl asked laughing.

"Nothing," I replied hastily. *"Rien."*

She held out the nightgown again. "Do you like it, then?"

"Yes. No. I don't know," I said. The girl shrugged and brought out another box. From it she took a beautiful blue gown with blue ribbons and lace.

"What size is your mother?" she asked.

"Size?" I muttered. "I did not ask. She is not big . . . she is not small . . . she is . . . in the middle."

"About my size?" the girl inquired.

I regarded the girl carefully. I almost forgot my shyness now that I was busy estimating and appreciating.

"Yes. Yes . . . but in the front . . . the . . . she . . is not so far ahead. *Comprenez-vous?* And in the back . . . there . . . she is not so far behind."

The girl laughed as if I had made a wonderful joke.

"Is she pretty, your mother? What kind of gown would she wish? Something simple? Or something wonderful, with lace and all?"

"Ah," I replied solemnly, *"Maman* is very beautiful. *Mais oui!* Papa says she is a queen."

"A queen? Then I have just the thing!"

She took a black nightgown from a box, one with bows and lace and so thin that when she held it before her I could see her face through the material.

"Ah, oui!" I said joyfully. "There we have it!" Feeling very grown-up now, I added, "You will charge it, please."

I gave her Papa's name, and she wrapped the gown. I picked up the large box and trudged slowly home. I was hot and tired, but I felt triumphant. I had done something I thought I was afraid to do, and I had done it for *Maman.*

When my mother slowly opened the box, her eyes became as big as black cherries. "What a wonderful thing!" she exclaimed. "And you picked it out all by yourself!"

"Oui," I said modestly.

"How did you happen to choose this one?"

I hesitated a moment and grinned a little foolishly. "Well," I explained, "it is because you are a queen and this is the nightgown for a queen. In the books of fairy tales the nightgown of the queen is always one which is high up at the top and very long at the bottom, and it is always full of lace!"

My mother hugged me to her for a long time, and I felt a small tear come down her cheek.

"Does it hurt, the rheumatism?" I asked.

"No, *bibi*. Nothing hurts just now. The tear is for happiness."

My Mother's Hands

There were more tears, of course, in the years that followed, but much happiness too. And then I was grown and *Maman* and *Papa* were old. And until a short while ago I wondered how elderly people who had been married for decades could still find in each other sources of surprise and wonder, even elements of excitement and provocation. I would visit my father and mother in their small apartment and chat about baseball, TV and happenings around town.

Now and then, sitting there, drinking the tea my

Gnarled and rough but as velvet
to my father (wrote Robert Fontaine),
the still young hands of a woman
he loved, a woman a long time in his heart,
a woman not really old. . .
(Sculpture by Henry Moore)

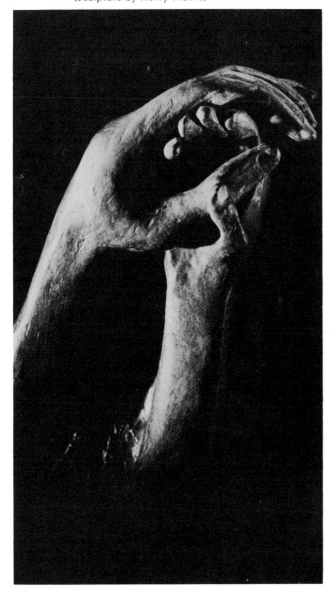

mother inevitably brewed for me and helping my father with the Sunday crossword puzzle, I would wonder how it was with them in their hearts; how they juggled the days and made them sparkle, or if they did.

Life is to be lived, savored, salted and consumed. But what do you dream about when you are almost 80 and have been in love for 50 years? Their lives were as quiet outside as one could imagine—as quiet as the snow or the rain or the rustle of trees in midsummer.

My father gets up at 7:30 and goes for a long walk. He knows many people—clerks, butchers, newsboys. He talks with them about the weather and the latest sports events. Then he buys a half-dozen doughnuts, goes home and takes a nap.

My mother markets and plays canasta with three friends once a week. Otherwise they watch television or listen to the radio. They never go to the movies. Years ago my father played the violin in movie theaters for silent pictures, and he is just as happy if he never sees a motion picture again.

So the life of my father and mother has flowed on, with me wondering, "What do they think about? Do they notice each other? Do they have strong emotions about each other? But how could they?" The blood has slowed down. The arms are inelastic. The eyes are dim.

Yet one morning when I called, I found them fighting, which in itself was most extraordinary. They were bickering and shouting about some obscure matter, something to do with an event some 25 years previous. They had different ideas as to how the event had turned out, and the discussion got hotter and hotter. At first I was amused, then alarmed. My father said, "That's the way you are, always so sure of yourself."

"I ought to know. I was there."

"I was there, too."

"Well, you don't remember then."

"My memory is perfect," my father shouted.

They kept at it like newlyweds for about 15 minutes. Finally my father took his hat and rushed out of the apartment slamming the door.

"Let him go," my mother said.

"I guess I'll have to. What were you fighting about?"

My mother shrugged. "I don't remember. He's just so stubborn. I keep hoping he'll outgrow it."

"If he hasn't now he never will."

"Well he better. I won't put up with it much longer."

I sat around for a while. I told my mother not to worry. She said, "Humph!" Finally I left.

Around dinnertime I called up. My mother answered and said my father had not come home yet or phoned. She did not sound as crisp as she had been. "I hope he doesn't do anything foolish," she said. "He's not a young man, you know."

"I know. I'll go look for him downtown."

Now about ten years ago my father had been disconnected from the last real job he held, as head of a music school. For the first time in his life he had decided to soothe himself with alcohol and had chosen the worst sherry ever made. Then he would become very talkative and a little belligerent, especially for a man five feet six, weighing 130 pounds neat.

After a while he got over it and never touched the stuff again. Yet I had a notion he had probably gone off again like a young, rebuffed lover. It was rather amazing to think of him, at his age, being sulky and irritated with my mother and she, for that matter, being wistful and lonesome like a girl at her first quarrel. In a way it was rather refreshing. I did not think they had it in them.

It was pouring rain as I began my walk, starting with the cheery hotel bars and working my way north to the more disreputable places. Once or twice I thought I had a glimpse of him, but when I got in out of the rain it was not he but some other sad old character.

At about 11:30 I gave up and went back to my mother's place. She was weeping gently now. "I believe he has really run away." She would stop weeping, square her shoulders and say suddenly, "I'll fix him." Then she would slump and weep some more.

I sat there with her, drinking tea, for a long time. We talked of the old days. She spoke as if they were all over and my father had deserted her for another woman.

At last the door opened and my father walked calmly in. He had a small package in his hand. He smiled quietly and said, "Hello."

"Where've you been?" I asked. My mother was forced to smile. She was so glad to see him.

"I went to a movie."

My mother was stunned. "A movie!"

"The Arcade. All in bright color. It hurt my eyes."

"What was it about?" I asked, to make conversation.

My father shrugged. "A lot of young, foolish girls and their mushy love affairs."

"Oh," I said noncommittally.

"You want some tea?" my mother asked. "You must be tired after all that color and those mushy girls."

"Sentimental stuff," my father said. "Movies don't seem to change much. They're just bigger and louder. Here!"

He handed her the package. It was a bottle of hand lotion, the sort that is guaranteed to make your hands soft as silk. My father hung his head a little and blushed. It was quite touching.

My mother beamed. "What a lovely bottle!"

"They say it keeps your hands like velvet," my father said.

My mother's hands have worked for me and others for many, many years; washing, baking, scrubbing, digging in a garden—they are gnarled and rough. To my father, though, they must have been the hands of a young woman, of a woman he loved, a woman who had stayed for a long time in his heart as precisely the same woman—and her hands were as velvet to him and he wanted to keep them that way.

My mother was weeping again but this time with pleasure and love.

I said, "Well, I've got to get along and you better go to bed."

So I left them to make up and to smile and to be alone. It was a moment, I am sure, when they preferred no company.

"Black Gold"
From Athabasca's Sticky Sands

At long last, northern Alberta's ocean of sand-imprisoned oil
is being tapped—and tiny Fort McMurray stands poised on the brink
of fame and fortune

By Harland Manchester

There's heady excitement in little Fort McMurray, a once-quiet northern Alberta outpost on the east bank of the broad Athabasca River at about the latitude of upper Labrador. For more than a century its hardy people, about one third of them of Indian blood, have won a meager living from the freighters which ply north toward the Arctic Ocean, and from fishing, trapping and logging. But now, its population up from 1200 to more than 5000 in four years, McMurray is on the brink of fame and fortune.

Walk down the road and you can smell the reason: a pungent, tarry odor, suggesting newly laid blacktop. Ride down the river in a motor launch, and you'll see streaks of black gunk exuding from the banks. The town rests upon a vast underground ocean of oil imprisoned in sand—the huge Athabasca tar sands deposit. This deposit has long been known as one of the world's greatest untapped oil reserves. The Alberta Oil and Gas Conservation Board estimates it contains about 626 *billion* barrels of the "black gold." Experts believe at least half can be recovered economically—enough to supply Canada and the United States, at current consumption rates, for 100 years.

This fabulous deposit has lured oil men for decades, and is now at last being opened and mined. At a bustling plant 20 miles downriver, close to 45,000 barrels of oil a day are being extracted. Processed into high-grade synthetic crude, the oil is shipped 266 miles by a new pipeline to a junction with existing pipelines near Edmonton. From there it is piped as far as Ontario for final conversion into gasoline and other consumer fuels. In this first commercial exploitation of the Athabasca field, Great Canadian Oil Sands Limited, backed by Sun Oil Company Limited, invested 235 million dollars; dozens of other firms have secured tracts and are making plans for large-scale production.

The sticky black sands were first seen by a white man in 1788, when Peter Pond, an explorer and fur trader, paddled down the river and scooped up samples. The Indians, he reported, used the tarry stuff to caulk their canoes. Government surveys of the Athabasca oil sands were made in the late 19th century and, ever since, scientists and prospectors have been speculating, experimenting with methods of recovery.

When you fly over this wilderness it is easy to see one reason why development has been so long delayed. There are stretches of swampy muskeg as far as the eye can reach. During the sub-zero winters the ground is rock-hard, the rivers are frozen three feet deep. Not long ago, cargo moved only by river boat and train. Now huge diesel monsters have slashed through forests to build a long highway over the ridge tops to connect with Edmonton.

Among the technical pioneers who made the old Athabasca oil dream come true was the late Dr. Karl A. Clark, of the Alberta Research Council, who began experiments with the black gunk more than 40 years ago. As a young engineer with the federal Department of Mines, he was assigned to study the oil sands as a possible road-making material. A railroad was built to a point near McMurray. Dr. Clark brought back a ton of oil sands and set to work in a laboratory to process it. Several miles of street and sidewalk were surfaced with the products of his research, but interest lagged, and research appropriations dried up with the Depression. Meanwhile, however, he had caught a glimpse of the real future of the deposit.

One of the big technical problems in processing the oil sand is its viscosity, or stickiness. Clumps of it stick to your boots, your hands get black from it and your clothes are soon ready for the cleaner. The oil adheres tightly to each tiny grain of sand. It will not separate easily from the sand and moisture, and it will not burn. (Throw it on a campfire and it puts the flame out.) But, after years of laboratory work, Dr. Clark and his group finally devised a separation process suitable for continuous large-scale production.

"Heat will release the oil," Dr. Clark explained. "But since the crude oil in the sand is heavier than water, we had to work out a trick to make it rise to the surface and float. We mix the sands with just enough hot water to make a pulp. Steam joins with the sticky oil to form bubbles, which rise to the top as a froth. Then a rotary paddle device skims off the froth, leaving the sand behind."

The process renewed interest among several large refiners, who sought permission to mine the sands. Alberta's provincial government officials said no, reluctant to promote a rival of the liquid petroleum fields, which are largely responsible for the province's booming prosperity. However, since there may someday be too little oil for global needs, the authorities finally, in September 1962, gave Great Canadian the green light to start tapping the oil-sand treasure. Athabasca's hour had struck.

Dr. Clark became a consultant to Great Canadian, and his process is now operating at the company's plant, which went into operation in the fall of 1967. It treats about 100,000 tons of oil sand per day, from which 45,000 barrels of synthetic crude are removed. In the gargantuan mining job, two immense, tractor-mounted "mining wheels," imported from Germany, chew into the vertical faces

Each hungry "mouth" gobbles almost a cubic yard of oil sand every time this huge "mining wheel" turns. Back to the separation plant daily go 100,000 tons of sand, from which 45,000 barrels of synthetic crude are removed.

This was Fort McMurray in 1964, soon after
Great Canadian Oil Sands obtained permission
to mine the Athabasca treasure. Population
went from 1200 to more than 5000 in four years.
The Athabasca River is at the upper left.

of the deposits. These digging machines have revolving multiple "mouths," or buckets, each taking a bite of almost a cubic yard. As they inch into
the hillsides, they feed the sand to conveyor belts or
automatic trains, which deliver it to the separation
plant.

Here hot water is added, the sand sinks to the
bottom and revolving wiper blades skim off the
frothy oil at the top. The oil then goes to a dehydra-
tion and deaeration plant, where all remaining sand,
air and water are removed. A further process before
the oil flows into the pipelines removes fractions like
petroleum coke, a cheap by-product, which fuels
the operation and also runs a sizable electric plant
to furnish power, light and steam for the whole
operation. Meanwhile, as the plant devours mountains of black oil sands, it spews out other mountains of gleaming white sand as fine and clean as
that found on any ocean beach. There is talk of a
local glass industry based on this by-product.

While there are oil sands enough near the surface to keep the strip-mining machines busy for
many years, other methods can be used to exploit
deep deposits hundreds of feet below. For several
years Shell Canada Limited, which has large leases
in the Athabasca area, has been experimenting with
a method of injecting hot steam and a chemical
down certain wells to emulsify the oil, which is then
carried along to other wells, where it is drawn up
by pumping. Shell is confidently prepared to develop this method at a total cost of 260 million
dollars. Other proposed methods include underground nuclear blasts, whose heat would create vast
caverns full of pumpable liquid.

So little Fort McMurray weighs its future. With
the opening of the oil-separation plant, a staff of
500 men, many with families, with a total payroll of
about $6,500,000 a year, descended upon the town.
Their demand for goods and services will attract
many more. A long, cement sidewalk has already
been laid past vacant areas, in anticipation of new
houses, streets, shops, hotels and public buildings.
Planning officials from Edmonton have made a survey to assist in zoning and growth regulation. The
region's 2700 miles of navigable water and innumerable lakes leaping with fish may lure sportsmen.
If all goes well, Fort McMurray on the Athabasca
will become a jewel of the North.

238

Quebec
Not Quite Europe, Certainly Not America

Four stories of *la belle province* from the pages of our French-Canadian edition
—hymns to its ancient capital city, its fiery autumn maples, its unique cuisine,
its bone-chilling, heartwarming winters

The Capital
By Ringuet (Dr. Philippe Panneton)
author of *Trente arpents*

The cities of North America are look-alikes, each much the same as the next: a little nearer perhaps, or a little farther, a little bigger or a little smaller, a little older or newer, richer or poorer, maybe more sun here than there, or more icicles. But they're all from the same mold, these North American cities, built with the same materials. Only Québec is different.

Look down. From the high Terrace, look down on the harbor, on Lower Town with its friendly, misshapen houses close-woven around the ancient church of Notre-Dame-des-Victoires. Look around.

See the great guns, silent sentinels from an explosive past, now a kind of jungle gym for the youngsters of la rue des Remparts, or a romantic prop for a honeymoon souvenir snapshot.

Oh, this unique old capital! Narrow streets, prim little houses, secret gardens amid the mysteries at the end of enticing *culs-de-sac*. . . And la rue du Parloir with its fringe of calm devotion, and old city gates whose great arches narrow the streets as if to discourage the unwelcome intrusion of car and autobus. . . And all this girdled by old granite walls which treasure the happy heart of the city of Montcalm and Dufferin.

Now look far out beyond l'Ile d'Orléans, through the immense door of the St. Lawrence, to the sea. It's as if you were on a bridge between two continents which met here in Québec, crossroads of the world, crossroads of the ages.

This is not quite Europe, but certainly not America any more. This moment is not yesterday, but neither is it really today.

Despite factories, apartment houses, posh motels and— alas!—a skyscraper, despite burgeoning suburbs like those of Hartford or Regina or all the Little Rocks of North America, despite all these, here is a charm and a fragrance that I find nowhere else.

This is Québec.

The Flaming Leaves of Fall
By Rina Lasnier
of l'Académie canadienne-française

Suddenly, in a great silent explosion of scarlet and gold, it happened: the fires of Canadian autumn raced and leaped across the countryside. And the strongest, warmest fire of all was in the leaves of maple.

Neither the narrow leaves of willow nor the oblong of elm, not the oak's rich Madeira nor the stately heart-shape of basswood nor the quivering leaves of trembling poplar . . . not even this cluster of young pines, straight and solemn like a children's choir . . . no tree, no leaf awakened the very soul of the land as did the blood-red maples. And this Canadian crimson, born of a long, slow kiss of sap and sun, makes us yearn for inward splendor in harmony with this majesty of the flaming leaves of fall.

The ancient purple of our martyrs, our heroes, our ancestors surges back to us. So alike, these leaves, but each different, each in its diversity enhancing the harmony of the whole. From the most delicately pale to the fieriest red, each leaf has triumphed over primitive bitterness, through a long night of struggle for survival. Now it lies stretched in a peace at once sweet and proud, a peace of victory: this color, this harmony.

This peace, the peace of autumn, lives on deep inside us, the peace of the heart, the peace of beauty. . .

La Cuisine Canadienne
By André Arnoldi

La cuisine canadienne has a character all its own— a delicate fragrance borrowed from France plus a rich flavor derived from the robust climate and geography of Québec and the appetites of hardy *habitants*.

Tradition shaped by loving and expert hands has given us *la soupe aux pois, le ragoût de pattes* and *la tourtière*. I love pea soup, "leg stew" and meat pie. But there's so much more.

Come, let's explore. You know our Gaspé salmon, of course. But you've turned up your nose at cod, haven't you? You were wrong because cod, when cooked with spices and herbs right after being caught . . . mmmm! And cod liver—whose oil you've despised since childhood, I know—and cod tongues; with these two the Gaspé housewife can make a gourmet dish. Served with potatoes and onions and with bread baked in the ancestral oven, *any* Gaspé fish is superb.

Now, what would you say to a roast leg of salt meadow lamb, the greedy lamb of the lower St. Lawrence which feed on salty grasses and seaweed in pastures which the sea floods at high tide. As the knife cuts into the crackling *gigot,* the delicately *rosée* meat stressed with garlic, you'll forget the more penetrating flavor of roast pork.

On we go. To Trois-Rivières and those wonderful little fish, the tommycod. To Lac Saint-Jean and blueberries so big that people say you need only "three to a pie"! Smother them in thick Lac Saint-Jean cream and you've got a feast for a king.

And now cheese. The strong refined cheese of l'Ile d'Orléans, the Oka cheese of the Trappists, the small cream cheese of Saint-Basile with its taste of filberts fresh as a new dawn.

Ah, yes, and so much more. Smoked eels from l'Ile d'Orléans and the Richelieu River—which Rome and New York put to better use than we do. *La tarte à la ferlouche,* with raisins, molasses and almonds. And buckwheat cakes, which Claude-Henri Grignon, in *Un homme et son péché,* condemns to undeserved indignity by making them a meal for a miser.

Well, I've not tried to teach. I simply meant to conjure up for you those feasts which were the daily fare of our youth. *Vive la cuisine canadienne!*

The Glittering Time
By Claude-Henri Grignon
author of *Un homme et son péché*

Marguerite Bourgeoys, that incomparable servant of God, sent from Troyes in 1653 to educate the young girls of New France, wrote home of "that harsh glittering winter that freezes the body but never the heart." Imagine the tiny school, built stone by stone with her own hands, and its blanket of snow on a holy Christmas night shining with stars and hopes. "There was so much snow that I was unable to push open the school door," she wrote. "And such cold, our Dear Lady, such cold!" But Marguerite Bourgeoys soon acclimatized herself and came to proclaim the splendor of winters. To her, the first snowfall each year always brought the same thrill.

Three centuries ago, pioneer settlers waged a desperate fight against the severity of the climate. Immigrants from the mild valley of the Loire or from the south of France, country of sunshine, perfumes and honey, they were afraid of the long, tedious, silent white season. But they came to realize that spring seems more beautiful, more comforting, after six months of frigid weather.

Our folk songs proclaim the poetry that filled the souls and hearts of these early Canadians when they heard the first bells of sleighs gleaming with snowflakes. Wintertime! It is still, in districts that have remained rustic and French, a season of rest and gaiety, of social gatherings and monumental meals.

God ordained that man should acclimatize himself to his native land. The Canadian, from lumberjack or trapper to big-city doctor or stenographer, dotes on winter. The terror of the early settler is now the joy of the skier, an invigorating sport amid incomparable scenery. Wintertime! It is all the poetry of our fair land. Sometimes, I admit, bodies are chilled and benumbed, but oh, what generous and warm hearts!

"And such cold, our Dear Lady,
such cold!" Wintertime
is "all the poetry of our fair land."

Calgary Whoops It Up

The Old West thunders again in this wild and famous Stampede

By Robert Christie

The Old West of cowboys and Indians cannot die so long as the annual Calgary Stampede lives on. It started in 1912 and still attracts visitors from every continent.

Cowboys come from as far south as the Rio Grande. Indians in bead-glistening buckskins and eagle feathers gather from half a dozen reservations. The RCMP, in ceremonial scarlet and gold, add their aura. More than 6000 exhibitors display everything from purebred livestock to oil paintings. Here in the shadow of the Rockies the nine-day Stampede draws an attendance of 800,000 people, well over double Calgary's population of 354,000.

Modern Calgary is the trading capital of a rich oil and cattle domain. But during Stampede week it pretends that no good-bys have ever been said to the Old West. This week has been called "the damnedest form of ancestor worship ever to put spurs on." The flag-hung streets are roped off against automobile traffic. Three dozen bands play for crowds of thousands that whirl from curb to curb in square dances. Chuck wagons from nearby ranches serve bacon and flapjacks free. Cowboys roam the streets on their ponies, and if a pretty girl takes a horseman's eye, down comes a lariat around her waist by way of introduction.

The Stampede itself is a battle between cowpunchers and outlaw horses, wild steers, Brahma bulls and slippery calves. The bucking stock is picked for meanness and toughness—for its ability to leave a rider sitting on a pile of fresh air. It is said that the show sprang from a violent argument back in 1912 as to whether Canada or the United States produced the best cowboys. A young Wyoming cowpuncher, Guy Weadick, persuaded four of Alberta's wealthiest ranchers to underwrite this cow-country Olympics to the tune of $25,000 apiece. The Stampede has never settled the debate. There are too many good men on both sides of the border.

During the 3½-hour afternoon shows the arena is in swift and constant motion. Loudspeakers bawl and in a whirl of sun and dust a young rider hurtles

244

The Stampede pits cowpunchers
against outlaw horses, slippery calves
and wild steers. Top professionals
make up to $30,000 a year
in this bone-crunching business.

A Calgary "first"—much copied elsewhere
—is the four-team chuck-wagon race,
a main Stampede attraction. With 20 men
and 32 horses, it's "a nightmarish traffic jam
moving at full throttle." Moving at virtually
no throttle at all, an unexcited buffalo
and its buffalo-skin-coated rider
parade on a downtown Calgary street.

out of a chute on a bareback horse. In a mere three
seconds man and animal go their separate ways. As
the cowboy's head and shoulders crunch into the
earth, other competitors run out and help him to
his feet. There's a doctor on hand if he's needed.

Another chute flies open and a calf sprints out,
heads for the safety of the catchpens at the far end
of the infield. A roper, his lariat whirling, thunders
after him. As the cow-pony closes in, the wily calf
swerves. Wise to these tricks, the rope-horse agilely
changes gait and pounds up behind the calf, slightly
to one side. Knowing that he has brought his rider
to an ideal distance for roping, he holds his place
and speed. The rider stands in his stirrups, drops his
loop cleanly over the calf's neck.

In a flash, the pony slides to a stop. The cowboy
leaps from his saddle and pulls himself hand over
hand along the taut rope to deal with 300 pounds of
calf. With a quick, muscular heave he flips the calf
down, whips the "piggin' string" from his own
teeth and, with a few swift motions, ties up three of
the little animal's legs. Then, throwing both arms
above his head, he signals the timekeepers that the

tie is completed. An experienced roper will have his calf thrown and tied 15 seconds from the time it breaks past the barrier.

The wild-horse race is one of the most exciting events. The chute gates swing back and 16 broncs plunge out with nothing on but halters. Each of 16 three-man teams (each rider-to-be has two helpers) tries to catch one of the horses, saddle him and put its rider aboard to cross the finish line. Roping is not allowed; the men must catch the horse by his halter-shank—a risky business, in view of what rearing broncs, flailing out with their forelegs, can do to a man. One of the two helpers, his heels grimly dug in, anchors the horse while his partner tries to saddle him.

The bronc snorts with rage as he feels the saddle drop on his back. He plunges and fights. The cinch is pulled tight by the third cowboy, whose next job is to get into the saddle. Now, a bronc tries to wipe off his rider and carries him murderously into a wire fence. Over by the chutes, two horses collide. One goes down and for a moment your heart is in your throat. After the place-winners have been decided, pickup men gallop in to take off any rider who may be stranded on the back of his horse.

Another event that stands your hair on end is the Brahma bullriding. A cumbersome-looking beast, with his heavy horns and enormous hump of muscle, a Brahma bull is docile when grazing on the range. But he is apt to become a killer the moment he feels a man on his back.

Watching one of these powerful beasts twist out of a chute, you see that the cowboy on his back is riding with only a rope tied around the animal's belly. A bell attached to the rope clangs with every plunge. The rider, to qualify, must hang on for eight seconds with only one hand and cannot change hands once he leaves the chute.

The Brahma spins, throwing himself in a tight, dizzying circle. The great head turns suddenly and tries to hook the cowboy with its fierce horns. When this doesn't work, the bull, his back arched

Stampede time is time for square-dancing
in the flag-bedecked streets
and for the music of three dozen bands
as Calgary pretends the Old West never died.

high, flings himself straight into the air. The rider loses balance, struggles to recover. The bull smashes down on his forehooves with tremendous force, and for a second appears to be doing a handstand. The cowboy is thrown almost directly in the Brahma's path.

Somewhere in the grandstands a woman screams. But as the bull snorts and paws the ground, a baggy figure hurries toward him. This is the bull-fighting clown. He fires a toy pistol in the Brahma's face and flags him, in comic imitation of a matador, with a cloak. The bull's attention is diverted from the fallen rider and he charges the clown. The agile buffoon steps aside as the animal expresses by. The Brahma whirls and with frightening speed returns to the attack. The clown leaps into a barrel. The animal butts the barrel into a spin. Now a second clown appears and claims the bull's interest. The animal then thunders toward clown number two. Eventually the clowns lure the Brahma into a catchpen.

"You may see funnier clowns," a cowboy remarks, "but you've never seen braver men. Lots of us owe our lives to them."

Cowboys flock to Calgary from as far as Texas.
Few ride to riches, and many are thrown and injured,
but the same men come back year after year.

In the wild-horse contest, each three-man team
tries to catch a bronc by his halter—
no roping is allowed—then saddle him
and race him across the finish line.

A tremendously popular event and one that is native to the Calgary Stampede, though widely imitated elsewhere, is chuck-wagon racing. Eight heats are run each evening around the half-mile track.

Four chuck wagons, each drawn by four horses, compete in each heat. Every chuck wagon has four outriders who must cross the finish line with their wagon. The wagons line up in the infield for the start, their stoves out on the ground, the fly tents up, the riders in each outfit grouped around the stove with their mounts behind them. When a pistol shot cracks, the men hurl the stoves into their wagons, and pack the tent poles. While the cowboys are running for their saddle horses, the chuck-wagon drivers already have their teams galloping in a figure eight around two barrels and jockeying for the careening dash onto the track.

The four wagons lurch out to the straightaway in a flying, dusty jumble of wheels, horses and men— a nightmarish traffic jam moving at full throttle. Followed by their shouting, galloping outriders, the wagons crowd, jockey and sway as they tear for the rail position on the first turn. A cloud of dust envelopes 32 horses and 20 men. Now space begins to show between the wagons, and the teams flatten out as they tip into the last curve and roll across the finish line, still at breakneck speed. There are few really serious injuries. Why is a mystery, for wagons have been known to explode into debris on collision.

Stampede participants gamble both their bodies and their bankrolls. Few come away winners; yet you see the same faces year after year. If a cowboy goes broke or is hurt, the other performers help him get to the next show where he may make a comeback. This spirit of live-and-help-live is a heartwarming feature of the whole business. For the good performers, of course, there is substantial money. Top professionals wind up a year of contesting with from $20,000 to $30,000 in their Levi's.

Regardless of past success, cowboys are superstitious. The oddest taboo in a long list concerns the peanut. Neither a contestant nor his wife will touch one because it's bound to bring disaster. A cowpuncher will have nothing to do with the number 30, and yellow is a color from which he will run screaming. He believes that injury is certain to claim him if a hat is carelessly tossed on a bed; that bad luck can come if he refuses a handout to a panhandler.

The Thanksgiving I Don't Forget

Not turkey but jackrabbit (with turnips) . . . the "pure Siberia" of those 40 acres
on a cold February morning . . . a poignant farewell to a son whose happy days of just being little
are suddenly over. Three warm accounts of the intangible joys of rural living

By H. Gordon Green

The Thanksgiving I remember most thankfully was the one when we had jackrabbit and turnips for dinner, when I was a boy on our farm at Arthur, Ont.

If Dad was ashamed of the dilapidated barns, the house he was always going to enlarge, the floor with pine knots that stabbed holes through the linoleum, the cookstove that let smoke into the oven, let me say now that it didn't matter. Sure, I remember winter mornings when a zero wind seeped through the cracks around the window. But I remember better the warm feel of our clothes when we took them down from the stovepipe where Dad had piled them.

We complained when we had to hurry home from school while the rest played ball, or when on a powder-dusty day we'd look up from the sweat and thistles of our hayfield to see other kids go singing up the road to the swimming hole. But our complaining never did run deep. Because Dad made us feel our work amounted to something.

Especially so at Thanksgiving. That was the day we made an inventory of everything on the place.

First Dad took us to the cellar with its barrels of fragrant apples, the bins of beets and carrots packed in sand, the mountain of sacked potatoes, the peas, corn, string beans, jellies, strawberries and other preserves which bowed down the shelves. Father had us inventory it all carefully. Then we went out to the barns and figured how many tons of hay there were in the mow and how many bushels of grain in the granary. We counted the livestock, chickens, turkeys and geese.

Dad wanted to see how we stood, he said. But he really wanted us to realize, on this feast day, how richly the Almighty had smiled upon all those hours of work we had so tearfully protested. And when we finally sat down to the feast which Mother had prepared, the grace was something we felt.

It may seem strange, then, to say that the Thanksgiving I remember most thankfully was the year we seemed to have nothing to be thankful for.

"And the home so rich for us all." Green's parents at their golden wedding anniversary.

The bad year had started off well enough. We had hay left over, we had lots of seed, and our four litters of pigs were as sleek as sausages. What's more, Dad had a little money set aside and thought we might finally afford a hay loader—that wonderful machine that simply trailed behind the wagon, lifted the hay and threw it on a rack at your feet.

It was the year, too, that electricity came. Not to us, because we couldn't afford it. The MacKillops had a party to show off their bright rooms and the iron that didn't have to sit on the stove. Mother looked a long time at the washing machine. If only we could afford to be connected.

It was a Monday night when Mother was doing her big wash that we found out what Dad had on his mind. He said, "My turn now." Mother protested but Dad took over the board anyway, and Mother turned to her knitting.

"Washing and knitting," Dad said to her. "You spend more time doing that than sleeping. Think we ought to break down and get this electricity?"

Mother came flying across the room and threw her arms around his neck and swallowed a tear or two as she thought of the hay loader that wouldn't be bought now.

So the line came up our lane, too, that year. Nothing fancy, but what wonder there was to that gleaming washing machine, and what unbelievable brilliance in the bulbs that dangled from each ceiling! The lamps went quietly off to the attic.

The coming of electricity was almost the last good thing that the year was to bring. The rains started just as the first oat spears began to put a pea-green haze over the country, and when the water finally drained away there wasn't a seedling left anywhere. We seeded again, but September brought more rains that beat the crops into the earth. The potatoes rotted in mud.

Dad sold a couple of cows that fall and all the pigs, and a lot of other livestock he had intended to keep. He got heartbreakingly low prices for them because everybody else had to do the same thing. About all we harvested that year was a patch of turnips that had somehow weathered the wet.

Then suddenly it was Thanksgiving again. "Maybe we'd better forget it this year," Mother said. "We haven't even a goose left."

But on the morning of the big day Dad brought in a jackrabbit. "These aren't half bad sometimes if you roast them with a hunk of fat pork," he said.

When we sat down to the rabbit that night I said, "It looks like a piece of old dead horse! I certainly don't want any." Mother cried.

Then Dad did a strange thing. He went up to the attic and got an oil lamp. He lighted it, set it in the middle of the table and told one of us to turn out the lights. When there was only the lamp again we couldn't believe our eyes. Could it really have been this dark before? How in the world did we ever see our way around in those days?

Dad said grace, and when it was over we were still quiet. In the humble dimness of the old lamp we were beginning to see clearly again.

It got to be a lovely meal. The jackrabbit tasted like turkey and the turnips were the mildest we could recall.

We can thank Father for that Thanksgiving. For that and all the other Thanksgivings we had with him. And for the home which, for all its want, was so rich for us all.

Years later when we descended upon him for Thanksgiving reunion, we came displaying the success which had come our way—we all had so many, many bright things now.

When it was time for the feast Father would bring out that old oil lamp, switch out all the rest and let it light our feast again. Maybe we need its humble gleam as badly in these days of our noisy success as we did that year of our poverty.

Why We Sold The Farm

I can't say that I blamed the children for not wanting to do the chores with me that cold February morning after the storm.

"This is pure Siberia!" said our 12-year-old Sydney. "We *work* like Siberia and it *looks* like Siberia!"

Then his younger sister, Marielle, started in. "Other people around here only have to worry about getting to the bus stop. But not us! Before we leave we have to feed pigs and cows and silly old hens that don't even lay eggs."

"All you have to do is to feed the chickens, Miss Huffy!" I said. "Now let's go!"

We kicked our way through the Quebec snowdrifts, shoveled out the stable doors and got the job done. But on the way back to the house, the one we call Big Fellow (because he's a head taller than I) began to talk. "Pretty stupid to go to all this agony year after year just for the privilege of losing money, isn't it?"

That was a sharp cut. Because we never had made any real money out of our part-time farm, north of Montreal, even with all our cows, hens,

"Well, one thing sure," says Gordon Green, "I got
a lot of work out of the farm—and muss
and worry. And laughs and satisfaction too."

pigs, sheep, ducks, geese, goats, turkeys and chinchillas. We are simply not practical enough. The monkey which runs around in our stable is embarrassing proof of that. Her only purpose seems to be to seize Sydney's cap from his head and toss it to the pigs.

It was my wife who shook me hardest that morning. "Why couldn't we be happy with just a nice home like the rest of the people around here?" she asked at breakfast. "Why don't we sell the farm? What do you get out of all that slaving?"

It was a question to which I gave a lot of thought as I went to my office in Montreal. And then the real-estate man dropped in to see me.

"Nine years ago," he reminded me, "you bought your 40 acres for $1000. We're offering $500 an acre. Cash."

I didn't say anything.

"Look at it this way," he said. "You're the last farmer left in your neighborhood, and the city people are coming in fast. They can pass laws. They can tax you out." He edged in closer. "You know as well as I do that the only way to make any money out of a farm today is to sell it for more than you paid. All this poetry about the joys of country life—it's an illusion. Why, I have half a hundred farms on my list just aching to be sold."

"I'll think it over," I promised.

What *did* I get out of my farm? I took the question with me to the barn that night.

Well, one thing sure, I got a lot of work out of it. Other men on my road get up only to catch the eight o'clock bus; I start the chores at six. For them the workday ends with supper (they call it dinner); for me there is still an hour or more of work in the barn—animals to feed and water, manure to be traded for fresh straw. And those are only the regular tasks.

With the work comes muss. In the summer the big lawns all down our road are neat, well barbered.

We have no lawn, only a huge rambling yard where the dogs dig, the geese squat and the children build feed-bag tents. We go into the house with animal husbandry stuck to our boots and our pants cuffs full of chaff. And in the kitchen there is all too often an orphan lamb to dart out from his nook behind the stove and cast aspersions on the wife's clean floor. Or a runt pig perhaps, or chilled chicks or a puppy.

I get a lot of worry out of my farm, too—about frost, thaws, rain, drought, hail, the rising price of hay and the sinking price of beef. Should there be an ailing animal, supper means little to me. I'll admit that I talk pretty loud about such trials. Yet for all its tribulations, the labor of farming has given me a satisfaction I have never found in any other occupation.

There is for instance the little shed on our farm, the chinchilla house, which the boys and I made. We went back into our woods one week in July and cut the trees ourselves. Our axes were dull, the alders switched our faces and the mosquitoes were the biggest we had ever seen. But we got the logs out, and helped Joe Gagnon load them onto his truck and away to the mill. Today when we look at the shed and remember the fearsome heat, the salt sweat, the pain of our stiffened muscles, this little nine-by-twelve structure becomes for us a victory monument.

I like the men that the farm makes, the way they talk and the things they laugh at. "That time you were going down the ramp with the case of eggs and the ram hit you from behind," we ask Joe Gagnon, "were you surprised?"

"By gar yes," Joe says. "My eyes pop out like a stomped-on bullfrog."

I like the neighborliness of such men. The time my boar nuzzled me with one of his tusks and opened me for 16 stitches, Joe and my father volunteered to take over for me. "Two old men are as good as one young one any day," my father said. And he was right.

"But you might have a heart attack," we told him that day he persisted in working with Joe in the haymow. (He was 74 then.)

Father didn't deny the possibility but he refused to worry about it. "When you've got to go, you've got to go." I don't suppose I could ever explain men like Joe and my father to my office friends, who are such serious, cautious men.

I like the thousand little things about a farm which can stop a man's heart in mid-beat. The trust of well-fed animals. The soft neighing of a mare to her exploring colt. The way a bitch looks up at you from the writhing mass of her first litter as if to ask you how in the world it ever happened. The sounds of the woods on the wild spring nights at mapling time and the smell of the fire-pink steam from the boiling sap. The power and the glory of a young bull as he blats and paws the earth to announce that he has now outgrown his age of innocence.

I like what the farm does for my children, and for the way a child can learn about creation without prudish hesitations. A few weeks ago there was quite a commotion at one of the neighboring homes. The center of the excitement was a cardboard box that the good lady of the house was trying to hide. But for all the precautions, a five-year-old boy managed a peek.

"Don't know why they're all excited," he said. "It's just the cat having kittens."

That enlightened boy, I am glad to say, started his education on my farm.

These were the thoughts which came to me during evening chores, as I pondered my wife's question.

But the more I thought the more I saw that all the reasons in the world couldn't save my little farm. Already there were people down the road who wanted to pass some kind of law that would prevent a rooster from crowing before seven in the morning. We might hang on another two or three years, but eventually our farm would have to succumb. One kind of life must cease so that another may thrive, and there was no use fighting the inevitable.

Frogs and snails for sure, and toads too,
and snakes. And for venturesome Barry Green,
on a sunny summer day on the farm,
a good-natured billy goat for a playmate.

Next day I saw the real-estate man. That night, I told the family. "The farm is sold. We're slightly rich. I hope you're satisfied."

There was a shocked hush, as if a funeral had unexpectedly come round the corner. "No!" my wife said finally. "You wouldn't!"

I was surprised at her. "But didn't you want it this way?" I thought she was going to cry.

The children had stopped eating, too. "But what will we do with all the animals, Dad?" Sydney asked.

"Sell them. What else?"

"Not my monkey, you won't!"

"Not my chinchillas, either."

The Big Fellow took a little more time to give me his opinion. "You might have asked me," he said. "I never did say that I didn't like farming. It was just that I didn't like the way we were doing it here and now."

And as I listened to them scolding me for being so impetuous, I saw that it was not as I had thought at all. Sure, my family had protested the battle of the farm—but in the same way I had. And, like myself, they loved it just the same. I felt a little ashamed, and very very happy.

Next day I called on the real-estate man again. "Some of these bigger farms you have on your list," I said. "Some of these places that are just aching to be sold—how about showing me a few?"

So the animals will only go to a new place and not to new owners. Which is why I am out in the barn now writing this as I wait through the cold dark hours with a lantern under my knees, beside a sow approaching the brink of maternity.

Good-By, Little Boy!

"Don't worry about my banties or my kittens, Dad," he said as he threaded his arms through the straps of his new schoolbag. "I'll look after them as soon as I come home!"

I doubt if Barry has even asked himself whether he likes this idea of commencing school. He merely knows that he is six now, and that this day is as unalterably in the scheme of things as the seasons are. He is ready to go down the lane toward the bus, leaving behind all those brimming, boisterous months when this farm has been his.

These days of surpluses and merciless markets are desolate for a family farm, and I confess that I often wonder if there is any point in trying to hang on. I find myself haunted by the miles of fence which must be rebuilt, the spavined barns whose bones must be straightened, the undernourished acres which need fertilizer and fresh seed. I think of the mountain of bills piling up for the few things we have done and say to myself, "Maybe the economists aren't so cold-blooded after all when they tell strugglers like me that we ought to get off the land and leave it to the big farmer, or to a firm which will regard farming as a business and not a way of life."

But on this day, when my last son stands ready for school, I am thankful that I haven't yet surrendered our farm at Ormstown, Que. For as I look at this sun-peeled, adventure-scarred young lad I am now turning out to the confusion of the world beyond, I know that whatever its faults, and no matter how impractical it may be, the farm is sending our son off to school with a magnificent education already completed.

No prince could have been more privileged, or had more willing subjects to worship his footsteps, than Barry in the short years that his legs have been long enough and free enough to follow his heart about this place. I have seen him walking across the fields on a sparkling morning with a half dozen dogs, a flock of sheep and his tomcat all bunched behind him as if he were the Pied Piper of Hamelin. I have seen the colts follow him so lovingly that he would sometimes stop to wipe their breath from the back of his neck. Or perhaps they keep nibbling at his back pockets until he turns around and shakes a

Confident, yes, but he has also learned
to wonder. Is there any place,
Green asks, where a boy's questions
reach so far as they do on a farm?

warning fist at them. One colt sometimes asks forgiveness at such a scolding, for he will rear up as if to embrace Barry and place his front feet on the boy's shoulders.

I have watched the shine of Barry's eyes as he has cupped a day-old chick in his hands and pressed its yellow fluff against the red of his cheek. I have heard him crawling through the chaff and the webs and the dark of the stable loft to find where the cat has hidden her kittens. I have watched him go to sleep, nose to nose with his favorite dog, as if he were determined to keep love beside him all through the night.

Is there any better lesson for a youngster to learn than how to love and be loved? And what parents can be so proud as to believe that *their* love is all that a child needs, and that *they* are all he ever needs to love? But love is not the only lesson this impractical farm has taught my boy. He has learned confidence, too. Perhaps there is a connection: perhaps confidence comes from love.

We have a 2000-pound Belgian mare in our pasture. If you've never seen a 2000-pound draft mare it will be difficult for you to imagine how any hide could be so full of horse. One almost needs a stepladder to get onto her back. And yet one day when that young lad thought no one was looking, he climbed the pasture gate and swung himself aboard. The mare took him for a little walk through the field and came back to the same gate. She hadn't even a halter on. Barry climbed off as easily as he had mounted and didn't think the adventure worth reporting. I wouldn't have known about it had I not just happened to look out the window at the right time.

He learned that confidence at a very tender age. Once when he was only four, we brought our sheep into the stable to check some ear tags, and Barry stood in the passageway to watch. One stubborn old ewe bolted, made straight for that passageway, knocked him down and sailed over the top of him. If you know sheep, you know the rest. Every animal

in the flock had to do the same. Fifty head of sheep sailed over him while he lay there. Another child might have gone into hysterics. Not Barry. When the last sheep had followed the leader he merely got to his feet and said, "Dad, them damn sheep all got out on me!"

Confidence like that, you may tell me, will make him unbearably sure of himself someday. I, too, might be afraid of that, were it not for the fact that he has also learned to wonder. And for the farm boy there is no limit to wonder. The crimson pulse in the gills of a fish. The yellow bubble the tree toad makes in his throat when he gets ready to beep. The taillights of the fireflies he catches in the long grass at night and puts in a jar to take to bed with him.

And is there any place on God's earth where a

small boy's questions start so early and reach so far as they do on a farm? Why does a cow put her tongue up her nose, Daddy? Why doesn't a dog wag his tail up and down sometimes, Daddy? How high is the sky? You couldn't lift the world as long as you have to stand on it, could you, Daddy? Why does a car battery make a hole in your pants when you sit on it?

Some of you worry that so much freedom and so few boundaries will deprive a boy of the lesson of discipline. But my son's life hasn't been all poetry. At six he has learned the meaning of work. He knows what it is to sweat and itch with his brothers in the hay. He has had to fight brambles and black flies to pick his share of blackberries. He has had chickens to feed, sap to gather, grass to cut.

On occasion, he still has had time to get into mischief and had to be punished. I recall the winter night when no amount of reasoning or threat could dissuade Barry from tearing around the living room as if he were a runaway horse. "Stop it this instant," I commanded, "or I'll throw you out the front door!" That was an interesting promise, and the runaway horse ran around faster than ever. I warned him twice more, then carried him kicking and squalling through the front door and dropped him into the nearest snowbank.

The result was electrifying. To the rest of the family as well as to the boy I had suddenly become the lowest form of animal life. "You wouldn't dare do a thing like that in the city!" my wife told me next morning. "The neighbors would have the police after you!"

Probably quite true. But it was enough for me to remember how, after he had cried out his wrath at me, Barry had quietly climbed to my knee, hugged me as close as he could and gone to sleep. What was the use of trying to tell Mother that this was a man's quarrel and that it had to be settled a man's way?

And now, my boy, your days of being little are all but over. I imagine that your mother will cry a bit when that school bus goes down the road, but a

"Nothing richer than the love, the confidence and the trembling sense of wonder. . ."

father isn't supposed to do a thing like that. He can only scribble a few thoughts in the middle of the night when there is no one around.

You are leaving the rowdy world of men and animals to go to school. And some lovely lady who doesn't know which end of a cow gets up first will teach you to be proper, will clean up your language, will tell you what she insists is most important for a boy your age to know. As the years pass, you will go on to other ladies who will pursue this ennobling process further, adding facts, facts, facts.

Your teachers and your mother will think me a heretic for saying this, Barry, but I don't much care how high your pile of facts may climb. I only hope that in these necessary years of fact-piling, you lose none of that education which is already yours.

For any of the wise poets, any of the mighty preachers, any of the men who have set this world on fire with great thoughts, would tell you gladly if they could that there is nothing a man can learn in all his lifetime richer than the love, the confidence and the trembling sense of wonder which you take with you when you go down my lane today.

Saskatchewan's Fabulous Potash Pile

A fantastic deposit of a vital fertilizer ingredient
promises new hope in the crucial race between human fertility
and soil fertility. A report on an epic mining adventure

By Lawrence Elliott

Late in the summer of 1955, a Saskatchewan newspaper reported, hopefully, that drill rigs were searching for oil in the southeast corner of that wheat-growing province. The story ended on what seemed an afterthought: "Commonwealth Drilling will do some potash coring at the same time."

Daydreams of an oil rush were quickly dashed—Commonwealth hit not a single gusher. But the mile-long rock cores that were drilled out launched a 100-billion-dollar mineral boom. For there, packed in a 450-by-50 mile subterranean sweep, was disclosed the world's greatest deposit of potash—enough to fertilize all the earth's arable land for the next 500 years!

Half a dozen companies, racing to pry the glistening crystal from the ground, committed 150 million dollars to an epic five-year battle against this hemisphere's most perverse geology. Finally, in September 1962, having achieved near miracles of mining engineering, International Minerals & Chemical Corp. (Canada) Ltd., jubilantly sent the first of the five-billion-ton lode to market. The importance of this discovery to a world of inexorably contracting farmland is incalculable, for only by increasing the food yield per acre can man win the race between human fertility and soil fertility.

Potash, a generic term for soluble minerals containing potassium, is as old as time and yet thoroughly up-to-date. As the only economic source of potassium, it is vital in the production of batteries, soap, television tubes, vitamin pills, fire extinguishers, even astronauts' breathing gear. Yet all these needs together do not match its importance as a fertilizer ingredient. Without potash, plant leaves would wither, crops shrivel, and, in a terrifyingly short time, all life on this planet would end. Thus, nine of every ten tons mined in Saskatchewan will go back into the soil. Small wonder that news of the potash corings stirred agronomists and governments around the globe.

Existence of potash deposits in Saskatchewan had been known for a decade. Just after World War II,

geophysicists charting the province's substrata had caught electronic echoes that revealed a potash bed more than 3000 feet down. But veteran mining men took one look at the stratigraphic profile and reported that the ore was not recoverable: ten underground rivers and water-saturated shale and limestone, a hard-rock miner's nightmare, intervened layer on layer above the potash salts. Now, however, the corings—20 test holes at $50,000 a hole—outlined a deposit far richer than had been suspected, and indicated that persistence, daring and a free flow of risk capital might just succeed in prying the much-needed stuff loose.

In June 1957, the directors of International Minerals & Chemical Corp., a U. S. business, took a deep

breath and voted, "Go!" A Canadian subsidiary was formed. Men dragged great rigs over the bush to make trails. Soon, ground for Yarbo Shaft No. 1 was cleared on a barren plain seven miles northeast of the little farming community of Esterhazy.

It was to be North America's toughest mining venture. To stabilize the water-laden ground, a huge refrigeration plant was built. A minus-20-degree brine solution was then pumped down through 34 freeze holes. Not until 300 feet of the shaft area was frozen solid could any excavating begin. It took a whole year to freeze and line the first 1200 feet with concrete—but the system seemed to be working.

Then, in June 1958, drillers reached the "Blairmore," a 200-foot belt of fluid quicksand under explosive pressure. To penetrate it was to risk the pent-up fury of the ages: water would come tearing through a dime-size opening with the velocity of a bullet.

For nine hard-slogging months the miners tried grouting their way through—a technique for displacing underground water by forcing a cement mixture into every rock pore and fracture. When they had pumped enough cement into the blotter-like Blairmore to lay a sidewalk from Esterhazy to Toronto, a pinhole leak suddenly flared wide. Water surged to within 120 feet of the surface before the pumps regained control and the leak could be sealed off. Back to freezing they went, a tedious 19-month effort—which was suddenly all undone by a rush

A cast-iron shaft lining—called "tubbing"
—was used to seal off a 200-foot layer
of quicksand in the IMC potash mine.
The quicksand was solidified by freezing.

of water bursting through 29 fractures in a thawing steel pipe.

Then Alec Scott, a strapping Saskatchewan native who had dug mines on the far side of the world, was named shaft superintendent. He promptly flew to Germany to confer with engineers about a new procedure for driving through water-burdened strata. Called "tubbing," it entails sinking a vertical tunnel whose walls are lined with massive rings of cast iron. IMC's last chance for success and a long shot at best, it would cost the company another two million dollars. But the German firm of Haniel & Lueg thought the technique might work against the relentless Blairmore, and sent a team of experts to Saskatchewan to help Scott.

For a full year, while 836 four-ton iron segments were cast to microscopic tolerances, the entire Blairmore was frozen into a 50-foot-thick pillar of ice. In

October 1960, the first five feet were gingerly mucked out, and 11 great sections were muscled into a ring against the frozen sand of the shaft wall. And so it was to go: dig and tub, dig and tub, five feet at a time for six nerve-racking months. Not a single stick of explosive was used, for fear of rupturing that precariously fashioned tube of ice. Instead, men wearing rubber suits against the minus-34-degree cold and working six-hour shifts around the clock used pavement-breakers to drill inch by inch into the heart of the pressure-pent Blairmore.

By now all of Esterhazy was holding its breath. Housewives out marketing stopped at the end of Main Street to study the huge, thermometer-like marker indicating the current depth of the shaft. The Kinsmen Club offered a $100 prize to the person who came closest to guessing the moment potash would be reached. "It was *our* mine now,"

The long-awaited big moment
came just before midnight
June 8, 1962. All Esterhazy,
"The Town with a City in its
Future," was as excited
as the ecstatic weekly *Miner*.

Two miners hold aloft a chunk of potash
to signal completion of a 3150-foot,
$10 million shaft which took
more than three years to complete.

said schoolteacher Jean Pask. "And the darn Blair-more was *our* problem."

The men finally drove down to the bottom of the Blairmore and 50 feet into the limestone below, tubbing all the way, linking the segments with 17,000 giant bolts. For the first time in history, the Blairmore was buttoned up, beaten.

It took five more months to grout the Three Forks strata and the Souris River, a rampant underground stream. Then, just before midnight of June 8, 1962, a handful of drillers broke through a layer of lime-stone 3132 feet beneath the silent prairie, snatched up fistfuls of glittering, rust-colored rock and wildly pounded one another's backs. After five heart-breaking years, IMC had a shaft down to the potash.

"WOWIE POTASH" headlined *The Esterhazy*

Miner, reflecting the jubilation of the entire area. From the company to each of 69 babies born in Saskatchewan that momentous day went a share of IMC stock. Value: $39. To Miss Winnie Piercy, Esterhazy's assistant postmistress, who had never been near the mine but had managed to outguess the experts, went the $100 Kinsmen Club prize. And to everyone in the 12 towns within the 700 square miles officially proclaimed as "Potashville" went some small sense of achievement: sprouting every-where were big red-and-white buttons with the triumphant tidings, "We Did It!"

It changed Saskatchewan. Gradually diversifying after years of being shackled to a beef-and-wheat economy, the province all at once had a huge new industry—and it has kept on growing. IMC now has two mines worth some $4,800,000 a year in taxes and royalties alone. More, IMC's dramatic success sparked the flagging hopes of others: eight more companies are now developing their holdings. Four mines are open, six others projected. As for Canada, from the IMC mines alone, the 100-billion-dollar potash pile contributes 60 million dollars a year

261

Three quarters of a mile underground,
a 52-ton "continuous miner," one of 13
in IMC's Esterhazy mine, backs off to take
another bite of potash ore. Esterhazy
sends 3½ million tons to market each year.

toward squaring up the nation's balance of trade, and adds another 45 million dollars in sorely needed railroad revenues.

But nowhere have the gains of the great potash strike been more dramatically reflected than in the once-drowsing rural crossroads of Esterhazy. IMC's two mines now employ 4000 persons, with a $9 million annual payroll. Esterhazy's population, 750 when the mine site was cleared, now is five times that. Its young people, once forced elsewhere to find work, now have opportunity at home.

One day I rode down the hoist into the mine with Alec Scott. We dropped at a stomach-fretting 22 miles an hour (the ore itself comes up twice as fast), whizzing past the iron tubbing that fends off the cantankerous Blairmore. When we reached bottom, our headlamps cast thin shafts of light out into one of the seemingly endless "drifts"—22-foot-wide tunnels hewn from the translucent, weirdly beautiful crystal ore. Alongside us clanked a conveyor belt, carrying ore to the shaft base.

We hitched a ride on a rubber-tired diesel truck

to a distant mine face. Here a monstrous, clawing 52-ton "continuous miner" bit into the glistening wall of ore in five-ton gulps, its massive rotating heads cutting a seven-foot circle with every pass, chewing out 19 inches a minute and throwing powder, chunk and boulder back into a shuttle truck, from which it would be loaded onto a conveyor belt. From the IMC mines these $250,000 continuous miners now send 3½ million tons of potash to market each year.

We followed a load of ore to the mill. In less than an hour, it was crushed, dumped into a slurry where the basic potash was separated from the salts, dried, screened and transported to one of four giant storage bins. It would not be there long: so intense is the worldwide demand for potash that IMC's people work three shifts around the clock, and 140 loaded freight cars leave every day.

"This is a particularly satisfying product to sell," IMC's president Thomas M. Ware said to me. "It can mean the end of hunger on this earth." That's not mere sales talk. From the dawn of civilization, crop failures have doomed men to starvation. Hunger has often been the final goad to violence and rebellion. And no country ever attained the standards of an industrialized society while the bulk of its men and women were bound to the desperate daily struggle to produce food.

As the world's greatest source of a vital fertilizer ingredient that can help to increase the yield of a mineral-starved acre many times over, Saskatchewan's potash pile is thus more than just an exciting and profitable discovery. It is a prime new weapon in the fight for abundance and human security.

Stress - A Factor in All Disease?

A Montreal doctor's fundamental research may add years to the human life span

By J. D. Ratcliff

The work of a Canadian researcher has opened dazzling vistas in medical science. It indicates there may be a common factor in almost all disease, whether it be a heart attack, a mild case of asthma or just the feeling of "being sick." Dr. Hans Selye of Montreal believes the factor is chemical imbalance in the body—*caused by stress.*

"If future events prove this concept correct," said *The Journal of the American Medical Association,* "it will be one of the most significant medical advances of this century." *The Lancet,* a leading British medical journal, agreed.

Chemical balance within the body is governed mainly by three tiny glands: the pituitary, which nestles under the brain, and the two adrenals, which sit astride the kidneys. All of them together weigh only about a third of an ounce, yet their unbelievably potent hormones have a huge influence on vital body functions. According to Selye's theory, their principal job is to adapt the body to all kinds of stress.

If you are chilled, hormones constrict the arteries and raise blood pressure, thereby providing greater warmth. When bacteria invade the body the glands

Hans Selye, a native of Austria,
came to North America on
a Rockefeller fellowship. In 1945
he became head of the Institute
of Experimental Medicine and Surgery
at the University of Montreal.

provide hormones to produce inflammation, which walls off infection. In case of severe injury they hasten the clotting of blood, lower blood pressure to control hemorrhage, increase blood sugar to provide quick energy, decrease sensitivity to pain. In sum, it is the task of the pituitary and adrenal hormones to combat stress and fight off any threat to the body's welfare.

It is Selye's belief that in a hurry-up world we are subjecting ourselves to too many stresses. We hurry constantly and worry incessantly. The businessman drives himself at his office all day, then worries most of the night. The housewife tries to run her home, maintain a social life, and participate in community activities—and at bedtime is so jangled that she needs a sleeping pill.

Glands attempt to adjust to the constant demands of stress. They pour out excess hormones to keep the body going. For a while they succeed. But in the end the defense mechanism itself breaks down. Arteries harden, blood pressure rises, heart disease or peptic ulcers develop, arthritis strikes. These and other diseases, according to Selye, are all part of the stress picture.

"The *apparent* cause of illness," says Selye, "is often an infection, an intoxication, nervous exhaustion or merely old age. But actually a breakdown of the hormonal-adaptation mechanism appears to be the most common ultimate cause of death." His study of this mechanism, via widespread experiments with animals, set the stage for his far-reaching discoveries.

Austrian-born of a family that has produced doctors for four generations, Hans Selye received his M.D. and Ph.D. from the German University of Prague. Later, when a Rockefeller fellowship brought him to North America, he studied at Johns Hopkins University in Baltimore and McGill University in Montreal. Since 1945 he has headed the University of Montreal's Institute of Experimental Medicine and Surgery.

As a medical student he pestered starchy German professors who loved to talk about specific diseases with specific causes, such as pneumonia and the microbe which produces it. "What about *nonspecific* disease?" Selye kept asking. "What about the feeling of just being sick?"

Professors had little patience with such nonsense. But Selye kept at them. Almost all diseases have certain common symptoms: pallor, loss of appetite, loss of weight, for example. "Don't these common symptoms *mean* anything?" he asked. "Don't bother with such things," he was told.

Selye did bother. In 1936, when he was studying at McGill, two female sex hormones were known. Selye thought he was on the point of discovering a third. To test the effects of a new extract he had produced, he shot it into female rats whose ovaries had been removed. He expected autopsy to show changes in the animals' sexual apparatus. Instead, the sight which awaited him was utterly baffling: his rats' adrenal glands were bloated to three times their normal size; their lymphatic systems had undergone degeneration; stomachs and intestinal tracts were dotted with ulcers.

Was it toxic material in his chemical juice that was wrecking the insides of the rats? To check, he shot some formaldehyde into a rat. A post mortem showed exactly the same picture: swollen adrenals, ulcers, wrecked lymphatic system. Clearly he was on a false trail in the search for a new hormone.

Then a momentous thought occurred: Would other things besides formaldehyde and his hormone juice wreck rats' insides?

He put caged animals on his windswept laboratory roof. They survived the winter cold for long periods but finally suffered the same kind of internal damage as the others. Next, he wore rats out in motor-driven revolving cages. The same effects occurred again. It seemed that *any* stress to which he subjected the animals produced the same symptoms: bloated adrenals, ulcers, decayed lymphatic system.

Selye thought back to his student days in Prague. What he was now looking at was nonspecific disease—not disease of a single organ, produced by a single factor. Almost any stress seemed to cause the conditions. Stress—could that be the key to everything?

In human beings there were no very good explanations of *why* heart disease strikes millions, *why* hypertension takes such a lethal toll, *why* arthritis and rheumatic fever wreak their devastations. Was it possible that all these things were mainly expressions, end results, of stress? Could it be that they resulted from hormonal imbalance within the body? It looked as if this might well be the case.

Sir Frederick Banting, the brooding genius who gave the world insulin, was visiting McGill. Selye told him about his experiments and his suspicions that stress might be the cause of many deadly illnesses. Banting listened attentively. "You may have something big," he said. "You will need money to pursue it. I believe I can get you a grant."

The grant came through: $500! It wasn't much, but Selye went ahead with his search, a lone man in a cubbyhole laboratory—one pioneer against traditional medical thinking with its emphasis on specific disease.

The first problem was to find why stress did such dreadful things to rats. Selye thought the pituitary

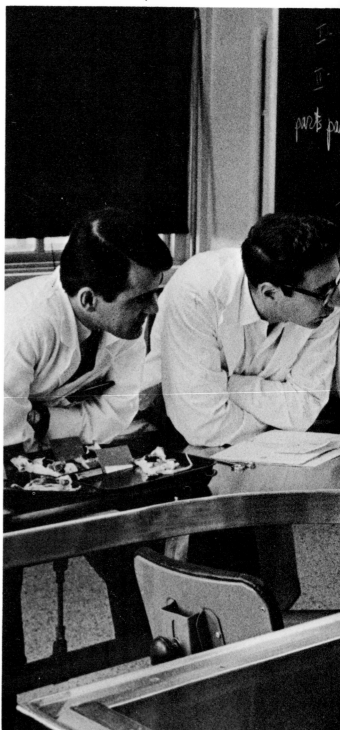

Once he worked alone in a tiny laboratory, with a grant of only $500, bucking traditional medical thinking. Now Dr. Selye and his stress theory are world-famous. About 5000 research papers on stress are published each year.

Heart attack, mild asthma or "just under the weather"—
the stress of modern hurry-hurry-hurry may be
a common factor in all disease, Dr. Selye believes.

might be responsible. He devised an exquisite technique for removing the gland with a device of his own invention. Then he subjected the pituitary-less animals to cold, heat, fatigue, noise, poisons. But with the pituitary gone the internal wreckage was even greater!

Next he removed adrenals but left the pituitary, and applied similar stresses. This time damage within the animals was again massive. So the adrenals, too, played a part in what Selye was beginning to call "the stress syndrome."

Gradually the whole picture began to unfold. When an animal was subjected to stress there was an alarm reaction. The pituitary poured out hormones which stimulated the adrenals to pour out others. If stresses continued, the alarm reaction was followed by a period of adaptation during which the animal learned to live with its stress. Eventually, however, the defense mechanisms wore out, the animals sickened and died.

Autopsy showed some striking symptoms. Generally, arteries were thickened and hardened, hearts and kidneys severely damaged. Some had arthritis-like diseases; others had diseases similar to rheumatic fever. In sum, they looked exactly like human victims of heart and circulatory disorders. Evidently the wreckage had been caused by the excess hormones produced by the pituitary and adrenal glands as an emergency defense against stresses applied outside the body.

There were, clearly, some remarkable parallels between what Selye had observed in his rats and what all of us have noted in ourselves. Under stress of worry, overwork, fatigue, chronic infections, many of us seem to get along well enough—for a time. Then the thin, quiet type, who keeps his worries bottled up within himself, becomes the victim of high blood pressure. The florid, hard-driving plant manager has his coronary. The always-tired, always-overworked housewife may become diabetic.

Selye wanted to check whether the wreckage he observed in his rats was caused or combatted by excess hormone production. Could similar wreckage be caused by *injecting* excess hormone or would it throw the body out of chemical balance and bring on disease?

He tries too hard, goes too fast,
pushes himself all day long—
and at home he worries most of the night.
Arteries, blood pressure or heart
are going to suffer sooner or later.

Stress strikes people of all ages,
under all circumstances, in peace
and war. These are Canadian airmen
soon after operations against the enemy.

The pituitary gland secretes a number of hormones which have specific purposes. Only one of them seemed likely to play a major role in the stress problem: STH (somatotrophic hormone), which is responsible for the body's growth. The adrenals produce about 30 hormones, but here again only one appeared a likely candidate: desoxycorticosterone—DCA for short.

To rats Selye administered walloping shots of DCA. In a short time they developed heart and kidney disease and high blood pressure. Their joints became swollen, inflamed, sensitive. With a naturally secreted bodily substance, Selye had produced some of the worst diseases with which man has to contend. Apparently, depending upon conditions, the stress hormones could either prevent or produce disease.

The next step was to see what STH would do. When given in excess it produced much the same diseases: a sickness like rheumatic fever, heart and artery disease, and diabetes. Now he was on the way! Selye reported these results to *The Journal of the American Medical Association.*

It was obvious that if STH and DCA could produce a host of diseases there must be other hormones which would neutralize them and counteract their effects. Otherwise we would all have arthritis, diabetes and heart and kidney disease. Thus Selye's work foreshadowed ACTH and cortisone five years before their actual discovery.

When cortisone and ACTH were announced in 1949 most physicians were astounded by their wide range of activity. How, they asked, could a single medicine such as cortisone be effective on a whole spectrum of apparently unrelated diseases—gout, asthma, skin ailments, arthritis, muscular diseases, eye diseases? To Selye the answer seemed clear

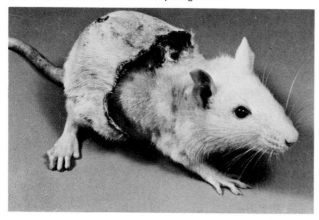

enough: the same types of diseases had been induced experimentally in his rats by excess DCA or excess STH. All ACTH and cortisone did was restore chemical balance; when it was restored, disease magically melted away.

Selye's work paved the way for other striking medical advances—in malignant hypertension, for example, where death is usually due to failure of an overworked heart, or to apoplexy caused by a burst blood vessel in the brain. Efforts to control malignant hypertension had a record of failure: doctors simply put patients to bed, told them to take it easy —and in a few months the patients were dead. But if the adrenals played a key role in hypertension, surgeons asked, why not remove them? Afterward, patients could be kept alive with cortisone, the most important of adrenal hormones.

The operation has been tried with eye-opening results on a few patients, most of whom were considered to be in the final months of life. About 75 percent survived the drastic surgery, and in almost all survivors sky-high blood pressures dropped to normal.

The interest aroused by Selye's stress concept is indicated by the fact that about 5000 research papers are published each year on the subject. More material evidence of acceptance comes from the financial support being given his research team, which now numbers 45, by foundations, individuals, pharma-ceutical firms and the Canadian and U. S. governments.

What lessons are to be drawn from Selye's discoveries? How can one avoid the stresses that so often lead to disaster?

It is simple to advise the hard-driver to take it easy, the worrier to let up—but the advice is difficult to follow. Everyone can be alerted, however, to the fact that stress is a killer—perhaps the greatest of all killers. As this realization grows we can take steps to minimize it. The businessman can find relaxing hobbies which will help him slow down. The housewife can learn that it might be more important to take a nap than to launder the guest-room curtains. We can all master any lesson once we know our lives are at stake.

If Selye's concept proves true, it is possible to foresee a day when people may get periodic checks of chemical balance just as they now get checks of metabolism, blood pressure and urine. If imbalance is discovered, perhaps the administration of hormones and other substances will restore the body to normal. When that day arrives Selye sees no reason why our life span shouldn't be upped to 100 years or more.

"The value of a theory," wrote the *British Medical Journal,* "lies in its capacity to weld together isolated facts, to stimulate research. No theory in living memory has possessed these virtues to a greater extent."

Jenny Butchart's Garden of Wonders

In an ugly old quarry near Victoria,
she created a bower of beauty
that enchants 500,000 visitors a year

By David MacDonald

Strolling at night in the Butchart Gardens near Victoria, B.C., you suddenly come to the edge of a cliff—and a breathtaking scene. Fifty feet below, in a vast bowl hewn out of solid rock, thousands of flowering plants, trees and shrubs create a wonderland of color, from pale pinks and purples to bright reds and blues—all framed in the soft glow of a hundred hidden lamps. A footpath leads you down and across emerald lawns, in shadow and light, past towering arbor-vitae to a lake banked in marigold. From the far rim of the bowl, hung with ivy, a silver waterfall glides into a pool where fountains trace lacy designs in the dark. The total effect is enchanting. "I've *seen* it," remarked one tourist, "but I still can't *believe* it!"

For it *is* incredible. Acclaimed as one of the world's most beautiful gardens, it was planted in what was actually an ugly place—by a woman who hardly knew a dahlia from a daisy.

Jenny Butchart was the wife of an Ontario cement manufacturer who moved west in 1904 to open a limestone quarry outside Victoria. Close to his digging site, Robert Butchart built a rambling mansion.

Within five years the quarry petered out, leaving a gaping mudhole beside their home. Jenny hated it. At 41, she was a plump, kindly little woman with a keen eye for beauty. To her, the old quarry was "a silent ghastly tomb"—so depressing that one day, staring into it, she burst into tears.

It was then that she caught a vision of what could be. "Why not put flowers there?" she urged her husband that night. "We've made it so ugly. Now let's try to make it beautiful."

"All right," Bob Butchart said. "You plant and I'll pay."

Over the next five years, while he poured his profits back into the quarry, Jenny transformed it into a glorious sunken garden. As word got round, people came to look—and the Butcharts shared their garden with all. They called their estate Benvenuto (Italian for "Welcome") and kept it open to the public all their lives. "The flowers are fleet-

273

ing," Jenny said once, "so people should enjoy them."

Many millions have done so. Today, though Jenny and her husband are gone, her flowers still rank among Canada's main tourist attractions. Now owned by their grandson, a former Naval officer named Ian Ross, the Butchart Gardens are visited by more than 500,000 people a year.

There is a lot to see. Jenny Butchart turned 30 of Benvenuto's 137 acres into four strikingly different gardens. There's an exquisite English rose garden, a formal Italian garden wrapped in hedges as finely sculptured as its Florentine statues, a Japanese garden with dwarf maples and rhododendrons, flowering cherries and a dainty teahouse nestling against a forest of giant Douglas firs. But most arresting of all is the four-acre sunken garden, Jenny's favorite. Her grandson calls it Topsy, because "it just growed."

It didn't, of course. It took years of painstaking work, hundreds of thousands of dollars and millions of plants to turn the old limepit into a beauty spot. Though her husband brought in laborers to help— including one Chinese who kept at it for 50 years —Jenny worked harder than any of them. She began by combing the countryside for good topsoil. As tons of rich loam were carted in, she spread it over the quarry floor. Then, clad in a muddy dress and gum boots, Jenny laid out flower-beds, seeded grass, transplanted saplings and forest ferns.

Gradually, with sweet peas and rambler roses that a friend gave her, the drab, gray quarry brightened. Jenny listened to experts in formal landscaping— then went her own informal way. For a novice gardener, she had a born artist's feeling for color, texture and form. By instinct, before a bud bloomed, she could see beauty in the contrast between rugged rockery and velvet lawns, between majestic evergreens and delicate blossoms like gypsophila and alyssum—names she didn't even know yet. And

Jenny Butchart's gardens,
"the handiwork of a woman who longed
for beauty in the wilderness,"
attract a half million visitors
each year. Mrs. Butchart's
transformation of an ugly quarry
was the start of Victoria's tourist trade.
Now the gardens have a full-time staff
of 50, among them two dozen gardeners.

what she imagined—a placid pool, a begonia bower
—Jenny made real.

Once, for example, she hit on the idea of gay
flowers cascading down the walls of the pit, so sheer
that no one could climb them. "Fine," said Bob
Butchart, "but how?" Next day Jenny hung over the
abyss in a bosun's chair, tucking alpines and ivy into
cracks and ledges.

Each winter, when her gardening stopped, Jenny's
husband took her abroad to look for more flowers.
She gathered rare species of plants, seeds and bulbs
from France, Holland, Italy, Spain, Alaska and the
Orient. On one trip the Butcharts were received by
the Emperor of Japan, who was so impressed with
Jenny and her undertaking that he later sent her
three cherry trees from his palace grounds.

On another occasion Jenny showed her flowers to
a British explorer, Frederick Marshman Bailey. "I

know one you haven't got," he said, "a poppylike herb named after me." She smiled and led him to a bed of sky-blue *Meconopsis Baileyi*. "Why that's impossible!" Bailey exclaimed. "I just discovered them myself, in Tibet." True enough. But he'd sent one plant to Edinburgh, where Jenny was the first to get seeds from it.

The rarest thing in her garden, however, was Jenny herself. Gracious, warm and unassuming, she was never too busy to take people around, even after Benvenuto's trickle of visitors grew to a torrent. When people didn't recognize her, Jenny enjoyed it all the more. Once, taken for a maid, she showed tourists through her home and was offered a tip. "No, thanks," she replied. "Old Mrs. Butchart doesn't let us accept money."

But there was no mistaking Robert Butchart. Thin and slightly stooped, he was always impeccably turned out in business suit and high starched collar. Though he knew little about flowers, he shared Jenny's enthusiasm for people. Together they held yearly outings for the aged and the poor at Benvenuto, where Jenny guided blind people through her gardens and described blooms they could only smell.

To make it easier for visitors to get there, Butchart paved the rutty mile-long side road to Benvenuto and lined it with 556 Japanese cherry trees—a glorious sight in spring. Family picnics were encouraged, with hot water and cups supplied at the Butcharts' kitchen door. A pond was stocked with goldfish, trained to eat out of tourists' hands, and tame peacocks strutted freely about the grounds. There wasn't a "Do Not" warning anywhere, although a diplomatic sign hung on one tree to protect the rest: "Please carve initials here."

The gardens, a public benefaction that cost the Butcharts a private fortune, were the start of Victoria's flourishing tourist trade. Yet in 1939, when they offered to sell Benvenuto *for one dollar,* neither the city nor the provincial government would pay for its upkeep. So they deeded it to grandson Ian Ross, a college student who was about to join the Canadian Navy. Even after moving into Victoria, where Robert died in 1943 at the age of 86, Jenny paid a skeleton staff to keep her gardens open to the public.

When Jenny herself died in 1950, at 82, her ashes, like her husband's, were cast on the waters of Tod Inlet, beside the gardens that still remain as their living monument.

By then, Ian Ross had come back to take over at Benvenuto, which had faded for lack of care during the war years. A graduate of law and the Battle of the Atlantic, Ross knew next to nothing about flowers, but he learned fast. And with experienced help from Dutch, English, Portuguese and Polish immigrants, he soon restored the gardens' former glory.

Only recently, however, has he pulled Benvenuto out of the red. "My grandmother never wanted anyone *paying* to see her gardens," he says. "But that has been the only way to preserve them." With a staff of 150 needed in peak months, there's now a small charge in spring and summer. "We make a small profit now," Ross says, "and plow it right back into the ground." Ross added highly effective touches of his own. In 1953, he put in four miles of underground wiring for an illumination system that has made Benvenuto as popular by night as by day—and even more lovely. In the sunken garden, Ross also installed a fountain that leaps 80 feet in the air and is illuminated at night. With his Chicago-born wife, Ann-Lee, he launched a series of free variety shows and Victoria Symphony sunset concerts, attended by crowds of 6000 and more.

To keep his showplace at its best, Ross employs a full-time staff of 50, headed by a retired RCMP sergeant named Walter Dodsworth. Two dozen gardeners produce flowers for all seasons—20,000 tulips in spring, beds of blazing red salvia in the fall—so that the gardens are an ever-changing kaleidoscope of color.

Each winter seeds are packaged for sale in the gardens' souvenir shop. Also sold there are huge amounts of film—Benvenuto is one of the most photographed spots on the continent—along with color slides, ceramics, flowered bone china and other mementos of generally high quality. "Mr. Ross

"The flowers are fleeting," Mrs. Butchart once said, "so people should enjoy them."

won't ever let this place become a tourist trap," said Mrs. Mabel Shiner, who went to work there in 1933. "Why, he once threw away hundreds of perfectly good postcards—just because they showed a willow tree that isn't here any more!"

In summer, Benvenuto's parking lot is jammed (U. S. license plates predominate) and 20 to 30 tour buses arrive each day. For many years to come, people likely will continue to visit and admire what the Victoria *Daily Colonist* called "the handiwork of a woman who longed for beauty in the wilderness."

A Great Canadian Art

By Claude Mélançon
author and naturalist

Canada's Pacific Coast Indians, inspired by an abundant mythology, created a unique art, an expression of the highest primitive culture on our soil. But its *raison d'être* was a social organization founded on devotion to honors and wealth. And the white man, by forcing profound changes on the customs of the coast tribes, dried out their artistic soul. Now the production of their works of art has stopped.

Coast artists were mainly sculptors. They expressed themselves in totem poles of the majestic cedar indigenous to their lovely homeland. But they also used argilite, animal horns, sea shells and the hair of wild goats. No matter what the material, one marvels at the extraordinary skill with which the abstract tale is told.

Totem poles, incidentally, were not idols. Princely families boasting the grizzly, killer whale or wolf as helper and adviser—when not claiming kinship with the Thunderbird or the Great Raven—wanted to advertise their good fortune. So a bear or whale or wolf totem pole was both a family coat of arms and a story about imaginary spirits and real-life animals.

But the totem pole alone does not illustrate the immense talent of these primitive Indian artists. Their canoes, carved from giant cedar trunks; their spoons, chiseled from the horns of wild sheep; their wooden dishes and the blankets woven by the Indian women . . . these are true masterpieces.

Canadian artists need not, as Picasso did, study primitive art in West Africa. They can find inspiration in an esthetic form which is part and parcel of their national inheritance.

The bold features (top left) in a relatively recent totem pole contrast with the "old man" look of a weather-worn sculpture (top right) carved more than 160 years ago. Many totems dating to 1800 still stand on Anthony Island in the Queen Charlotte group off the British Columbia coast. Less well preserved than newer totem poles (center and lower right), they are nonetheless of great artistic importance.

Metro: Toronto's Answer to Urban Sprawl

The concept of municipal government that saved one great city from chaos offers hope to other metropolitan centers heading for disaster

By James Nathan Miller

Toronto, with a population close to 2,000,000, is the 13th largest metropolis in North America and world-famous as a demonstration of how the problems of undisciplined urban sprawl can be cured. Its government is a federation of the central city and its suburbs. Together, they provide certain key services through a metropolis-wide unit. Toronto's had it since 1954.

Before that the city was in bad shape. "Toronto isn't a city," wrote *Maclean's* in 1951, "but 13 cities piled haphazardly on top of each other like a child's stack of wooden blocks." Its separate local governments faced financial disaster. Some suburban municipalities had to pay such high interest rates for municipal bonds—5¾ percent compared to the City of Toronto's low of 3 percent—that their borrowing ability was severely impaired.

The inadequacy of sewers was highly dangerous, and the water supply was so limited that in some neighborhoods there was no tap water at all on summer afternoons. Transportation outside the city limits was chaos, with 30 disconnected transit lines. Each municipality built roads with little or no thought to the problems it might be creating in adjoining areas. Summed up *Maclean's*, "Toronto is a particularly hideous illustration of all that can be bad about urban living."

In 1953 Toronto was so close to a true breakdown of many of its governmental services that drastic action was imperative. Some kind of metropolis-wide government was needed—but the various governments couldn't agree on *what* kind. The City of Toronto wanted to expand its 35-square-mile area to encompass the whole 241-square-mile region. The suburban governments were strongly opposed to such a "takeover." Finally, the Province of Ontario stepped in and dictated a solution: a federation of governments. "If this had not been done," says Lorne Cumming, chairman of the Ontario Municipal Board when it drew up the new government, "they might still be arguing."

First, Ontario established a new 241-square-mile

Arterial roads like the Don Valley Parkway
are metropolitan highways
under Toronto's trail-blazing system
of municipal government. One area-wide
authority administers services which
used to be handled—much less adequately—
by 13 individual municipalities.

Not only transportation
but also sewage, water
and land-use planning
are *metropolitan* concerns,
dealt with since 1954
on a metropolitan basis.

Municipality of Metropolitan Toronto, with all the functions that the old governments were incapable of performing adequately: police, water, sewage, regional roads, transportation, finances, regional parks, land-use planning. Second, the new plan let the old governments keep their local councils, school boards, zoning committees, road crews, building inspectors, fire departments, garbage trucks. Local citizens continued to pay only a single tax—to their old municipal governments, which then passed on a portion to the metropolitan government.

"Metro," as it's called, took over on January 1,

1954. Since then, said Prof. Daniel Grant of Vanderbilt University, who studied the federation under Ford Foundation auspices, "it has accomplished an amazing number of things that would have been impossible under the old system." Indeed, Metro almost transformed Toronto physically. Yet the taxes there rose no faster than in other Canadian and U.S. cities.

For instance, it made possible the world's only metropolis-wide system of traffic control. Buried at several hundred spots in the streets of the metropolitan area are magnetic vehicle detectors that feed information on traffic density and speed into a cen-

One of the biggest metropolitan areas in North America, Toronto was sprawling its way to chaos when Metro was introduced in 1954. Now Metro is world-famous as proof that big-city problems *can* be resolved.

tral computer in the old city hall. By measuring traffic far out on the suburban feeder roads, the system can meter cars onto the arterial highways. For rush-hour commuters, it has eliminated up to two thirds of the traffic-light stops they formerly had to make.

The system cost $5 million. But the basic fact about it is that under the old governmental setup this kind of central control would have been financially, bureaucratically and legally impossible to install.

As soon as Metro was authorized to ignore the intermunicipal boundaries, it began enlarging its

sewage-treatment plants and running giant trunk sewers to every municipality in the area. Few houses today depend on septic tanks, and no new house can be built without a sewer connection. The water problem has been solved with a $60-million building program of reservoirs, purification plants and more than 100 miles of mains that have eliminated the need for private wells.

When one of the local governments wants to borrow, it is no longer forced by its limited tax base to pay a high interest rate. Metro does the borrowing for the municipalities, lumping all local borrowing into one big package backed by the full credit of the

Local municipalities retain
many boards, committees and services
—and still levy taxes, part of which
is passed along to the Metro government.

Detectors buried in Toronto streets
feed data to this computer.
It controls signal lights
and helps speed traffic.

entire metropolitan area. The resulting lower interest rate means savings of millions of dollars. Metro has top municipal credit rating among investors.

The routes, schedules and fares of every bus, streetcar and subway train are part of a single interlocking scheme, regarded as one of the world's finest municipal transportation systems. Arterial roads are spliced together into continuous metropolitan highways; a cross-Metro trip that used to take two hours can be made in 30 minutes.

Here are the main lessons that metropolitan areas can learn from Toronto:

Certain municipal services—transportation, sewage, water, land-use planning—can not be ade-quately performed on an every-government-for-itself basis. These services must be provided by an area-wide government, and this can be done without gobbling up all the local governments. But *some* local governments will have to go. Generally, the experts consider a municipal population of 50,000 about the minimum desirable. In 1966, Toronto found that seven of its 13 municipalities were so small—ranging in population from 8000 to 20,000—that they simply couldn't play in the same league with the others, which ranged from 93,000 to 692,000. So the seven small ones merged into the bigger ones. Today Metro consists of six efficiently sized municipalities: the city and five boroughs.

Most important, to get metropolitan reform, leadership is needed at a higher governmental level. The crucial factor in Toronto's success was that the Province of Ontario forced the issue. Without this vital act of political leadership there would be no Metro today.

Canada's Game Scores Abroad

From Los Angeles to Leningrad, from Germany to Japan,
our lusty but lovely national sport is exciting millions of new fans

By David MacDonald

During a National Hockey League game in Montreal in 1965, Gordie Howe of the Detroit Red Wings went gliding down the ice with long, flowing strides and took a quick pass in front of the Canadiens' nets. As goalie "Gump" Worsley came sprawling out to block him, the 200-pound six-footer spun delicately on his skates, drew back his stick and drove the puck home with a whoop of joy. It was Howe's 600th goal in NHL competition—a previously "impossible" record—and such a thrilling moment that even Montreal's 15,000 wildly partisan fans were moved to cheer the Detroit superstar.

Two minutes later, however, they were scream-ing for his scalp. For when a Canadien slammed him into the rinkside boards, Howe lashed back with an elbow and broke the rude chap's cheekbone. "It may seem crazy," as Howe had reflected once before, after belting another player into hospital with an awful but lawful body check, "yet that's what I'm paid to do."

Crazy or not, the lusty yet lovely game he plays so well is now the world's fastest-growing team sport, a rousing spectacle of speed and color that is exciting crowds from Los Angeles to Leningrad.

Indeed, as NHL pros wage it, no contest outside the bullring provides such a stirring, improbable

Montreal Canadiens' big Jean Béliveau—
"all grace and Gallic élan," writes
David MacDonald—cuts around
Detroit defenseman Gary Bergman
and beats goalie Roger Crozier. Part
of the puck can be seen
on the ice near the right-hand goalpost.

blend of beauty and brutality. Montreal's Jean Béliveau is all grace and Gallic élan, a swooping skater whose crisscross passing plays dazzle the eye. Chicago's explosive Bobby Hull rockets around so fast (44 feet per second) and shoots so furiously (120 m.p.h.) that the Chicago *Tribune* has called him "the most exciting athlete in sports today." When Toronto goalie Johnny Bower does the splits, into a swirl of oncoming blades, he's a nerveless Nureyev. And slam-bang bruisers like Boston's Ted Green and New York's Arnie Brown bring fans to their feet by bouncing opponents on their rears.

Refined from the ancient European game of bandy, a formless free-for-all that 19th century Canadians took up to ward off the winter cold, ice hockey has become one of the hottest commodities in North American professional sport. According to New York *Times* columnist Arthur Daley, the National Hockey League is "the most productive moneymaker in the entire history of athletics." The game itself has been likened to "a combination of soccer, golf, prizefighting and tong war."

Yet hockey is uniquely itself. "There is no game that moves so swiftly, so continuously and so poetically," author Paul Gallico once noted. "It is played by a group of the most violent and reckless men on the face of the globe."

"Hockey's great appeal to spectators," says Dr. John Lohrenz, a Montreal psychoanalyst who used to coach the game, "is the thrill of speed and danger, without the risk."

Thus, while NHL team-owners often deplore rough play and fisticuffs, by *other* teams, they know better. "If we don't stamp out that sort of thing," a Toronto official mused after one rousing brawl, "we'll have to print more tickets."

Indeed, such is the clamor for hockey's thrills and spills that the NHL extended franchises to six major U.S. cities—at $2,000,000 a throw—and became a 12-team league in 1967.

From Canada, where hockey is a national mania, the game has spread to 30-odd lands—even to

Great names in Canada's great national sport:
left to right—Jean Béliveau, Bobby Orr,
Allan Stanley, Henri Richard, Johnny Bower.

Superstar Gordie Howe of Detroit,
nearing the end of a great career,
seems to have all the fire and stamina
of a rookie as he fights for the puck
along the boards in a Red Wing game
with the Toronto Maple Leafs.

Mexico and Japan—and won millions of avid new fans.

In 1946, Russia had no hockey players; today she boasts 500,000, and crowds of 50,000 often pack Moscow's huge open-air rink at −30°. Second only to soccer in popularity in Sweden, hockey has become *the* game in Czechoslovakia and Finland. For the World Amateur Hockey Tournament in Yugoslavia in 1966, most of the important matches were sold out the year before. "It's a sign of our times," remarked Helge Berglund, head of the Swedish Hockey Federation. "People want things to happen fast."

Hockey's playing surface, 200 x 85 feet of glare ice, is the fastest in sport. The players are chosen for their ability to skate swiftly and shoot hard; to improvise instant ploys and, insofar as a lenient rule-book allows, to clobber the other guys. When two such teams square off, each intent on firing the puck into the other's goal, the action is bound to be exciting for all concerned. "During a hockey game," runs one maxim, "the only sane person in the rink is the referee."

Perhaps so. For when otherwise normal people play the sport, or merely watch it, strange things happen. In a New York amateur league, whose four teams compete for the sheer love of it, a truck driver had a stick broken over his head—by a Columbia University math professor.

It was ever so. During "King" Clancy's first term with the Toronto Maple Leafs, in 1930, a priest talked him into donning a cassock and helping out as a ringer in a game between two Catholic seminaries. "By Heaven," recalls Clancy, one of the hardiest pros of his day, "that was the roughest game I've *ever* been in."

Rough as it may be, hockey has edicts against slashing, boarding, tripping and such, plus graver felonies like fighting and deliberate bloodletting. If a man's offense is noticed by the referee, he's banished to a penalty box that is unique in sport. There, until lately, players who flayed together stayed together, still packing their shillelaghs. Predictably, some of the game's biggest brawls have begun in the "cooler." Now penalized players are forced to sit apart.

"Even when we only go to *watch* hockey," says psychoanalyst Lohrenz, "we unconsciously prepare to *play* it. Blood pressure rises, adrenaline flows faster. In short, we build up steam. When that lets go, even timid people can become tigers."

Another reason why hockey fans get carried away is that they're close to the action, in relatively small arenas, where they can hear and almost feel a thumping body check. "They're not just spectators," says NHL President Clarence Campbell, "—they're *participants!*"

As such, all scream, cheer or gnaw their nails. Some have pelted the enemy forces with eggs or ink —a Detroit man once threw an octopus!—while a few fight in the stands. But most patrons vent their fury in purely vocal ways.

In the heat of battle, hockey teams rarely hear— or need—incitements to mayhem. Once, however, before a minor-pro game in Quebec City, a visiting player hurled hunks of raw meat into the hostile mob. "You wolves have been howling for blood all year," he shouted. "Maybe this will keep you quiet."

Still, according to Dr. Lohrenz, hockey provides a healthy outlet for repressed tensions. "More than in most sports," he says, "the fans identify with the players. To a woman, say, a burly defenseman may represent her domineering husband; when he's knocked down, she feels better. And when Jean Béliveau scores for Montreal against an English-speaking goalie, it's a triumph for *all* French Canadians."

While hockey is easy to understand, it is possibly the hardest of all sports to master. Like most top athletes, an NHL player needs speed, stamina, split-second reflexes, agility, balance and strength— plus an instinct called "hockey sense."

Above all, because hockey is a punishing business, it requires rugged individuals who shrink not from pain nor the sight of blood. A true pro is rec-

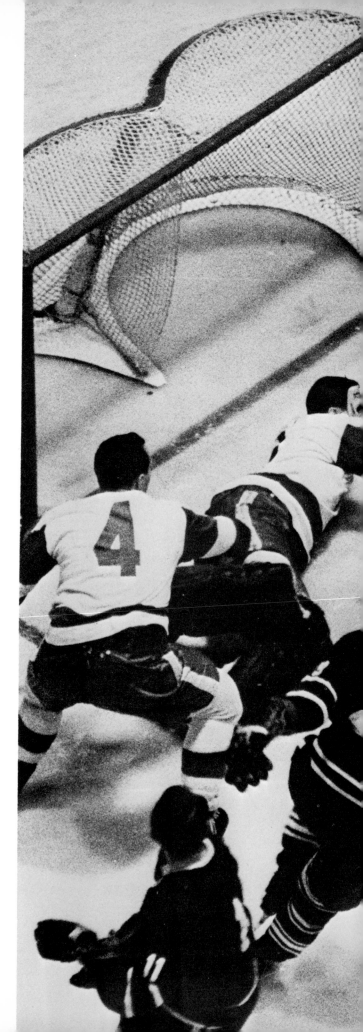

ognizable by the stitch-marks on his face—Detroit defenseman Bill Gadsby retired with 500!—and by his pearly dentures. "You're not really a hockey player," says one veteran, "until you've lost a few teeth."

During the NHL playoffs in 1963, Bobby Hull played one game for Chicago with a broken nose so badly swollen that he could hardly see past it, yet he scored three of his team's four goals and set up the other. Another time, in 1964, Boston's Dean Prentice was tripped from behind and crashed into the boards. Not until he'd scored on a penalty shot would he leave the ice—with a fractured back. "You know," former New York goalie Chuck Rayner once remarked to the rink physician who was sewing up a four-inch gash in his face, "a fellow could get hurt in this job."

Goaltenders are a breed apart. Their task, the most hazardous in sport, is to brave slashing sticks and blades—merely incidental risks of the trade—in order to throw themselves at flying pucks that can break bones and scramble their features. This calls for quick hands, the audacity of a Kamikaze pilot, and some 40 pounds of protective gear. Even so, blistering shots have torn the huge gauntlets from goalies' hands and bruised them through four-inch leg pads.

Apart from physical harm, goaltenders are prone to edgy nerves. Detroit's brilliant Roger Crozier earned an ulcer as a 17-year-old junior player, while veteran goalie Glenn Hall still gets nauseated before most games. Small wonder. One mistake, or a fluke of fate, can be disastrous.

In an overtime period to end the 1954 Stanley Cup finals, Montreal goalie Gerry McNeil was about to catch a long, easy shot when one of his own defensemen swung in front, screened his view and accidentally knocked the puck past him—at a cost of $1500 in bonuses for each member of the team. After stewing all summer over that one shot, McNeil gave up his $15,000 job. "No money," he said, "is worth that misery."

The strain of their last-ditch responsibilities tends to make goalies age fast. Once, watching Terry Sawchuk in the Detroit nets, an old NHL hand asked, "How old is that boy?"

"Twenty-four."

"Next year," he said sadly, "he'll be *thirty*-four."

If working conditions are less than ideal for the 216 players in big-league hockey, the hours and wages are excellent. In fact, the average income of NHL players tops that of any other profession in Canada—$25,000, including bonuses and awards, for seven months' toil—and some earn twice that much. Mere rookies become household names, glamour boys.

The most glamorous of all, golden-haired Bobby Hull, was a muscular young farm boy of 13 when a Chicago scout first spotted him on an outdoor rink. Not yet 30, he earns about $100,000 a year in salary and fringe benefits, and gets more fan mail than most movie stars.

Yet even Hull hasn't approached the adulation heaped on Maurice "The Rocket" Richard. In 18 years with Montreal, the fiery superstar became a French-Canadian idol, unable to walk down the street without stopping traffic. In 1960, slowing to the speed of ordinary stars, The Rocket was paid $25,000 *not* to play, lest his luster dim with age.

The plain fact of the matter is that Canadians, divided by language, are united by a deep love for their nation's best-known art form. "Hockey isn't just a game," one Canadian columnist wrote, "but an essential element of our culture."

In Toronto, English Canada's greatest city, the NHL Maple Leafs have filled their 15,000-seat rink for every game since 1946. There's a waiting list of 10,000 for season tickets—so prized that they've been left in wills. And in Montreal, heart of the French minority, *Le Club de Hockey Canadien* is revered to the edge of fanaticism. In 1955, after the beloved Rocket Richard was suspended for attacking a referee, a riot resulted which caused $100,000 damage.

All across the country, each Saturday night from October to April, 8,000,000 Canadians watch NHL games on TV. It's a sacred rite, not to be denied. When Ottawa police were summoned to a rowdy domestic fight, the husband pleaded extreme provocation: "She turned off the hockey game!"

In their passionate dedication to the sport, Canadians sometimes reach weird and wonderful heights. As far back as 1906, in a memorable grudge match between Cobalt and Haileybury, Ont., a Cobalt lawyer bet $45,000—a fortune then—and went broke. The happy Haileybury sponsor, who won $50,000, rewarded his team handsomely—with a silver mine. More recently, in Glace Bay, N.S., 5000 coal miners chipped in to build a rink for their own semipro team, then threatened to strike when their star goalie was disqualified on a technicality.

Hockey fans are notoriously fickle. For years, for example, Toronto partisans cheered Gordon Drillon, a high-scoring forward with a deceptively lazy style. Then, abruptly, they razzed him for loafing on the job. When a newspaper photo showed six Maple Leafs serving as pallbearers at the team doctor's funeral, one wag sent it to the coach with the query: "Is Drillon carrying his share of the load?"

When helter-skelter Eddie Shack joined the Leafs in 1961, he was rumored to be illiterate. But no. Once, as he was barging up the ice, a Detroit coach shouted, "G'wan, stupid, you can't even spell." Seconds later Shack scored, then skated back to the Detroit bench. Leaning over the rail to face the coach, he declaimed, "G-o-a-l."

Big-league hockey is essentially as serious as any other multimillion-dollar industry. Its raw material grows wild, on thousands of playground rinks where most Canadian boys start skating as soon as they can walk. Like other industrial recruiters, NHL scouts beat the bush leagues for talent, ranging all across Canada, into U. S. hockey hotbeds like Massachusetts, Michigan and Minnesota—even as far afield as Sweden.

At the Forum in Montreal. Top left: New York
Rangers' Orland Kurtenbach and Montreal goalie
Rogatien Vachon reach for a flying puck
as Canadiens' defenseman Ted Harris comes
to Vachon's assistance. Behind Kurtenbach
is Bobby Rousseau. Right: the moment
of truth between speeding forward
and slow-moving goalie—Gump Worsley
of Montreal slides out from his net
to meet Chicago Black Hawks' Bobby Hull.
Below: Glenn Hall of the St. Louis Blues,
one of that goaltending breed who must have
"quick hands, the audacity of a Kamikaze pilot,
and some 40 pounds of protective gear."

Canada's game it may be but Canada's prestige
in international hockey competition
has slipped. Her best players do too well
at home to be much bothered
about defending Canada's honor abroad.

They especially watch for speed, size and spirit. Toronto's Conn Smythe once hired a hard-driving athlete named Syl Apps after watching him play only one game—of *football*. "Anyone with that kind of spirit," he said, "*has* to become a great hockey player." Sure enough, Apps is now in the Hockey Hall of Fame.

By the age of 15, a promising prospect may have several NHL scouts bidding for his services. Once signed by New York, say, the prodigy starts climbing up through various farm teams from junior to minor-pro, hoping to reach Madison Square Garden.

For developing pro hockey to its present high degree, however, Canada has paid a stiff price in prestige at the World Amateur Hockey Tournament, which, begun in 1920, has lately become a not-so-cold war.

For years, Canadians so dominated the game that they could win the international title with almost any third-rate amateur team. But in 1954, at Stockholm, Russia competed for the first time—and won. Canadians were stunned, their pride sorely hurt.

One year later, in Germany, a stronger Canuck team regained the championship by blanking the Soviet upstarts 5-0. Since then, however, Russia has taken over again, winning regularly. In 1965, when Canada finished a dismal fourth, newspapers

cried "Shame!" and pointed questions were even raised in Parliament.

One answer is that Canada's best players—600 admitted pros and hundreds of excellent amateurs —are too busy making money at home to defend the national honor abroad. (Canadian teams in world and Olympic competitions are composed of college students and a few superpatriots.)

In Russia, dozens of farm teams cultivate talent for the Soviet national squad. Standout players are sworn in as Red Army officers, then posted to Moscow and paid to practice together all year. The result is better teamwork than many Canadian pros display.

Oddly enough, there's bitter rivalry between Russia and satellite Czechoslovakia, which has 80,000 hockey players. When the favored Czechs lost to the U.S.S.R. in 1964, angry citizens of Prague demonstrated outside the coach's home.

The third big power in European hockey is Sweden, whose players have multiplied from 3000 to 175,000 since 1948.

In the United States, too, hockey is booming as never before. The number of all-weather artificial-ice rinks grew from 96 to 2000 in 15 years, and has meant a proportionate increase in schoolboy teams. So popular is one hockey clinic, in Princeton, N.J., that many fathers enroll their sons at birth to make sure they get in. Minor-pro hockey thrives in such unfrozen places as Memphis, Tenn., and Houston, Tex.

The game's excitement is winning thousands of fans in—lo!—Mexico City. Hockey was introduced there in 1948, by graduates of Canadian colleges. "The fire and action of hockey appeals to Latins," says junior-league president Jaime Roberts, whose grandfather came from Canada. "For big games, we need lots of police."

As hockey continues to spread, the day may come when we'll see a truly *world* playoff for the Stanley Cup, the NHL championship bowl. If a Cup playoff should ever pit Russian against Canadian pros, it probably wouldn't supplant Brotherhood Week. For the Soviets play, as *Sports Illustrated* has noted, "as though the future of the communist world depends on their sticks and blades." As for Canadians, their commitment to success in hockey knows no bounds, not even family ties.

Not long ago, a Montreal player who flubbed an easy shot was pained to hear his own son razzing him from the stands. Later, at home, he demanded an explanation.

"When you score, you're my father," the lad replied. "But when you miss an open goal, Daddy, you're a bum."

The Corner Rink

By Michel Normandin
For many years "the voice of hockey"
on radio in French Canada

It's the end of November and Quebec crackles at the first icy touch of winter. Days are ever shorter and in the long evening an army of boys toils to build the rink where parochial league games will be played this new hockey season. Quick, *mes amis!* December's nearly here.

This year the rink is in the schoolyard. The boards have been up for a month now—a fence not two feet high but *four* feet, thanks to a better-than-average take from the benefit euchre in September.

Tomorrow, after school, the flooding starts. If the pump won't work, after the harsh weather of the past couple of years, they'll use molasses barrels from the general store—if necessary, even washtubs—for that first coat of ice on the frozen ground. That'll go on night after night and, with the help of a few good blows from the northeast, they'll soon take on the team from the next parish and avenge that 6-0 shellacking at the end of last season.

But the thousands of corner rinks in Quebec cities, towns and villages are for hockey players of *all* ages. Look at this little fellow, barely big enough to

The Béliveaus and Richards of not many seasons hence, Canadian youngsters learn the hockey art on corner-lot rinks across the country.

walk but his eye already on the NHL. If he's from Bordeaux he knows that Maurice "The Rocket" Richard got his start on this same rink. East-end Montreal? On *this* rink Emile Bouchard threw *his* first body check. If this is Chicoutimi, this youngster will try to imitate Georges Vézina or Johnny Gagnon.

On his blue, white and red sweater he wears No. 9—The Rocket's hallowed number. In his stockings, mind you, two mail-order catalogues serve as shin protectors.

In a few years he'll be in a junior league. Then on to intermediate. His name will appear in the local paper. He'll be a neighborhood hero and get a chance in senior competition. And after ten years of hockey—perhaps 300 league games, thousands of hours of practice, dozens of lumps and bruises and cuts—this little Maurice or Emile or Jean will be big Maurice or big Emile or big Jean of *les Canadiens*.

And back in Bordeaux or Montreal's east end or Chicoutimi, other men will say: "*Moi,* I played on the same team he did!"

Expo 67: The Billion-Dollar Birthday Party

The country's first world's fair drew millions to Montreal to
honor the centennial of Confederation. But it did more than that: it
created a new, dynamic image of Canada, for herself and for the world

By David MacDonald

When Canada began preparing to stage a world's fair at Montreal in 1967—the nation's centennial—many skeptics scoffed. And no wonder. Though most expositions have been seven years abuilding on solid ground, Canadian planners had less than four years to complete theirs in a place then lying partly beside the St. Lawrence River, but mainly *under* it. "You're crazy!" one engineer told them, after a computer predicted that Expo 67 couldn't possibly be ready before '69.

But the electronic oracle reckoned without one vital factor: human ingenuity. For, as 50 million visitors saw, Canada produced the biggest and the best world's fair in history.

Covering 1000 acres, the stunning Expo site took in a peninsula and two lagoon-laced islands—all

largely man-made—which British architect Sir Basil Spence acclaimed as "a modern Venice in the St. Lawrence." All it required was $40 million, enough rock and soil to match the Great Pyramids, plus 15 months of hard work. After completing this "impossible" task, moreover, the Canadians sold a record 70 nations on joining in a billion-dollar spectacular as boldly imaginative as its setting. "Man can do amazing things when he tries," said Pierre Dupuy, commissioner-general of the exhibition. "And that's what Expo is all about."

The first major fair ever sanctioned in the Americas by the 31-member International Exhibitions Bureau, which spurned New York's recent show for crass commercialism, Expo 67 was an exciting progress report on "Man and His World."

In a wonderland of futuristic pavilions, this global gala provided a rare review of the achievements of *Homo sapiens,* and fascinating glimpses into years ahead. It was instant education, plus a feast of fun. "See the life of your time," the posters urged, "and have the time of your life."

Life, at Expo, was well spiced with variety. In surroundings as disparate as America's vast geodesic dome and tiny Thailand's gilded shrine, exhibits ranged from a Dead Sea Scroll to—stand in line!—Elvis Presley's guitar. You could see a tiled Tunisian mosaic from the 2nd century, or a model city planned for the 21st; watch primitive African dances, walk across a mock-up lunar landscape, match wits with a machine, hear the babel of Spanish, Hindi and Greek. Whether you wished to gaze

at priceless paintings, sail in a Chinese junk, ride an Indian elephant, eat Arabian couscous, drink Danish akvavit, hear La Scala or ogle *le strip,* it was all there, only eight minutes by subway from the heart of the French-Canadian metropolis.

"Expo has something for everyone," said Montreal's go-getting Mayor Jean Drapeau, who won the Exhibition Bureau's okay for it late in 1962, after Moscow gave up a prior claim to the 1967 world's fair. "There's never been anything like it." He was right.

Free-wheeling architects made Expo
a wonderland of futuristic shapes
and patterns. West Germany's roof
of translucent plastic and steel mesh
(right) looked in close-up like a parade
of circus tents.

But Expo was a treasure house also
of ancient things cherished by modern man,
like the pre-Hispanic stone work (below)
at the Mexican pavilion.

Most eye-catching of Expo's bright pavilions
was the transparent geodesic dome which enfolded
the U.S. display. Twenty stories high,
this $9,300,000 bubble is a filigree of steel tubing
with an acrylic "skin" that glistens by day
and radiates a golden glow at night.

The Man in the Community building, one of the theme pavilions, had a hexagonal spire (above) of British Columbia fir.

Deep blue sky accentuates the clean and simple lines of a corner of the Indian pavilion. Expo's 300 structures were called "the most exciting collection of buildings on earth." This world in not-so-miniature was only eight minutes by subway from the heart of Montreal.

Maybe nobody had as great a time as the kids. For busy teenagers at the Boy Scouts of Canada pavilion, for younger fry just soaking up sun during a pause in an Expo playground, for youngsters from a score of countries (and for Montreal boys and girls who went back dozens of times) . . . to be a kid who went to Expo was to have a never-to-be-forgotten time of your life.

You could eat Norwegian smoked reindeer, drink Siberian wine, listen to Jamaican steel bands. Expo was a hundred languages and dialects, a thousand specialties. People of every country, like these Ethiopians, celebrated their special national day.

Where to next? There was *so* much to see and do and, for most visitors, so little time. Many planned each hour of each precious busy day and sometimes had to choose between, say, a Swiss glassblower (below) and a trip by Venetian gondola. Another Expo choice: 70 restaurants and almost as many snack bars.

Fifty-five Expo pavilions made extensive use
of film, and used everything from standard,
single-screen devices to enormous, multiscreen
projections like this one in the Czechoslovak
pavilion. Each of the 112 cubes in the rectangular
screen had its own projection equipment. Fifteen
thousand slides were used in a 14-minute show
called *The Creation of the World*.

There was something for everybody,
and 50,306,648 people visited this
greatest-ever exposition. Some of
the best fun was to settle under a
big umbrella and watch other people.

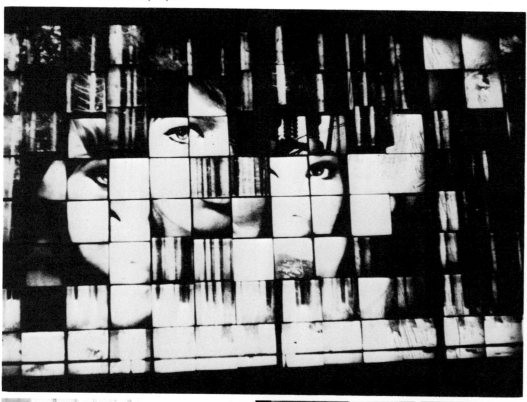

In the U.S. pavilion (left) was a record of U.S. advances in many fields, from electronics to toys. Visitors could inspect a buglike craft for landing men on the moon, or Elvis Presley's guitar, or giant photographs of Hollywood stars like Valentino and Garbo.

From old masters by the world's greatest painters to the exciting work of modern young sculptors, Expo's art was a remarkable exhibition in itself.
These enormous figures, fashioned from aluminum by Mario Armengol, were in the British pavilion.

Imagine yourself about to land
on the moon (not the U.S. pavilion).
Doesn't that look like the earth
(not the moon) 'way off there in space?

Expo at night was a fairyland of light
and color. Dominating this photo (below)
of Ile Notre-Dame is Russia's $15-million
glass-walled edifice, its upswung roof
seeming poised for flight.

And everywhere the Minirail,
driverless and leisurely, traveling
endlessly and tirelessly on
a track which walked stilt-legged
over water, through buildings,
past parks and above people.

... strolling *chansonniers*, Quebec
handicrafts and dancers, while-you-wait
portraits and silhouettes and caricatures...

Expo's main amusement center was La Ronde,
a swinging place of laughs and thrills
and screams and popcorn and candy floss,
a 135-acre funland with an international
shopping bazaar, a 300-yacht marina, daily
water-ski shows, nightly fireworks...

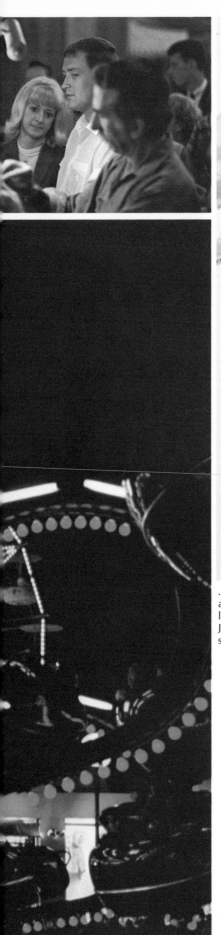

. . . and clutches of thrill rides,
a children's funfare, clowns,
logrolling, a replica of a
Jacques Cartier ship and a
staggering array of French bistros.

Habitat, the newest concept in big-city housing,
consists of three 12-story pyramids built of precast
concrete boxes forming one- to four-bedroom apartments.
Designed by Israeli architect Moshe Safdie, Habitat
was built by the Canadian Government as an experiment
in mass-produced housing. Expo, said the editor
of *Architectural Forum,* "may be remembered chiefly
because of Safdie's concrete boxes, just as people recall
the great Paris Exposition of 1900 because of Eiffel's tower."

It is remembered for a thousand wonderful things—
the happy roofs of La Ronde, for instance, which some wonderful
grown-up shaped and colored like children's blocks.

Biggest and costliest of all Expo
pavilions was Canada's, a $21-million,
11-acre complex topped by a 109-foot
inverted pyramid called Katimavik,
an Eskimo word for "meeting place."
Six million dollars' worth of exhibits,
from covered wagons to computers, showed
how Canadians used human and natural
resources to create a rich society
in an enormous land that Voltaire
once wrote off as "so many acres of snow."

Fittingly surrounded by water,
Britain's pavilion consisted
of a vast hall as white as
the cliffs of Dover,
and a 200-foot tower designed
by Sir Basil Spence to look "tough,
craggy and uncompromising." The top
was deliberately not finished
—a sign that Britain isn't, either.
On Expo's final day, planes
flew over the site in a colorful
windup to Canada's birthday party.

AN
ACT
OF FAITH

See what an empire is here, surely the best
in climate, soil, mineral, and other productions
in the world, and peopled by such a race as
no other country under heaven can produce.
No, Sir, here are the bundle of sticks;
all they want is to be united.

Thomas C. Haliburton (Sam Slick), 1855

An Act of Faith and…

By A. R. M. Lower
Canadian historian

Canada, with its divisions of race, presents no common denominator in those profundities which normally unite, in race, language, religion, history and culture.

If a common focus is to be found it must come out of the common homeland itself. If the Canadian people are to find their soul, they must seek for it not in the English language or the French but in the little ports of the Atlantic provinces, in the flaming autumn maples of the St. Lawrence valley and the portages and lakes of the Canadian Shield. They must seek for it in the sunsets and the relentless cold of the prairies, in the foothill, mountain and sea of the West and the vastness of the North.

From the land, Canada, must come the soul of Canada. That it may so come is not as fanciful as some might think. When the experiment was begun in the northern wilderness no one foresaw the strong state that was to be. Canada has been built in defiance of geography. Its two coasts were bridged by a transcontinental railway almost in defiance of common sense. Canadian statesmen reconciled the irreconcilable when in the 1840's they joined dependence to independence. They accomplished one of the greatest acts of state-building in history when in 1867 they brought together scattered provinces and two peoples into one country.

Though the extremists would more than once have wrecked it, the structure built has never failed in crisis to rally to it the support of moderate men from both races.

It has stood through two world wars. In every generation Canadians have had to rework the miracle of their political existence.

Canada has been created because there has existed within the hearts of its people a determination to build for themselves an enduring home. Canada is a supreme act of faith.

…a Language to Learn

By Arnold Toynbee
British historian

Most Canadians speak only one of the two national languages and refuse to learn the other. What an opportunity they have been missing!

The Canadians' two mother tongues happen both to be also world languages. What a godsend! Why not take advantage of it? And would this not also help all Canadians to achieve their common aim of maintaining their national individuality? A bilingual Canadian people would have a much better prospect than the present di-lingual Canadian people has of saving itself from being absorbed into the United States.

The Swiss have set an example that the Canadians ought to take to heart and copy. In Switzerland there are four national languages that enjoy parity —and in Switzerland a foreigner notices that, when one Swiss citizen meets another whose mother tongue is not his own, he at once begins to talk in his fellow citizen's mother tongue. This psychological equality of the four Swiss language groups is a remarkable achievement; for they are most unequal in numbers and in economic strength.

If the English-speaking Canadians are to rise to the Swiss standard of linguistic good manners, they must start young. Why should not the Canadian educational authorities in both the Canadian language groups invite a party of Swiss educationists to study the present systems of education in the two parts of Canada and to make recommendations for improving them?

One needed improvement is to revise the biased accounts of the English-speaking Canadian community's history in French-Canadian school books, and vice versa. But the chief educational reform needed is to make all Canadians, from coast to coast, bilingual in French and English.

Canada Won't Go Yankee

A generation ago, in 1936, a great humorist-economist
made his own statement of faith in his country's future

By Stephen Leacock

Every now and then English newspapers break out
into a discussion of the "Americanization of Canada"—based on a sort of underlying fear that
Canada is getting a little too close to the United
States. It is the same sort of apprehension as is felt
on a respectable farm when the daughter of the
family is going out too much with the hired man.
The idea is that you can't tell what may happen.

In the case of Canada, the danger symptoms are
supposed to be that Canada is "flooded" with American newspapers, "deluged" with American broadcasts, "permeated" with American ideas; that American tourists cross the border in an unending stream,
and Canadian tourists go back with them like a
receding tide; that education is almost indistinguishable as carried on at Harvard or at Toronto. All
these things, and a hundred more, are produced as
terrible portents.

In other words, a relationship which should stand
as a bright example for less fortunate nations, as a
hope for distracted Europe, is turned against Canada
as a mark of under-patriotism and lack of national
spirit.

To my mind, the situation is exactly the other
way. If Canada is being Americanized, then what
England needs is to be Frenchified, and what France
needs is to be Anglicized—and both of them to be
Germanized. If then one might take the resulting
amalgamation and Italianize it a little, and even
give it a touch of Czechoslovak shellac rubbed on
with a piece of old Russian Soviet, the world would
be on the way to peace on earth.

That the Canada-U.S. relationship should end
in a political union is just a forgotten dream. Long
ago, of course, things were different. When the
Loyalists from the United States came to British
North America in 1784-90, future union was a natural idea. Even in the War of 1812 some of the
settlers of Upper Canada were only half-minded
about the British flag.

Later, the relative poverty and stagnation of Canada contrasted with the onrush of civilization in
the United States—the hip-hurrah of the roaring
Forties with canals building, cities rising, forests
falling—a vociferous age, shouting with conscious
potentiality. No wonder that many merchants of
Montreal signed a petition for annexation in 1849,
or that many farmers of Upper Canada—of Massachusetts and Virginia stock—would have taken
annexation gladly if it came with peace and honor.
The Maritime Provinces, too, were close to the
United States: they sold their fish in Boston and
bought their education at Harvard, though they
kept their souls in Scotland.

But history has left all that behind. When the
curtain that had concealed the vast resources of the
Canadian Northwest was drawn aside, there rose
the vision of a Commonwealth as wide as a continent. The whistle of the locomotive was heard in
the Rockies. Canada began to fill the West. It
reached out to pluck the Maritimes from the commercial embrace of the United States. It saw a new
idea in the Union Jack; not subservience to England,
but single sovereignty across a continent. People
with such a vision before them do not amalgamate
with anything. Canada has firmly embraced its own
political ideal and means to keep it.

The political destinies of America and Canada
lie apart but our social and cultural relations are
close. We read a flood of American newspapers because to us an American newspaper is today's, and
an English paper belongs to the week before last.

The cities of America and Canada lie side by side.
We read the news over one another's shoulders.
More than that, a lot of our news is common property. If the barometer falls to a new low in Montana, we have to watch out. If a farmer is reported
frozen in Kansas, we may lose a couple up near
Sudbury. If the Ohio floods Cincinnati, it is likely
that the Grand River will flood Galt, Ont. We *have*
to watch the American newspapers.

Hordes of Canadians spend Easter in New York,
and rough-looking, rich Americans flock here to
fish in the Gatineau.

The Thousand Islands International Bridge crosses the St. Lawrence River between Clayton and Alexandria Bay in New York and Ivy Lea, Ont., between Gananoque and Brockville. It was dedicated in 1938 by Prime Minister Mackenzie King and President Franklin D. Roosevelt. At about that time, Stephen Leacock wrote: "The best hope for European countries is to get into the kind of mutual relationship now fortunately held between the United States and Canada."

And more than that—for those are things on the surface—our language and culture run close together. Let us make no pretense to talk the best English, because everyone knows that that is spoken only by the Scotch—or even to talk good English. But at any rate, Canadians and Americans talk the same kind of bad English, and a common language is a powerful bond. A lot of our customs in Ontario came with the Loyalists and are with us still—our school system, our local government, our Thanksgiving Day, our New Year calls, our logging bees and spelling bees.

The international good will that exists between Canada and the United States is what all the world must achieve, or perish. With war so devastatingly mechanized, it is universal peace or nothing—and world amity can never be brought about by treaties and sanctions, but only through unity of ideas, of interest, of understanding.

In past history, such unity did not matter. Men out of arm's reach could not hurt one another. A little nation in a valley sat snug: a people on an island lived in peace; a castle gathered in its brood like chickens. But all this is gone. An island is nothing. Men must unite or die; and the only hope for their union lies in what would be academically called "the interpermeation of culture." In other words, nations have got to know each other.

Now the Canadians and the Americans know each other. That places the Canadians as a sort of halfway element between the Americans and the British people—creates as it were the nucleus of a world union: not in a sense of an alliance to menace the world, but as a first area of solidarity from which it may spread abroad. In this alliance, we Canadians have the lesser part. But in the great arch of British-American solidarity we are the keystone. Don't shake us out.

The First Century: Success or Failure?

Bruce Hutchison compares the dream of the Fathers of Confederation
with the trials and triumphs of the great nation they founded

On that first day of July 1867, church bells pealed, bands played, soldiers marched and bonfires burned in every Canadian town to celebrate the birth of a nation. But it was a nation in name only, a paper declaration not yet impressed on the empty earth. Four disparate little British colonies, with some 3.4 million scattered people, had joined in an unlikely confederation of unknown boundaries stretching across half a continent.

Everything conspired against this wild experiment—geography, climate, economic forces and deep divisions between English-speaking and French inhabitants. Its future, seemingly, must be hard, poor, quarrelsome—and brief. Even now, after a century of nationhood, most Canadians can't quite realize how much we've accomplished, or grasp the greater prospects ahead.

But while Canada is now measuring its progress by impressive statistics of population, wealth and physical growth, perhaps there is a more authentic measurement. How would the Fathers of Confederation judge their work if they could see it now? What would they say about Canada's success or failure?

From John Alexander Macdonald, whose genius put Confederation together, we would hear one of those wry, twinkling speeches that made his listeners

chuckle and think furiously by turn. Like them, we could not escape the peculiar charm of this slim, gangling figure in flashy clothes, the mane of black curls, the purpled nose and the cheerful grin masking inner sorrows.

His lifelong enemy and brief partner, George Brown, would speak in chiseled antique idiom, the huge body heaving, the red whiskers bristling, the great arms flailing. Then, in bubbling French accent, the staccato jests of Georges-Etienne Cartier, Quebec's brisk terrier; the bulldog growls of Charles Tupper; the financial facts pouring from Alexander Galt's infallible memory and the Irish whimsy of young Thomas D'Arcy McGee. These daring visionaries would surely confirm our faith in Canada. They would also tell us where we have faltered.

Imagining their verdict, we should remember that the Fathers had the advantage of a boundless hope undimmed by the smoke of the past century. Unlike their heirs, they did not confront a global revolution that no one understands, much less a world menaced by its birth rate or by the threat of nuclear suicide.

Their disadvantages, fortunately, were not measurable. They had no statistics to guide them, scant economic learning, little knowledge of the territory

Georges-Etienne Cartier, facing right, stands
next to John A. Macdonald (seated) in a photograph
of delegates to the 1864 Charlottetown convention
which led to union of the British colonies
in North America. A century later, as conflicts
beset the Canadian experiment, provincial premiers
and federal cabinet ministers meet in Ottawa.
The Fathers of Confederation, says Bruce Hutchison,
would be "incredulous, indignant or amused
that some impatient Canadians have rejected
Confederation as a failure and propose to split
a thriving, prosperous country into two
or more separate states assured
of a mean life and probably a swift death."

west of Ontario. Possibly their ignorance was their greatest asset. For had they seen how hard the westward road ahead would be, they might have trod instead the easier road south to join the United States.

Their minds were set on an intangible purpose that they could never put precisely into words. But we can gauge the Fathers' estimate of their chances from the governor-general's speech to the joint Parliament of Upper and Lower Canada on January 19, 1865. Submitting the Confederation scheme, Lord Monck proclaimed in rotund Victorian terms: "With the public men of British North America it now rests to decide whether the vast tract of country which they inhabit shall be consolidated into a state combining within its areas all the elements of national greatness."

National greatness! Here was a challenge—and a question only Canadians could answer. Would their answer be as bold as their ambition?

Some politicians hesitated to plunge into the unknown even after the constitution was ratified. Joseph Howe, Nova Scotia's troubled tribune, denounced Confederation as "The Botheration Scheme." Antoine Aimé Dorion, the Quebec opposition leader, described the British North America Act as "absurd from beginning to end." But despite such voices of regional suspicion, the perilous experiment began.

The Fathers would hardly be surprised to find it firmly established now as a going concern. They *would* be surprised, however, to find within it one of the world's most affluent societies, with other ethnic groups now making up 25 percent of its population. Surprised, too, by the rapid expansion of provincial powers, contrary to their plans, by government's growing intervention in private business, by all the Keynesian tools as unknown to them as automobile and television. And they would be amazed to hear that they themselves are now regarded as towering giants who dwarf their 20th-century heirs.

Still, they *were* giants, by any standard. They showed as much ability as the men who drafted the U.S. Constitution. They may look smaller in retrospect, but only because they had less material to work with.

With their native intelligence, doubtless they would soon grasp the new economics, having effectively used their own crude tools of national credit to build railways from Atlantic to Pacific. They would understand why Canada is respected—and sometimes overestimated—throughout the world.

Canada's successes would not surprise the founders
of the country. But they *would* be surprised
to find within Canada one of the world's most affluent
societies, with ethnic groups other than French
and British now making up 25 percent of the population.
Immigrants have come from most countries. Some
posed (below) for photographs after disembarking
at Quebec in 1911: a German family,
a young Austrian, a Dutch couple and their baby.

And they would comprehend the present confusion
of our politics, since they had known nothing else
themselves in pre-Confederation times. Probably
they would tell their successors that this malaise
must pass, as it passed in 1867, once a big enough
decision retests the nation's wisdom and courage.

But if the Fathers were here now we would have
to ask them candidly whether their political system
had improved or deteriorated after a century's experience. Both Macdonald, an old hand at manipu-
lating the seamy side of politics, and Brown, who
never ceased to damn the corruption of all governments, would agree that the public life is immacu-
lately honest now compared with the open bribery
and rigged elections of the old days. And they would
agree that there has been a great refinement in the
arts and instruments of government. If we have
fallen behind the pace of history here, so have all
nations. Macdonald might say of our times what he
said of his own: "The wheel is revolving and we are
only the fly on the wheel."

Though he and his generation could adjust to our
revolutionary age, certain ideas now astir in Canada
would completely baffle its architects. They would
be incredulous, indignant or amused that some impatient Canadians have rejected Confederation as a
failure and propose to split a thriving, prosperous
country into two or more separate states assured of a
mean life and probably a swift death. You can almost hear Macdonald's retort to the separatists
across the House: "Gentlemen, you are mad!"

Brown said much the same thing to those who
opposed Confederation in the great debate of 1865:
"No man who has a true regard for the well-being
of Canada can vote against this scheme unless he
is prepared to offer some better remedy for the evils
and injustices that have so long threatened the
peace of our country."

"There," Cartier cut in, "is the question!" And so it is today. The few Canadians who would dissolve the nation are bound to suggest a better alternative. They cannot, because there is none.

While the Fathers would waste no time on separatism, they would blink in amazement at Canada's national inferiority complex. At first, they too suffered from it. As British colonists they stood in awe of the famous figures then strutting the world's stage at London. But they quickly began to outgrow this feeling of subordination. As early as the Washington conference of 1871, Macdonald did not hesitate to quarrel openly with the British government when he saw Canada's commercial interests sold out to the United States. For all his reverence for British institutions, he had become a Canadian, and he never lost his suspicion of "overwashed Englishmen, full of crotchets."

Now that Canada has long since won full independence from Britain, he would realize that our primary international concern—a mixture of assets and liabilities—is the next-door presence of the world's greatest power. This was his besetting anxiety, too. And it looked far more dangerous in his time, because the United States then resented Canada as a nuisance.

Always a hardheaded realist, Macdonald would have to admit that the colossal American neighbor has far outstripped Canada in power and per capita wealth, in the public arts and sciences. But he would never understand why we should feel inferior to anyone in the private art of living when no nation's general life is superior to our own. That secret sense of failure haunting many Canadians must move the Fathers to laughter, or tears. Let us confess the truth: in self-confidence, and in self-confidence alone, we have gone downhill since 1867. Such is the price that a small nation must pay for the big neighbor's presence and protection. But it isn't the only price. Canada pays also in envy, sometimes in distrust or even anger.

The Fathers would fully understand, because they

The biggest buildings and the brightest
are the buildings of Detroit, across the
river border from Windsor, Ont. (foreground).
Macdonald would admit the United States
has outstripped Canada in power and per capita
wealth, in the public arts and sciences. But,
says Hutchison, Sir John A. would never understand
"why Canadians should feel inferior to anyone
in the private art of living when no nation's
general life is superior to our own."

penetration, so alarming to modern Canadians, could be contained only by his people's independence, courage and ingenuity. The nation would succeed or fail on its own merits.

This is the sovereign test still facing us after 100 years. While it may be forgotten temporarily in the clamor of politics, no national policy can avoid it. The test has not always been wisely met, either in public policy or in the individual Canadian mind, but the Fathers would see no excuse for the despair, the inferiority complex, afflicting some of their successors.

As they would see it now, the nation possesses just about everything necessary for even greater success, except a sound perspective. That lack has recently produced a native cliché which would puzzle and irritate the Fathers. Canada, we say, is seeking an "identity."

No such word appears in Confederation's first great debate because no one saw any need of it. The Canadian identity was accepted then as a natural condition beyond argument or complaint, like the cruel northern weather, the wilderness, the solitude and the daily struggle against these harassments. That many Canadians are trying to discover or invent a synthetic identity would be dismissed as a harmless joke, or a harmful waste of energy.

The nation's builders had inherited an identity from more than two centuries of war, massacre, hunger and dumb endurance on the Canadian earth. Identity showed varying facets in a far-flung and diverse country, and two primary elements, Anglo-Saxon and French. Like all the precious things of life, it was cherished in silence and did not require public inspection. Yet it was there. Otherwise these men would not have decided to build a nation in poverty when they could join another, already opulent. From the beginning, when the victors and vanquished of the British conquest at Quebec were working as equals to create a purely Canadian nationality, Brown had asked: "Where, sir, in the page of history shall we find a parallel to this?"

knew and often exploited the familiar anti-American syndrome which still appears among Canadians. To win his last election campaign, the dying Macdonald used the old specter quite cynically: he accused his political opponents of "veiled treason" for proposing free trade with the United States. Yet if he were here now he would say again, as he always said, that a successful Canadian state cannot live on fear and hostility. Macdonald's approach to the future was based on a *positive* Canadianism, a trust in his own people, not a hatred of foreigners.

He would tell us, as he told his generation, that the vital cement of Confederation must be the Canadians' love of their own land and their own ways. At the same time, he knew that peaceful American

322

On a bridge in rural Quebec, the battle cry of the separatist. Below a statue of Georges-Etienne Cartier, the white splotch of protest—and Cartier's words: "We are of different races not for strife but to work together for the common welfare." Writes Hutchison: "The few Canadians who would dissolve the nation are bound to suggest a better alternative. They cannot, because there is none."

While the debate on the new state's constitution was complex and stubborn, nobody asked whether the Canadian person was identifiable and thus worth preserving; he had identified and preserved himself since Champlain's arrival at Quebec. After this, why should he now appoint solemn royal commissions of inquiry or beat his breast as a demonstration of national character? It had been written legibly across a continent for all men to read. Why should amateur physicians take the people's pulse every day until they begin now to think they must be sick?

Canada's basic health would not trouble our ancestors. Of course, they would worry about the conflicts agitating our politicians, economists and psychologists. But they overcame similar stresses in their time and would expect no less from us. Strain is the eternal price of freedom.

You can study the records of Confederation's second great debate, now under way. You can explore Quebec's grievances and the Anglo-Saxon reaction to them, read the speeches of frenzied bigots on both sides. But you will find there nothing of importance that the Fathers overlooked, no more reliable guide than Macdonald's simple letter to an English-speaking friend:

"The truth," he wrote, "is that you British Canadians can never forget that you were once supreme.

No man in his senses can suppose that the country can, for a century to come, be governed by a totally unfrenchified government. If a British Canadian desires to conquer he must 'stoop to conquer.' He must make friends of the French without sacrificing the status of his race or religion. He must respect their nationality. Treat them as a nation and they will act as a free people generally do—call them a faction and they become factious."

This from the Scottish immigrant boy who, with an instinct deeper than knowledge, had grasped the inward nature of his adopted land. Macdonald knew that in a psychological sense, though not in a

British-Canadian prime minister and French-Canadian
successor, custodians of the Confederation wrought
by Macdonald. "No man in his senses," Sir John A.
wrote a century ago, "can suppose that the country
can . . . be governed by a totally unfrenchified
government." A British-Canadian "must make friends
of the French," he said, "without sacrificing
the status of his race or religion. He must respect
their nationality. Treat them as a nation and
they will act as a free people generally do—
call them a faction and they become factious."

constitutional way, French Canada must always be
a nation, as distinguishable, durable and proud as
any in the world. He also knew, better even than
some modern French Canadians, that this nation
could not long survive, in English-speaking North
America, outside a larger structure of national
government strong enough to protect its two
essential ingredients.

So did Cartier, an unalterable French Canadian if
ever there was one. "We are of different races not
for strife," he said, "but to work together for the
common welfare."

The Macdonalds, Cartiers and Browns would re-
joice in the present growth of English-speaking
Canada and the surging renaissance of Quebec. But
they would be dumbfounded and saddened to hear
from some Canadians that Quebec's progress is a
threat to the dual society, from others that French
Canada cannot continue to progress inside it. In this
concept, as nowhere else, the Fathers would see
that their plans have not yet succeeded.

Long ago the Fathers heard the familiar cries of
extremists in both camps and took them for what
they still are—the voices of self-destruction, loud
and shrill, but never convincing enough to halt the
Canadian march. Yet the nation's makers would
tell us that their work must ultimately fail altogether unless the sensible majorities on both sides
can master the dominant fact of Canada: its double
nationality of language, culture and mind.

To master that fact we need no new discovery, no
new method, no magic unknown to the men who
gave us our fair estate. We need only to rediscover
their method and, above all, the impulse behind it.
They knew, and we must learn, that the paramount
Canadian question is not political or economic. It is
wholly human. It cannot be answered in favor of a
permanent nation unless ordinary human beings, no
better or worse than the pioneers, are sufficiently big
to finish their task.

One thing is certain: if we fail to solve our internal problems we cannot survive as an independent

The work of the nation's makers, writes Hutchison, "must ultimately fail altogether unless the sensible majorities on both sides can master the dominant fact of Canada: its double nationality of language, culture and mind . . . the paramount Canadian question is not political or economic. It is wholly human."

state. The Canadian experiment can be endangered by no one except its own sons. Such was the lesson at the beginning and its outcome was Confederation. Such is still the lesson today. As the Fathers would rightly ask, have we really learned it? And, if so, how do we intend to employ it?

Brown might have been speaking today, not 102 years ago, when he demanded of his companions: "Shall we then rise equal to the occasion? Shall we approach this discussion without partisanship and free from every personal feeling but the earnest resolution to discharge conscientiously the duty which an overruling providence has placed upon us?"

Those words have an old-fashioned ring in our sophisticated ears, but they are just as valid and relevant today as when Brown uttered them.

The response that must determine Canada's tomorrow will not come from statesmen, economists or other experts. It will come from the 20 million obscure individuals who call themselves

Canadians and, in their unrecorded workaday lives, will make or unmake the nation's life. If, after a century, we can't make a success of racial accord in our uniquely fortunate land, who on earth can?

It was easy to throw a modest birthday party in 1867. It was easy to throw a lavish party in 1967, and easy to pay the immediate bill. But there will be another bill to pay, a bill recurring with every generation and payable in the very different coin of intelligence, tolerance and decent neighborly behavior. Poor as they were, the Fathers gladly paid that bill and trusted us, who are rich, to pay it again. From Canada, if it is to have the future planned by them, history will take no lesser payment.

An Indian Prayer

Of all the "centennial projects" in Canada in 1967, ranging from small-town parks to a gigantic world's fair, one of the most heartening was the Canadian Interfaith Conference.

Set up under the nation's Centennial Commission, the Conference embraced 34 religions—a strong expression of Canada's long yearning for unity through diversity. Among its own projects: an anthology of 185 prayers to be recited in churches and synagogues across the land.

Perhaps the simplest and most beautiful entry in the booklet was this ancient Blackfoot prayer, which speaks to the hearts of all men as much as to the Great Spirit worshipped by the first Canadians.

O Great Spirit, Creator of all things;
Human beings, trees, grass, berries.
Help us, be kind to us.
Let us be happy on earth.
Let us lead our children
To a good life and old age.
These our people; give them good minds
To love one another.

O Great Spirit,
Be kind to us.
Give these people the favor
To see green trees,
Green grass, flowers and berries
This next spring;
So we all meet again.

O Great Spirit,
We ask of You.

Acknowledgments

The condensations reprinted in this book are used by permission of, and special arrangement with, the publishers holding the respective copyrights.

In Search of Canada, by V. S. Pritchett, *Reader's Digest*, July '65, condensed from *Holiday* (April '64), © 1964 by The Curtis Pub. Co., Independence Square, Philadelphia.

Sir John A., Master-Builder of Canada, by Bruce Hutchison, *Reader's Digest*, Nov. '61.

Ottawa, A Queen's Choice, by Gustave Lanctôt, *Sélection du Reader's Digest*, Nov. '47.

"The World's Best Doctor", by Richard Match, *Reader's Digest*, April '53 and Oct. '61, condensed from *New Liberty* (July '52), © 1952 by Liberty of Canada Ltd., 73 Richmond St. W., Toronto.

Alexander Mackenzie, First Across Canada, by Bruce Hutchison, *Reader's Digest*, May '66, condensed from *The Kiwanis Magazine* (Dec. '65-Jan.'66), © by Kiwanis International, Chicago.

He Discovered the Treasure of Great Bear Lake, by Francis and Katharine Drake, *Reader's Digest*, Sept. '49 (The Treasure of Great Bear Lake), condensed from *The American Mercury* (Sept. '49), © by The American Mercury, Inc.

"In Flanders Fields", by Bernhard Ragner, *Reader's Digest*, April '38, © 1938 by The New York Times Company. Reprinted by permission.

"He Taught Us How to Live", by Frank Germann, *Reader's Digest*, Feb. '67 (The Unforgettable Father Murray).

Wilder Penfield, Explorer of the Human Brain, by Murray Teigh Bloom, *Reader's Digest*, July '58, condensed from *The Elizabethan* (June '58), © by Universal Publications (Quebec) Ltd., 1255 University St., Montreal 2.

The Man Behind the New Montreal, by David MacDonald, *Reader's Digest*, Nov. '66, condensed from *Winnipeg Free Press* (Oct. 8, 1966), © by David MacDonald, published by Winnipeg Free Press Co., Ltd., Winnipeg 2.

How We Discovered Insulin, by Dr. Charles H. Best as told to J. D. Ratcliff, *Reader's Digest*, March '64, condensed from *Today's Health* (March '64), © 1964 by American Medical Assn., 535 N. Dearborn St., Chicago, Ill. 60610.

Sheepdog Navy, by J. C. Furnas, *Reader's Digest*, April '43 (Canada's Sheep-Dog Navy), condensed from *The Nautical Gazette*, April '43, © The Nautical Gazette.

A Million Fingers in the Dikes, by Carl B. Wall, *Reader's Digest*, Oct. '50, condensed from *The American Mercury* (Oct. '50), © The American Mercury, Inc.

Fighting the Wild Atoms at Chalk River, by David O. Woodbury, *Reader's Digest*, March '55.

The Big "Bump" at Springhill, by Joseph P. Blank, *Reader's Digest*, Jan. '60.

The Man Who Refused to Die, by Lawrence Elliott, *Reader's Digest*, Nov. '67.

Wilderness Mother, by Mary E. Matheson, *Reader's Digest*, March '39, condensed from *The Atlantic Monthly* (Jan. '39), © 1938, The Atlantic Monthly Co., 8 Arlington St., Boston.

Klondike Stampede, by Jo Chamberlin, *Reader's Digest*, April '40, condensed from *The Kiwanis Magazine* (April '40), © 1940 by Kiwanis International, Chicago.

He Created Dan McGrew and Cremated Sam McGee, by Wallace Reyburn, *Reader's Digest*, Oct. '51, condensed from *Everybody's* (April 21, 1951), published by Everybody's Publications, Ltd., 34-35 Farringdon Street, London, E.C. 4.

The Good Samaritan of Labrador, by David MacDonald, *Reader's Digest*, Oct. '67.

Longest Main Street in the World, by Lawrence Elliott, *Reader's Digest*, July '66.

The Amazing Crusoes of Lonesome Lake, by Leland Stowe, *Reader's Digest*, Feb. '57, condensed from *Crusoe of Lonesome Lake*, © 1957 by Leland Stowe, published by Random House, 457 Madison Avenue, New York 22.

The Flying Judge From Yellowknife, by Lawrence Elliott, *Reader's Digest*, March '65, condensed from *Winnipeg Free Press* (Dec. 12, 1964), © 1964 by Winnipeg Free Press Co., Ltd., Winnipeg 2.

The Remarkable Eskimo Artists of Baffin Island, by Lawrence Elliott, *Reader's Digest*, Sept. '62.

The Land, Always the Land!, by Bruce Hutchison, *Reader's Digest*, June '68, condensed from *Western Windows*, © 1967 by Bruce Hutchison, published by Longmans Canada, Ltd., 55 Barber Greene Rd., Don Mills, Ont. An excerpt from this essay appeared in *Maclean's* (Oct. '67).

Meet "Mr. Canada", by Robert Collins, *Reader's Digest*, Dec. '67.

The Men Before Columbus, by Farley Mowat, *Reader's Digest*, Nov. '66, condensed from *True, The Man's Magazine* (Aug. '66), © 1966 by Fawcett Publications, Inc., 67 W. 44 St., New York, N.Y. 10036.

Unbeatable *Bluenose*, by David MacDonald, *Reader's Digest*, Oct. '66 (The Unbeatable *Bluenose*), condensed from

Winnipeg Free Press (Sept. 3, 1966), © by David MacDonald, published by Winnipeg Free Press Co., Ltd., Winnipeg 2.

People of the Sea, by Farley Mowat, *Reader's Digest*, July '67 (Newfoundland Centennial: "T'ree Hunnert Year Gone By"), condensed from *Century* 1867-1967, © Century 1867-1967, published by Southam Press Ltd., 321 Bloor St. E., Toronto 5.

The *Draveurs:* Cowboys of the Forests, by Ira Wolfert, *Reader's Digest*, March '61, condensed from *Commerce* (Feb. '61), © 1961 by Ira Wolfert, published by Commerce Inc., 14 est, rue St. Jacques, Montréal 1.

Man of Laughter, by Leslie Roberts, *Reader's Digest*, June '61 (The Most Unforgettable Character I've Met).

How We Kept Mother's Day, by Stephen Leacock, *Reader's Digest*, May '50, condensed from *The Leacock Roundabout*, © 1926 by Dodd, Mead & Co., 79 Madison Avenue, New York, N.Y. 10016.

Unforgettable Ma Murray, by Georgina M. Keddell, *Reader's Digest*, May '67.

For the Love of *Maman*, by Robert Fontaine, *Reader's Digest*, May '50 (A Nightgown for the Queen), condensed from *The Happy Time*, © 1945 by Robert Fontaine, published by Simon & Schuster, Inc., 630 Fifth Avenue, New York, N.Y. 10020.

My Mother's Hands, by Robert Fontaine, *Reader's Digest*, May '57, condensed from *The Atlantic Monthly* (March '57), © 1957 by The Atlantic Monthly Co., 8 Arlington St., Boston.

"Black Gold" from Athabasca's Sticky Sands, by Harland Manchester, *Reader's Digest*, Feb. '65.

The Capital, by Ringuet, *Sélection du Reader's Digest*, July '47.

The Flaming Leaves of Fall, by Rina Lasnier, *Sélection du Reader's Digest*, Oct. '48.

La Cuisine canadienne, by André Arnoldi, *Sélection du Reader's Digest*, Aug. '50.

The Glittering Time, by Claude-Henri Grignon, *Sélection du Reader's Digest*, Jan. '48.

Calgary Whoops It Up, by Robert Christie, *Reader's Digest*, July '55, condensed from *Winnipeg Free Press* (April 30, 1955), © 1955 by Winnipeg Free Press Ltd., Winnipeg 2.

The Thanksgiving I Don't Forget, by H. Gordon Green, *Reader's Digest*, Nov. '56, condensed from *Farm Journal* (Nov. '55), © 1955 by Farm Journal, Inc., Washington Square, Philadelphia 5. This story also appears in *The Faith of Our Father*, published by McClelland & Stewart Ltd., 25 Hollinger Rd., Toronto 16.

Why We Sold the Farm, by H. Gordon Green, *Reader's Digest*, Sept. '60, condensed from *Farm Journal* (May '58), © 1958 by Farm Journal, Inc., Washington Square, Philadelphia 5.

Good-By, Little Boy!, by H. Gordon Green, *Reader's Digest*, Sept. '63.

Saskatchewan's Fabulous Potash Pile, by Lawrence Elliott, *Reader's Digest*, May '64 (Saskatchewan's 100-Billion-Dollar Potash Pile), condensed from *The Rotarian* (May '64), © 1964 by Rotary International, 1600 Ridge Ave., Evanston, Ill. 60201.

Stress—A Factor in All Disease?, by J. D. Ratcliff, *Reader's Digest*, Jan. '55 (Stress—The Cause of All Disease?).

Jenny Butchart's Garden of Wonders, by David MacDonald, *Reader's Digest*, June '66 (Canada's Garden of Wonders).

A Great Canadian Art, by Claude Mélançon, *Sélection du Reader's Digest*, Nov. '55.

Metro: Toronto's Answer to Urban Sprawl, by James Nathan Miller, *Reader's Digest*, Aug. '67.

Canada's Game Scores Abroad, by David MacDonald, *Reader's Digest*, March '66, condensed from *Hockey Pictorial* (Feb. '66), © 1966 by David MacDonald. *Hockey Pictorial* is published by Hockey Illustrated Ltd., 1434 St. Catherine St. W., Montreal.

The Corner Ice Rink, by Michel Normandin, *Sélection du Reader's Digest*, Jan. '49.

Expo 67: The Billion-Dollar Birthday Party, by David MacDonald, *Reader's Digest*, April '67.

An Act of Faith, by A. R. M. Lower, *Reader's Digest*, July '66, excerpt from *Colony to Nation*, © 1946 by A. R. M. Lower, published by Longmans Canada, Ltd., 55 Barber Greene Road, Don Mills, Ont.

A Language to Learn, by Arnold Toynbee, *Reader's Digest*, Oct. '65 (The Case for a Bilingual Canada), condensed from *The Observer*, © 1965 by The Observer (London) Foreign News Service.

Canada Won't Go Yankee, by Stephen Leacock, *Reader's Digest*, Oct. '36, condensed from *The American Mercury* (Sept. '36), © 1936 The American Mercury, Inc., 570 Lexington Ave., New York.

The First Century: Success or Failure?, by Bruce Hutchison, *Reader's Digest*, July '67 (Canada's Century: Success or Failure?).

An Indian Prayer, *Reader's Digest*, June '67.

INDEX

Photo Credits

146 - Bruce Larsen (2),
Mrs. I. G. Turner (right)

151 - Leland Stowe, Ralph Edwards

154 - Ralph Edwards, Bruce Larsen

162-3 - Carl Iwasaki, LIFE Magazine (c)
Time Inc.

164 - Carl Iwasaki, LIFE Magazine (c)
Time Inc. (left), J. H. Sissons

165 - J. H. Sissons

166, 170 - NFB (John Feeney)

171 - NFB (West Baffin Eskimo Co-op)

167, 169, 175 - TDB

168 - M. F. Feheley

172-4 - Fred Bruemmer—except 173 top
right, NFB (Doug Wilkinson)

176 - M. F. Feheley, TDB

177 - M. F. Feheley

178, 181, 183 - B.C. Government

182 - Bill Halkett

185 - Chuck Diven

186 - CBC (Gilbert A. Milne) (top left),
CBC (Henry Fox) (center right),
Canadian Centennial Commission
(bottom left), John Fisher (remainder)

188 - John Fisher

189 - Malak

190 - Canadian Centennial Commission

192 - Painting by Christian Krohg, The
National Gallery, Oslo; photo by
O. Vaering

195 - The Royal Library, Copenhagen

196 - Norwegian Embassy, Ottawa;
Thomas E. Lee

197 - Thomas E. Lee

198, 200-1, 203 - MacAskill Collection

199 - G. P. Backman

204 - CGTB (John de Visser)

205, 207 - CGTB (Pierre Gaudard)

206 - CGTB (Malak)

208 - CGTB (Ted Grant)

209 - NFB (John de Visser)

210, 212, 214-5 - Malak

213 - George Hunter

217 - Beny

218, 220, 222, 224 - Karsh

219 - McGill University

221 - PA

227 - *Alaska Highway News*

228, 229 - Georgina M. Keddell

230 - Horst Ehricht

233 - Sculpture courtesy Dominion Art
Gallery, Montreal; photo by
Albert Krafczyk

235, 237-8 - Sun Oil Company Limited

239 - Pierre Gaudard

240 - NFB (Freeman Patterson)

243 - Cicot

245-8 - Calgary Stampede

249 - CGTB (Jack Delorme)

250, 252, 254, 256-7 - H. Gordon Green

258 - Beny

259-63 - International Minerals &
Chemical Corporation

264 - NFB (Jack Long)

265, 270 - University of Montreal

267 - Pierre Desmarais Inc.

268 - NFB (Pierre Gaudard)

269 - Brian M. Smith, DND

271 - I. Comtesse v. Schwerin

272 - Bob and Ira Spring

274 - Butchart Gardens

275 - Toby Rankin, Butchart Gardens

276 - Bob and Ira Spring,
Butchart Gardens

277 - Toby Rankin

278 - Chuck Diven

279 - Chuck Diven (top right), B.C.
Government

281-2 - Boris Spremo

283 - Lockwood Survey Corporation Ltd.

284 - Boris Spremo, Toronto Real Estate
Board (Bill Huffman)

285, 291 - Boris Spremo

286, 293 - David Bier

288-9 - Graphic Artists

294 - André Sima

295 - *Montreal '67*

296 - Brian M. Smith

297 - Toby Rankin (top), Arnott Rogers
Batten, Brian M. Smith

298-9 - Brian M. Smith (3 top) and
Rudi Haas

300 - Arnott Rogers Batten (top left),
Rudi Haas (top right), Hilary G. W.
Richards

301 - Brian M. Smith (top) and
Arnott Rogers Batten

302-3 - *Montreal '67* (top left) Brian M.
Smith (bottom left, center), Hilary
G. W. Richards

304-5 - Brian M. Smith

306 - Hilary G. W. Richards, Malak (top)

307 - Brian M. Smith (top)
Toby Rankin (2 right)

308 - George Hunter, Toby Rankin

310-1 - Brian M. Smith

312 - NFB (Pierre Gaudard)

314-5 - NFB (Ted Grant)

317 - CGTB (George Hunter)

318, 320-1 - PA

319, 324 - NFB (Chris Lund)

322 - NFB (Ted Grant)

323 - NFB (Richard Sexton),
Brian M. Smith

325 - NFB (Pierre Gaudard),
Arnaud Maggs

327 - B.C. Government

328 - George Hunter (Summer sails,
Lake Ontario)

335 - Malak (Saskatchewan wheat)

337 - NFB (Egon Bork) (Tree line,
Northwest Territories)

338 - Paul Baich (MacMillan Park,
Vancouver Island)

340 - Boris Spremo (Toronto balconies)

Following page - TDB (Arctic modern)

Inside back cover - Graphic Industries
(Al Kipnes) (Vancouver skyline)

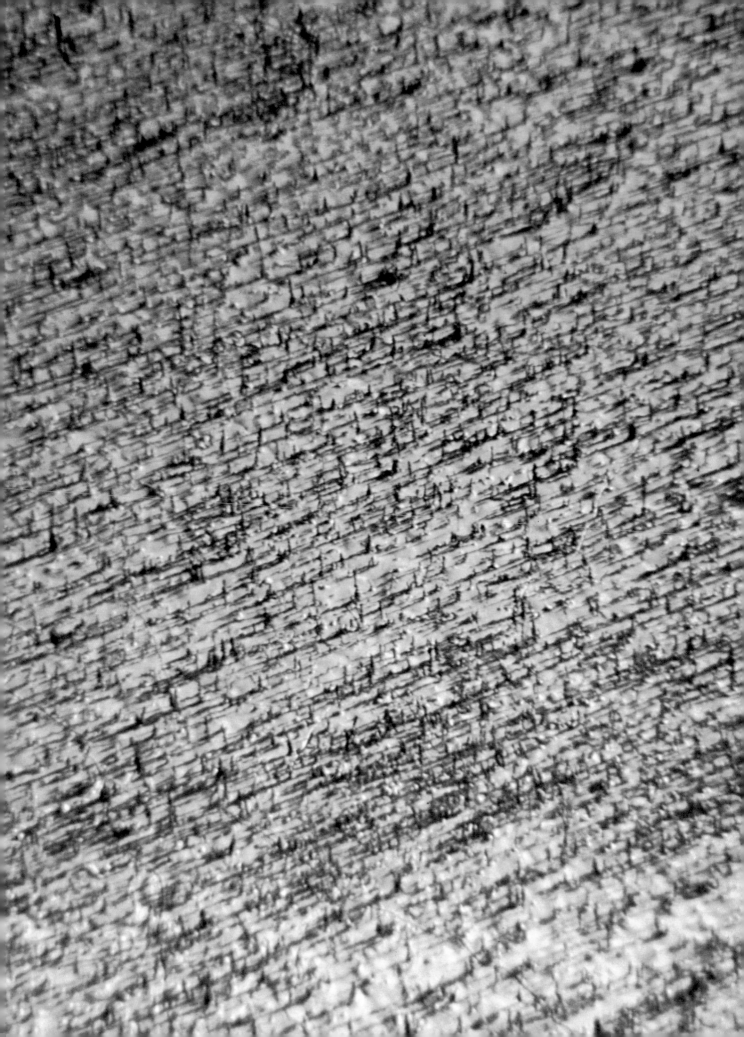